Home and Identity in Nineteenth-Century Literary London

Edinburgh Critical Studies in Victorian Culture
Series Editor: Julian Wolfreys

Recent books in the series:
Rudyard Kipling's Fiction: Mapping Psychic Spaces
Lizzy Welby

The Decadent Image: The Poetry of Wilde, Symons and Dowson
Kostas Boyiopoulos

British India and Victorian Literary Culture
Máire ní Fhlathúin

Anthony Trollope's Late Style: Victorian Liberalism and Literary Form
Frederik Van Dam

Dark Paradise: Pacific Islands in the Nineteenth-Century British Imagination
Jenn Fuller

Twentieth-Century Victorian: Arthur Conan Doyle and the Strand Magazine, 1891–1930
Jonathan Cranfield

The Lyric Poem and Aestheticism: Forms of Modernity
Marion Thain

Gender, Technology and the New Woman
Lena Wånggren

Self-Harm in New Woman Writing
Alexandra Gray

Suffragist Artists in Partnership: Gender, Word and Image
Lucy Ella Rose

Victorian Liberalism and Material Culture: Synergies of Thought and Place
Kevin A. Morrison

The Victorian Male Body
Joanne-Ella Parsons and Ruth Heholt

Nineteenth-Century Settler Emigration in British Literature and Art
Fariha Shaikh

The Pre-Raphaelites and Orientalism
Eleonora Sasso

The Late-Victorian Little Magazine
Koenraad Claes

Coastal Cultures of the Long Nineteenth Century
Matthew Ingleby and Matt P. M. Kerr

Dickens and Demolition: Literary Afterlives and Mid-Nineteenth-Century Urban Development
Joanna Hofer-Robinson

Artful Experiments: Ways of Knowing in Victorian Literature and Science
Philipp Erchinger

Victorian Poetry and the Poetics of the Literary Periodical
Caley Ehnes

The Victorian Actress in the Novel and on the Stage
Renata Kobetts Miller

Dickens's Clowns: Charles Dickens, Joseph Grimaldi and the Pantomime of Life
Jonathan Buckmaster

Italian Politics and Nineteenth-Century British Literature and Culture
Patricia Cove

Cultural Encounters with the Arabian Nights in Nineteenth-Century Britain
Melissa Dickson

Novel Institutions: Anachronism, Irish Novels and Nineteenth-Century Realism
Mary L. Mullen

The Fin-de-Siècle Scottish Revival: Romance, Decadence and Celtic Identity
Michael Shaw

Contested Liberalisms: Martineau, Dickens and the Victorian Press
Iain Crawford

Plotting Disability in the Nineteenth-Century Novel
Clare Walker Gore

The Aesthetics of Space in Nineteenth-Century British Literature, 1843–mc1907
Giles Whiteley

The Persian Presence in Victorian Poetry
Reza Taher-Kermani

Rereading Orphanhood: Texts, Inheritance, Kin
Diane Warren and Laura Peters

Plotting the News in the Victorian Novel
Jessica R. Valdez

Reading Ideas in Victorian Literature: Literary Content as Artistic Experience
Patrick Fessenbecker

Home and Identity in Nineteenth-Century Literary London
Lisa Robertson

Forthcoming volumes:
Her Father's Name: Gender, Theatricality and Spiritualism in Florence Marryat's Fiction
Tatiana Kontou

The Sculptural Body in Victorian Literature: Encrypted Sexualities
Patricia Pulham

Olive Schreiner and the Politics of Print Culture, 1883–1920
Clare Gill

Victorian Auto/Biography: Problems in Genre and Subject
Amber Regis

Gissing, Shakespeare and the Life of Writing
Thomas Ue

Women's Mobility in Henry James
Anna Despotopoulou

Michael Field's Revisionary Poetics
Jill Ehnenn

The Americanisation of W.T. Stead
Helena Goodwyn

Literary Illusions: Performance Magic and Victorian Literature
Christopher Pittard

Pastoral in Early-Victorian Fiction: Environment and Modernity
Mark Frost

Edmund Yates and Victorian Periodicals: Gossip, Celebrity, and Gendered Spaces
Kathryn Ledbetter

Literature, Architecture and Perversion: Building Sexual Culture in Europe, 1850–1930
Aina Marti

Oscar Wilde and the Radical Politics of the Fin de Siècle
Deaglán Ó Donghaile

Manufacturing Female Beauty in British Literature and Periodicals, 1850–1914
Michelle Smith

New Media and the Rise of the Popular Woman Writer, 1820–60
Alexis Easley

For a complete list of titles published visit the Edinburgh Critical Studies in Victorian Culture web page at www.edinburghuniversitypress.com/series/ECVC

Also available:
Victoriographies – A Journal of Nineteenth-Century Writing, 1790–1914, edited by Diane Piccitto and Patricia Pulham
ISSN: 2044-2416
www.eupjournals.com/vic

Home and Identity in Nineteenth-Century Literary London

Lisa C. Robertson

EDINBURGH
University Press

Edinburgh University Press is one of the leading university presses in the UK. We publish academic books and journals in our selected subject areas across the humanities and social sciences, combining cutting-edge scholarship with high editorial and production values to produce academic works of lasting importance. For more information visit our website: edinburghuniversitypress.com

© Lisa C. Robertson, 2020, 2022

Edinburgh University Press Ltd
The Tun – Holyrood Road, 12(2f) Jackson's Entry, Edinburgh EH8 8PJ

First published in hardback by Edinburgh University Press 2020

Typeset in 11/13 Adobe Sabon by
IDSUK (DataConnection) Ltd

A CIP record for this book is available from the British Library

ISBN 978 1 4744 5788 0 (hardback)
ISBN 978 1 4744 5789 7 (paperback)
ISBN 978 1 4744 5790 3 (webready PDF)
ISBN 978 1 4744 5791 0 (epub)

The right of Lisa C. Robertson to be identifiedastheauthorofthisworkhasbeen asserted in accordance with the Copyright, Designs and Patents Act 1988, and the Copyright and Related Rights Regulations 2003 (SI No. 2498).

Contents

List of Illustrations vii
Series Editor's Preface ix
Acknowledgements xi

1. Housing Crisis: Home and Identity in Nineteenth-Century Literary London 1

Part I: Structures of Authority: The Model Dwellings Movement

2. 'Out of its torpid misery': Plotting Passivity in Margaret Harkness's *A City Girl* 19

3. 'More making the best of it': Living with Liberalism in Mary Ward's *Marcella* 36

4. Labour Leaders and Socialist Saviours: Individualism and Collectivism in Margaret Harkness's *George Eastmont, Wanderer* 55

Part II: Chambers, Lodgings and Flats: Purpose-built Housing for Working Women

5. Irritating Rules and Oppressive Officials: Convention and Innovation in Evelyn Sharp's *The Making of a Prig* 75

6. The Kailyard Comes to London: The Progressive Potential of Romantic Convention in Annie S. Swan's *A Victory Won* 95

7. Fugitive Living: Social Mobility and Domestic Space in Julia Frankau's *The Heart of a Child* 111

Part III: 'Thinking Men' and Thinking Women: Gender, Sexuality and Settlement Housing

8. 'Vital friendship': Sexual and Economic Ambivalence in Rhoda Broughton's *Dear Faustina*   133

9. 'Twenty girls in my attic': Spatial and Spiritual Conversion in L. T. Meade's *A Princess of the Gutter*   154

Part IV: Homes for a New Era: London Housing Past and Present

10. 'To make a garden of the town': The Nineteenth-Century Legacy of the Hampstead Garden Suburb   175

Epilogue   192

Bibliography   196
Index   211

List of Illustrations

2.1 Katharine Buildings, Cartwright Street, front elevation. Designed by Davis & Emmanuel for the East End Dwellings Company (built 1884; photograph 1970). Image courtesy of London Metropolitan Archives (City of London). 22

2.2 Katharine Buildings, Cartwright Street, rear elevation. Designed by Davis & Emmanuel for the East End Dwellings Company (built 1884; photograph 1970). Image courtesy of London Metropolitan Archives (City of London). 25

3.1 Passmore Edwards Settlement, C. C. Brewer and A. Dunbar-Smith (1895). Illustration from *Academy Architecture and Architectural Review*, 9 (1896), p. 29. Digital image courtesy of Getty Research Institute, Los Angeles (84-S1354). 50

4.1 Architect's drawing of the Artizans' Buildings (or Corporation Buildings), Petticoat Square. Designed by William Haywood for the City of London Corporation (1885). Illustration from *The Builder*, 26 September 1865, pp. 425–6. Digital image courtesy of the Getty Research Institute, Los Angeles (85-S815). 61

5.1 North-west elevation, Chenies Street Chambers. Designed by J. M. Brydon for the Ladies' Residential Dwellings Corporation (1887). Illustration from *Scribner's*, 2 (July–December 1887), p. 601. Digital Image Courtesy of Cornell University Library Collections. 87

5.2 Interior entranceway, Chenies Street Chambers. Designed by J. M. Brydon for the Ladies' Residential Dwellings Corporation (1887). Illustration from *Scribner's*, 2 (July–December 1887), p. 601. Digital Image Courtesy of Cornell University Library Collections. 88

7.1 'Soho Club & Home for Working Girls', advertisement from *The Story of Old Soho* (London: T. Pettit & Co., 1893), p. 26. © British Library Board, General Reference Collection 10349.ff.35.   118

7.2 Front elevation, Artillery Mansions, Victoria Street, Westminster. Designed by John Calder (built 1895; photograph 1971). Image courtesy of London Metropolitan Archives (City of London).   121

8.1 Physical drill at Lees Hall, Canning Town Women's Settlement. Photograph from George R. Sims (ed.), *Living London*, vol. 2 (London: Cassell, 1902), p. 269. Digital image courtesy of the John M. Kelly Library, University of Toronto.   144

10.1 Waterlow Court, Hampstead Garden Suburb. Designed by M. H. Baillie Scott (1909). Photograph by Eric de Maré, 1960. Image courtesy of the Architectural Association Photograph Library.   181

Series Editor's Preface

'Victorian' is a term, at once indicative of a strongly determined concept and an often notoriously vague notion, emptied of all meaningful content by the many journalistic misconceptions that persist about the inhabitants and cultures of the British Isles and Victoria's Empire in the nineteenth century. As such, it has become a by-word for the assumption of various, often contradictory habits of thought, belief, behaviour and perceptions. Victorian studies and studies in nineteenth-century literature and culture have, from their institutional inception, questioned narrowness of presumption, pushed at the limits of the nominal definition, and have sought to question the very grounds on which the unreflective perception of the so-called Victorian has been built; and so they continue to do. Victorian and nineteenth-century studies of literature and culture maintain a breadth and diversity of interest, of focus and inquiry, in an interrogative and intellectually open-minded and challenging manner, which are equal to the exploration and inquisitiveness of its subjects. Many of the questions asked by scholars and researchers of the innumerable productions of nineteenth-century society actively put into suspension the clichés and stereotypes of 'Victorianism', whether the approach has been sustained by historical, scientific, philosophical, empirical, ideological or theoretical concerns; indeed, it would be incorrect to assume that each of these approaches to the idea of the Victorian has been, or has remained, in the main exclusive, sealed off from the interests and engagements of other approaches. A vital interdisciplinarity has been pursued and embraced, for the most part, even as there has been contest and debate among Victorianists, pursued with as much fervour as the affirmative exploration between different disciplines and differing epistemologies put to work in the service of reading the nineteenth century.

Edinburgh Critical Studies in Victorian Culture aims to take up both the debates and the inventive approaches and departures from convention that studies in the nineteenth century have witnessed for the last half century at least. Aiming to maintain a 'Victorian' (in the most positive sense of that motif) spirit of inquiry, the series' purpose is to continue and augment the cross-fertilisation of interdisciplinary approaches, and to offer, in addition, a number of timely and untimely revisions of Victorian literature, culture, history and identity. At the same time, the series will ask questions concerning what has been missed or improperly received, misread, or not read at all, in order to present a multi-faceted and heterogeneous kaleidoscope of representations. Drawing on the most provocative, thoughtful and original research, the series will seek to prod at the notion of the 'Victorian', and in so doing, principally through theoretically and epistemologically sophisticated close readings of the historicity of literature and culture in the nineteenth century, to offer the reader provocative insights into a world that is at once overly familiar, and irreducibly different, other and strange. Working from original sources, primary documents and recent interdisciplinary theoretical models, Edinburgh Critical Studies in Victorian Culture seeks not simply to push at the boundaries of research in the nineteenth century, but also to inaugurate the persistent erasure and provisional, strategic redrawing of those borders.

Julian Wolfreys

Acknowledgements

The research for this project, which is based on a doctoral thesis, was made possible by the award of a Chancellor's International Scholarship from the University of Warwick. I am grateful for the support of the Department of English and Comparative Literary Studies at the University of Warwick, and in particular Emma Francis, who supervised my research. I am also indebted to Laura Schwartz and Nadia Valman for their encouraging and structured feedback on an earlier version of this project. The earliest stages of research benefited from the involvement of Lawrence Phillips, Lorna Jowett and Janet Wilson; I also owe particular thanks to Ruth Livesey and Mary Elizabeth Leighton, whose support at a critical stage of this project was decisive in its continuation. I also wish to express my gratitude to the Society of Architectural Historians of Great Britain for their generous support. The kind assistance and perennial patience of librarians at Senate House Library, the Bodleian Library, the British Library, the London Metropolitan Archives, and the Architectural Association Photo Library and Archive was crucial in the processes of locating a number of obscure editions and illustrations.

While this project was typed in the collective solitude of various libraries, it was written in the course of discussion and debate with friends and colleagues. I owe particular thanks to Emily Gee, of English Heritage, who replied to my tentative enquiry about women's residences with enthusiasm and uncommon kindness. Both the Literary London Reading Group and the Literary London Society have, for many years, fostered an environment of informed but informal discussion, and for this I am grateful to Jenny Bavidge, Martin Dines, Nick Bentley, Richard Dennis, Matthew Ingleby, Lara Atkin, Michael McCluskey, Luke Seaber – and especially Eliza Cubitt and Peter Jones. I am also grateful to Flore Janssen, Terry Elkiss and Deborah Mutch, whose collaborations on a number of projects related to Margaret Harkness have been invigorating and productive. My thanks also to Helena Goodwyn, Terri Mullholland, Lisa Mullen,

Helen Goodman, Ryan Powell, Tim Bell and Sarah Knor for illuminating discussions in cities around the globe, and at all times of day (and night); and also to Sara Lyons and Noah Moxham, for many years of intellectual support and engagement, as well as innumerable excellent meals and much general amity.

My thanks also to Stephanie Bannister, Eliza Cubitt, Terry Elkiss, Flore Janssen, Sara Lyons, Lisa Mullen and Terri Mullholland for their comments on the final draft of this book. I am immensely grateful to Michelle Houston, Ersev Ersoy and Julian Wolfreys at Edinburgh University Press for their interest and support of this project through all of its stages, as well as to the anonymous readers who provided important comments and insights on the manuscript.

My greatest debt is to my grandmother, D. Sylvia Stephenson, who insisted that any book with a child in it was suitable for children – and thus encumbered me with much of Dickens at a young age. While my interest in literature was established by the collections of nineteenth-century authors in her library, it was her own stories of life in London – and elsewhere, through two world wars – that captivated me most. This book is for her, with my eternal gratitude and admiration.

Chapter 1

Housing Crisis: Home and Identity in Nineteenth-Century Literary London

London's spectacular growth over the course of the nineteenth century produced an urgent problem: how people might live together, efficiently and harmoniously, in a congested urban environment? This problem, however, also presented an opportunity for architectural and literary innovation. By the turn of the twentieth century, new models of housing spanned the city's districts, from the open spaces of Hampstead Heath to those of Peckham Rye, and extended to all facets of society: workers' hostels offered affordable shelter for itinerant labourers; model dwellings companies provided improved housing for the working classes and workers' cottages for the upwardly mobile artisan classes; suburban expansion made available low-density neighbourhoods and individual gardens to the burgeoning middle classes; and in the city centre, apartment buildings provided accommodation for a metropolitan demographic diverse enough to include both thespians and parliamentarians. Yet the task of reinventing domestic space was not restricted to architects and urban planners: philanthropists, politicians, novelists, dramatists and pundits all turned their attention to reconceptualising the ways that people might live together in the city.

This book examines the relationship between literary representation and new forms of urban domestic architecture in London between 1880 and 1920. In principle, it is concerned with mapping rhetorical shifts on to the reimagining of household practice and the physical reconceptualisation of domestic space during this period. It treats architectural and literary forms as texts that both require exegesis, the rendition of which reveals the interconnectedness of material and ideological realms. The four decades around the turn of the twentieth century were a period in which there existed a comprehensive social effort to design domestic buildings that diverged from the conventional household model, which based its spatial organisation on the nuclear family unit. As Caroline Morrell explains, the Census Report of 1871 stated that 'the natural family is founded by marriage, and consists, in its complete state of husband, wife and children'.[1] Yet during the late nineteenth century, public interest and critical opinion were attentive to the growing diversification of domestic relationships in urban centres. A variety of models of housing that emerged in the latter half of the nineteenth century addressed this diversification, including the four that are the focus of this book: model dwellings, women's residences, settlement housing and the garden city.

Writing Identity

The architectural innovations that produced new models of domestic space were responses to a range of social and political changes in the city, but so too did each new space provoke shifts in the material experience and ideological imaginings of home. Close examination of such dynamics reveals that the relationship between material and ideological space is not unidirectional nor deterministic, but is instead is complex, shifting and mutually effective. This process has been mostly clearly articulated by Daphne Spain, who in *Gendered Spaces* (1992) refers to the 'mutual reinforcement of [spatial] processes', and Doreen Massey, who proposes that space and social relations are 'mutually constitutive'; that, to quote Massey, material space 'effects and has effects back' on the construction of social and political ideologies.[2] Both Spain and Massey have found this materialist approach productive when considering the complex nature of identity, and gender identity in particular. While the built environment – a phrase that this book uses to refer to all non-organically produced social and cultural spaces – represents and reinforces status differences based on identity, domestic architecture is especially generative for examining the dynamic shift in conventional ideologies of gender, sexuality and class that occurred at the end of the nineteenth century. Housing is, as the work of Alice T. Friedman and Annmarie Adams demonstrates, a highly charged site of personal identity, and one that articulates the dynamics of intimate relationships.[3] Housing necessarily engages with the normative values of social and political thought; this is not to say, however, that it must always capitulate to them.

Critical attention to the relationship between material and ideological space has proliferated since the publication of Henri Lefebvre's *La Production de l'espace* (1974; translated into English in 1991), but nineteenth-century critics were themselves cognisant of the multivalent effects and dimensions of the built environment. John Ruskin is perhaps the best-known figure to have called attention to the relationship between material and psychic space, and as he explains, '[a]ll architecture proposes an effect on the human mind, not merely a service to the human frame'.[4] What effects, then, did new designs for urban housing have on the subjectivities of inhabitants of late nineteenth-century London? An important task of the following chapters is to examine how new and often radical designs for nineteenth-century housing are represented in the period's literature, but also to consider how these representations shifted consciousness and social practice. Such an investigation reveals how housing, rather than providing a stable or consistent framework for shifting concepts of identity and changing social practices, engages with their very formation. Emily Cuming's valuable study *Housing, Class and Gender in Modern British Writing, 1880–2012* reveals how categories of identity – including class, gender, sexuality and race – are regularly forged in relation to access to resources such as housing.[5] Any examination of identity therefore demands attentiveness to the complexity of its intersecting categories, the nature of which produces different and regularly unequal access to forms of social power.

A range of literary representations of new forms of urban housing feature in this book, both fiction and non-fiction, but each chapter foregrounds a novel in which the relationship between gender and housing, in particular, is a central concern. The sustained focused on gender is deliberate, as one of the objectives of this book is to define ways to understand women's imaginative and material contributions to the construction of the city. The methods of intersectional feminism reveal the ways in which concepts of identity involve deeply imbricated social categories that cannot be teased apart, and must be examined collectively. In this sense, any consideration of a social category such as gender must also be attentive to divisions of, for instance, race, class, sexuality, ability and ethnicity. As an analytical tool, intersectionality aims to foreground complexity – and while the intersection of gender alongside class and sexuality comes into focus in this book, other aspects of identity remain on the periphery. This is not, to be sure, an indication of their insignificance. An examination of the ways in which nineteenth-century racialised thinking shaped the design and construction of new forms of urban housing – and literary responses to these spaces – is a project that demands careful investigation. It is, however, also a project that in its complexity requires more nuanced consideration than is possible within the parameters of the current study. *Home and Identity in Nineteenth-Century Literary London,* in this sense, does not aim to exhaust discussions of the multivalent relationships between identity and domestic forms during the nineteenth century, but rather to indicate ways by which the complex nature of relationships between material and ideological spaces can offer important insight into the processes of social change.[6]

Writing Cities

The development of feminist criticism in the latter decades of the twentieth century stimulated considerations of the ways in which women have been historically denied participation in the production of urban environments, both through professional exclusion and social marginalisation. Building on work by cultural historians such as Elizabeth Wilson, who suggests that during the nineteenth century, 'women's very presence in cities [was] a problem' as their existence outside the home 'overturned a symbolic natural order', architectural historians such as Sarah Deutsch and Jessica Ellen Sewell reveal how women, in Sewell's words, 'negotiat[ed] the gaps between the urban landscape as it was built and as it was imagined to be'.[7] The transgressive nature of women's very presence in the city was also established by cultural historians such as Judith Walkowitz and literary scholars such as Deborah Epstein Nord, whose *Walking the Victorian Streets* (1995) marked the advent of a series of investigations into the intricate relationship between gender, urban space and literary representation that has endured in the nearly twenty-five years since its publication.[8] These studies are indispensable for their attention to the diverse and creative ways that women have historically learned to navigate the urban spaces in which they are not privileged subjects.

What remains to be examined in greater detail are women's active contributions to the production of the built environment, both imaginatively and materially.[9] That these contributions have historically been obscure is not to say, of course, that they have been absent. Elizabeth Darling and Lesley Whitworth's *Women and the Making of Built Space in England, 1870–1950* (2007) is one study that effectively re-evaluates women's active historical contributions to the production of the built environment. The essays in this collection recognise that many women were instrumental in professional positions that affected the design and management of cities and housing; women who were historically dismissed as amateurs, and whose activities were often derided as commonplace, have here made their way to the forefront of debate about the production of urban space. *Home and Identity* similarly works to establish women's historical role as contributors to the urban environment, but takes – first and foremost – literature for the subject of its analysis in order to concentrate on new architectural forms of domestic space, and the ways in which representations of these spaces contribute to the reformulation of conventional categories of identity.

Writing Housing

Architectural experimentation was necessary to accommodate London's population, which increased in size and diversity in the final decades of the nineteenth century. These experimental new designs for housing, although atypical, were conspicuous on account of their novelty and influential owing to their presence in the most populous areas of London. As a result, these new domestic spaces appear with relative frequency in the period's literature and pose a distinct challenge to the cultural centrality of the middle-class family home. This book highlights four new architectural forms that took shape in the latter half of the nineteenth century as exemplary of such shifts in domestic space: model dwellings, women's residences, settlement housing and garden cities. Each example of these individual types that this book considers was purpose-built and different in physical properties and dimensions to the conventional family home, which was designed for the 'natural family' as outlined by the Census Report of 1871. Although such conventional family homes did not always house nuclear families – which themselves may have included extended members or servants – the buildings themselves were nevertheless ordered around the family unit, whether country house, cottage, city terrace or back-to-back.

The new architectural forms of domestic space that this book examines were each designed as deliberate alternatives to conventional housing, and for this reason these buildings differ structurally and spatially. Model dwellings, while designed to accommodate some families, also included communal facilities and were structured as aggregate domestic space. The nature of poverty meant that a single-room dwelling might accommodate an extended family, or a two-room flat might be shared by several independent lodgers. This was in part made possible by the flexible space provided by many of these model dwellings, which often included between one and three rooms in addition to a scullery. Women's residences accommodated single women, and this was therefore a domestic model designed along the lines of gender segregation; and depending on the economic position of the resident, they might be single or shared occupancy (described in the period as co-flatting). Settlement housing was also most often gender-segregated, and as a model of communal living it drew influence from monastic and collegiate residential design. Garden cities incorporated aspects of earlier experiments in urban housing into a comprehensive civic pattern, but did so with the purpose of eschewing the less salubrious aspects of urban centres. Each model of housing, therefore, offers a new structural model of domestic space. For this reason *Home and Identity* does not engage with adapted residential structures such as boarding houses, nor does it consider the institutional spaces that Jane Hamlett so productively examines in *At Home in the Institution* (2016). While institutional homes such as schools or hospitals provided alternative domestic spaces to the family home, the impetus for their design and construction was different to the new forms of architecture that this book examines.

The new forms of housing that this book highlights have received limited attention in historical or architectural scholarship. A developing interest in nineteenth-century socialist history and labour politics during the post-war period and into the 1960s resulted in several studies of working-class housing, such as John Nelson Tarn's *Working-class Housing in 19th-Century Britain* (1971) and *Five Per Cent Philanthropy* (1974). Tarn's work remains unrivalled in its attention to architectural detail and analysis of the social and political conditions that gave rise to these new forms of housing.[10] There have been equally few architectural studies of the settlement movement and its housing. Deborah Weiner's groundbreaking *Architecture and Social Reform in Late Victorian Britain* (1994) makes important observations about the architecture of both Toynbee Hall and the Passmore Edwards Settlement, but there has been no attempt by scholars since its publication over twenty years ago to delve deeper into the important material that Weiner unearthed.[11] The form of housing that has received the least attention is women's residences. Although brief discussions of these buildings appear in Martha Vicinus's *Independent Women* (1985) and Annmarie Adams's *Architecture in the Family*

Way (1996), Emily Gee's research offers the only sustained architectural examination of these buildings over the roughly forty-year period when they were most popular.[12] And while the garden cities movement has long been of interest to architectural historians, there is little work that considers its representation in literature, particularly with respect to its nineteenth-century origins.

This book examines these new forms of housing – model dwellings, women's residences, settlement housing and garden cities – as an architectural sequence, rather than as discrete experiments. This sequence is one that offers continuity across the city's perceived geographic and economic boundaries. Although 'housing' and 'home' are both used throughout this book, the former term appears more regularly, as it emphasises the collective and relational status of the structures at the centre of its investigation. In public discourse, 'housing' is, as Cuming points out, regularly used as an abstract term to denote the obverse of 'self-identity, affect, and comfortable seclusion', concepts that seem bound to notions of home. Yet its semantic complexity as both noun and verb also indicates 'complex issues of agency and power'.[13] While 'home' as a place of habitation is regularly discussed in relation to the formation of individual identity, particularly in recent years by way of domestic material culture, *Home and Identity* focuses on the connections and dislocations between individuals, buildings and communities – a relational system that Alison Blunt and Oliva Sheringham describe as one of multiple scales – in order to interrogate how these scales are related to categories of social power.[14]

In *Architecture and the Modernism of Private Life* (2008), Victoria Rosner proposes that literary texts articulate the values and social hierarchies encoded in the domestic spaces in which they take place.[15] Literature plays an important role, Rosner points out, in 'imagining a [. . .] reorganization of private life to accord with changing social customs'.[16] The examination of new forms of urban housing presented in this book confirms Rosner's claim, but equally reveals that such a 'reorganisation of private life' is not restricted to the twentieth century. Rosner asserts that during the era of modernism, private life became dominated by disorder, which was a response to the altogether too orderly systems of the Victorian home. The 'peace and stability of the Victorian household deteriorated', she suggests, 'deformed by the pressure of changing social, sexual, and cultural mores. What took its place was a far more provisional, more embodied, more unstructured kind of private life – the kind of life we still call "modern".'[17] The new forms of housing that this book foregrounds suggest that the 'metamorphosis' Rosner describes was underway by at least the middle of the nineteenth century, a period antecedent to that which she describes as 'modern'.[18]

The purpose of this book's examination of new domestic spaces in the context of this project is not, however, to stage a historical argument about the point at which domesticity became recognisable by modern standards; and certainly, the rethinking of domestic space in response to changing social customs is not a phenomenon unique to one era. Instead, it offers an examination of new architectural forms that is grounded in the relationship between text and context. It is not a historical study, but aims to unpick the ways in which cultural context is related to language and language use – and interrogate how the forms of language and architecture become methods by which social divisions based on identity are both reified and challenged. This book reveals how the specific social and political circumstances of the late nineteenth century provoked a reconsideration of domestic space and corresponding shifts in social beliefs and practices, but it does so in order to suggest a methodology by which other historical periods and their artefacts, both architectural and literary, can be reinterpreted. Oddly, for a study that purports to examine architecture, Rosner suggests that '[i]t was interior design – and not architecture – that articulated a visual and spatial vocabulary describing the changing nature of private life'.[19] A range of nineteenth-century literary responses to the changing nature of domestic life reveals the ways in which such shifts are legible in the period's emergent architectural forms.

Home and Identity gives priority to literary representations of new models of domestic space, and as a result important figures in the history of London's housing such as Octavia Hill and Beatrice Webb are treated as ancillary. Yet these individuals – and others – loom on the margins to inform this book's evaluation of the ways in which philanthropic and political discourses shaped the design and construction of domestic space. In its concentration on fiction, this book aims to bring into focus the ways in which imaginative writing participates in the discursive process of producing the ideological and material spaces of home. Matthew Taunton refers to the creative experiments of writers as 'fictions of the city', narratives that 'frequently contain projections about the ways in which that city could be improved or perfected, or go to wrack. In this regard novels [. . .] about urban life form a continuum with treatises on urban planning, architectural manifestoes and social reform tracts.'[20] This continuum of discourse on urban practices that Taunton describes is particularly apposite in an examination of the late nineteenth century, as it was only in the last twenty years of the century that the professions we now associate with the material production of urban space – architects and urban planners – came to be regulated by professional bodies and, consequently, to be defined as the professions we understand them to be today. Taunton's exploration of mass housing in two nineteenth-century cities, Paris and London, demonstrates how fiction is a form of culture that participates in the discursive construction of domestic space. Yet this argument can be developed further still, in an examination of the relationship between discursive and material practice. Jane Rendell's work on site-writing is immensely useful in this sense: we might ask not how we write *about* housing, but how we write housing, and in so doing perform important critical and political interventions into urban space.[21] This book, then, is an investigation into the ways in which nineteenth-century novels build houses.

Representing Crisis

The emergence of slum fiction and investigative journalism in the latter half of the century – given impetus by the 'Condition of England' novel, which reached its peak at mid-century – represents housing crisis in its depiction of insanitary homes and the condition of abject poverty. Yet this material reality also caused a crisis of representation: novels written during this period represent urban housing, but are simultaneously preoccupied with the extent to which representation can capture lived experience. This representational difficulty is made more complex by the novel's attempt to grapple with the dislocations that emerge from the genre as a predominantly middle-class form, but one that attempts to represent spaces that diverge from the image and experience of conventional middle-class domesticity. The formal challenges that arise from the attempt to render these spaces legible to largely middle-class audiences are evident not only in the representation of urban slums or working-class housing, but in other representations of domestic spaces that depart from the conventional family home.

This book identifies a range of novels that present to the reader evidence of such representational difficulties in their depiction of unfamiliar models of housing and unconventional domestic relationships. Although the representation of these new spaces and social relations is varied in its treatment across these novels, what is common to all texts – albeit in different ways – are formal dislocations that emerge in the rendition of these spaces. In some instances, such as L. T. Meade's *A Princess of the Gutter* (1895), these disruptions emerge in the representation of characters and ambiguous romantic relationships; in others, such as Margaret Harkness's *A City Girl* (1887) or Evelyn Sharp's *The Making of a Prig* (1897), formal dislocations are evident in the narrative trajectory; and in novels such as Rhoda Broughton's *Dear Faustina* (1897), disruptions are present in the manner of omissions that exist in the very language of the novel itself. There are many novels, such as Margaret Harkness's *George Eastmont, Wanderer* (1905), in which a number of representational difficulties are evident in both form and content; there are others, such as Annie S. Swan's *A Victory Won* (1895), which more comfortably align with the generic conventions of the nineteenth-century novel. *Home and Identity* elucidates these disruptions in its analysis and explores the ways in which they coincide with a historical period that manifested new architectural forms that challenged the paradigm of the middle-class family home. If femininity itself is a product of domestic ideology as represented in fiction, as Nancy Armstrong suggests, then this book makes a related claim: that the omissions or aberrations that emerge from representational challenges in these novels are textual spaces that allow for the emergence of new identities and paradigms of thought.[22] These novels engage with new experiences and architectural forms, and in so doing open up novelistic space in which new possibilities for representation emerge.

This book has three related aims: first, to examine the ways in which the literary representation of new urban housing reveals formal dislocations in the late nineteenth-century novel; second, to interpret the process by which the articulation of these textual spaces produces new psychic structures that, in turn, affect the material environment; and third, to suggest how these textual spaces allow the emergence of new definitions of home and identity. The first part of this book offers a consideration of the nineteenth-century political and legislative developments that initiated slum clearance and city improvement projects, and that led to the construction of model dwellings and early local authority housing. Chapter 1 investigates the origins of the model dwellings movement and elucidates its social, political and architectural significance by focusing on Margaret Harkness's novel *A City Girl* and its representation of life in a block of model dwellings in London's East End. Chapter 2 examines the ways that Mary Ward's novel *Marcella* (1895) engages with model dwellings to present readers with an exercise in nineteenth-century liberal thought. Chapter 3 offers an analysis of the ideological tensions between individualism and collectivism in Margaret Harkness's *George Eastmont, Wanderer* – and particularly the development of the socialist and labour movements – alongside which the model dwellings movement emerged.

The second part traces the origins of purpose-built housing for women and considers its treatment in contemporaneous novels and journalism. Increasing opportunities for education and employment in the latter half of the nineteenth century encouraged many women to move to London with the aim of establishing an independent livelihood. There was, however, a dearth of respectable accommodation for middle-class women who were seeking clerical and professional positions. Chapter 4 examines the origins and development of middle-class women's residences, also known during the period as ladies' chambers, and focuses on Evelyn Sharp's *The Making of a Prig* in order to demonstrate the representational conflicts associated with women's housing both in the novel and in society more generally. While *The Making of a Prig* makes use of the discourses of realism in order to unpick the complex and often compromised social position of independent working women, Annie S. Swan's *A Victory Won*, which is the focus of Chapter 5, engages with the sentimental traditions of the Kailyard school of fiction in order to foreground the progressive and mutually supportive relationships between women that ladies' chambers could also foster. Chapter 6 shifts its focus to examine residential buildings for working-class women, most often known as 'girls' clubs' or 'women's hostels'. It focuses specifically on Julia Frankau's *The Heart of a Child* (1908), a form of *bildungsroman* that follows a woman who moves from an East End slum, to a room in a girls' club, and finally to her own flat in a block of residential mansions. This chapter argues that these new forms of housing were a response to changing social and material factors, but also served to destabilise conventional gender ideologies and broaden dominant notions of domesticity.

The third part of this book examines how the settlement movement challenged conventional notions of home and labour by studying its representation in two novels that construct these concerns within discussions of sexuality. Chapter 7 considers the ways in which Rhoda Broughton's *Dear Faustina* intervenes in debates about new forms of urban housing, including settlement housing, to indicate how shifts in domestic design and practice reveal the relationship between economic and sexual power. Chapter 8 examines the ways in which L. T. Meade's *A Princess of the Gutter* suggests that settlement housing had the capacity to reinvigorate religious belief in a period when urban poverty – and the processes of looking at and writing about this poverty – threatened religious conviction and commitment. The chapter argues that although each novel differs in its representation of the settlement movement and its housing, each text gives expression to the ways in which new social and spatial arrangements brought into question the nature of women's relationships with community and with each other.

The final part of this book examines the garden cities movement as a realised utopian response to the nineteenth-century housing crisis, both in terms of a reassessment of domestic space but also in the context of broader revisions to urban planning. Chapter 10 investigates the development of Hampstead Garden Suburb through the language of Mary Gabrielle Collins's *Garden Suburb Verses* (1913), and the ways in which its design synthesised the experimental housing forms of the nineteenth century into a comprehensive city plan. It focuses especially on the residential buildings in Hampstead Garden Suburb that offered alternative models of domestic space to conventional family households, to reveal how the garden city model engaged with radical nineteenth-century housing but integrated these projects into both landscape and community. The Epilogue revisits key themes and ideas unearthed over the course of the book to suggest how nineteenth-century representations of new forms of domestic space might provide imaginative resources to address the housing crisis that London faces in the twenty-first century.

Writing London's Housing Crisis

Today, it is clear that we have not solved the nineteenth century's housing crisis, nor have we moved beyond the concerns of its authors and activists. London's current housing crisis, as David Kroll explains, 'has already taught us we are not above repeating failures of previous generations and could probably learn from their successes'.[23] There are rhetorical consonances that unite the nineteenth-century housing crisis with that which London faces today: overcrowding, immigration, slum landlordism, as well as the quality and safety of social housing, are all subjects that continue to shape discussion. Whereas nineteenth-century housing debate regularly focused on social need, discussion today is most often fixated on commodity value. This is an interpretation reinforced across popular and political culture:

from television programmes that glamorise the housing market and ennoble those who are affluent enough to engage with it, to the introduction of the 'help-to-buy' programme in 2013 – a partial retronym of and intentional allusion to the controversial right-to-buy scheme introduced in the 1980s – which presupposes that widespread home ownership somehow engenders a more equitable society.

To establish such consistencies across the social and political problems of different eras also offers valuable resources at a moment when the value of historicism is being debated and revalued in the disciplines of English Literature and Cultural Studies. As Martin Hewitt has suggested, historicist studies do not merely attribute textual interpretation to context but instead treat history as a canvas that requires a 'three-dimensional approach' to a text; that is, meaning and interpretation extends beyond its own formal structures. Equally important, Hewitt suggests, is that these narratives provide 'resources for action' both at the moment of their creation and the instance of their deployment.[24] This book does not use a historical narrative of London's housing crisis in order to suggest a particular ideological interpretation of the present. It does, however, wish to call attention to the consonances and dissonances between the nineteenth-century housing crisis and that which London faces in the twenty-first century – a subject that the Epilogue of this book revisits. The novels examined here, active in their own engagement with contemporary attempts to grapple with London's housing crisis, remain relevant today and offer readers new resources in thinking through the ways in which reconceptualising domestic space specifically in relation to social need rather than market value offers opportunities for civic progress. In doing so, each novel offers a new foundation and impetus for historical and present-day debate.

Notes

1. Cited in Morrell, 'Housing and the Women's Movement 1860–1914', unpublished thesis, pp. 31–2. This definition, as Morrell acknowledges, is narrow, as it 'excludes members of the extended family or other people not related by blood or marriage, it also overlooks the changing and differing nature of "family" relationships'. Nevertheless, this narrow definition became a mean against which alternative models were measured and judged. For a more thorough discussion of the relationship between dominant concepts of family, home and household during this period, see ibid. pp. 26–45.
2. Spain, *Gendered Spaces*, p. 79; Massey, *Space, Place, Gender*, p. 225.

3. Friedman, *Women and the Making of the Modern House*; Adams, *Architecture in the Family Way*.
4. Ruskin, *The Seven Lamps of Architecture*, p. 8.
5. Cuming, *Housing, Class and Gender in Modern British Writing*, p. 16.
6. One indication of the form such investigations might take shape can be found in Terri Mullholland's examination of the ways in which the space of the boarding house in the twentieth century served as a site that was 'complicated by negotiations of race and nationality' (*British Boarding Houses in Interwar Women's Literature*, p. 17). See ibid. pp. 118–50.
7. Wilson, *The Sphinx in the City*, pp. 5, 33; Sewell, *Women and the Everyday City*, p. xiii. See also Deutsch, *Women and the City*.
8. Walkowitz, *City of Dreadful Delight*; Nord, *Walking the Victorian Streets*. See also Parsons, *Streetwalking the Metropolis*; Liggins, *George Gissing, the Working Woman, and British Culture*; and Parkins, *Mobility and Modernity in Women's Novels*.
9. See, for example, Matrix Feminist Design Cooperative, *Making Space: Women and the Manmade*, which was one of the earliest interventions into the ways that cities are gendered. Elizabeth Grosz has explored the ways in which cities produce gendered and sexualised bodies in essays such as 'Bodies – Cities'. Subsequently two other anthologies brought together scholars across disciplines to address the complexities of gendered identity in urban and non-urban spaces. See Coleman, Danze and Henderson (eds), *Architecture and Feminism*; Bordain, Penner and Rendell (eds), *Gender Space Architecture*.
10. The most crucial text here is Thompson, *The Making of the English Working Class*. Another important study that built on Thompson's work is Stedman Jones, *Outcast London*. This interest also inspired research on urban poverty and the slum. See, for instance, Wohl, *The Eternal Slum*. This concern was also visible in literary studies, albeit slightly later. See Ingle, *Socialist Thought in Imaginative Literature*, and Klaus (ed.), *The Rise of Socialist Fiction*.
11. Weiner, *Architecture and Social Reform in Late-Victorian Britain*. There have been two notable studies dedicated exclusively to the history of the settlement movement in the UK to date: Beauman, *Women and the Settlement Movement*, and Scotland, *Squires in the Slums*. Lucinda Matthews Jones is currently preparing a monograph entitled *Settling: Domesticity, Class and Urban Philanthropy in the British University Settlement Movement*.
12. Vicinus, *Independent Women*, pp. 295–9; Adams, *Architecture in the Family Way*, pp. 153–9; Gee, '"Where Shall She Live?"', unpublished thesis. Ladies' chambers receive comparatively brief treatment in Parsons, *Streetwalking the Metropolis*, pp. 111–12, and Liggins, 'Having a Good Time?', pp. 98–110.
13. Cuming, *Housing, Class and Gender in Modern British Writing*, pp. 3–4.

14. Blunt and Sheringham, 'Home-City Geographies: Urban Dwelling and Mobility', p. 16. For the ways in which domestic material culture relates to identity, see Hamlett, *Material Relations*, and Holmes, *In Bed With the Victorians*.
15. Rosner, *Architecture and the Modernism of Private Life*, pp. 1–2.
16. Ibid. p. 2.
17. Ibid. p. 3.
18. Ibid. Rosner acknowledges that a discomfort with conventional notions of home is evident in much New Woman fiction of the 1880s and 1890s, but her examples (Thomas Hardy's *A Laodicean* [1881], George Gissing's *The Odd Women* [1893], and Grant Allen's *The Woman Who Did* [1895]) focus on reactions to the family unit without considering what forms – both architectural and social – were already beginning to take its place.
19. Ibid. p. 9.
20. Taunton, *Fictions of the City*, p. 1.
21. Rendell, *Site-Writing*, p. 7.
22. Armstrong, *Desire and Domestic Fiction*, pp. 3–5.
23. Kroll, introduction given at 'Mobilising London's Housing Histories: The Provision of Homes Since 1850', Centre for Metropolitan History, Institute of Historical Research, 27–28 June 2013.
24. Hewitt, 'The Poverty of Anti-Historicism', paper given at BAVS Talks 2015, Oxford Research Centre in the Humanities (TORCH), 12 May 2015.

Part I

Structures of Authority:
The Model Dwellings Movement

Chapter 2

'Out of its torpid misery': Plotting Passivity in Margaret Harkness's *A City Girl*

Given Margaret Harkness's commitment to progressive causes and, particularly in her early life, her support of socialist politics, it is perhaps surprising that her first novel *A City Girl* (1887) so derides the efforts of an important antecedent to the state provision of housing in Britain: the model dwellings movement. Initiated by a philanthropic interest in improving the housing conditions of the industrious working classes, the model dwellings movement was equally given its impetus by a string of legislative changes to housing policy from roughly mid-century. The creation of the Metropolitan Board of Works in 1856 gave local councils the authority to condemn and demolish insanitary dwellings, but there was little provision for councils to replace the housing of those who were evicted under such city improvement projects – which were often little more than forms of social cleansing. The Labouring Classes Dwelling Houses Acts of 1866 and 1867 provided some coherence in legislation across London's municipal boroughs, and offered an incentive for positive rather than negative provision. The Acts allowed model dwellings companies to borrow money from the government's Public Works Loan Commissioners below market rate in order to finance the purchase of clearance sites and the construction of working-class housing.[1] Most model dwellings companies, of which there were approximately thirty operating in London in the latter half of the century, promised investors an annual dividend of roughly 5 per cent and thus the business model earned the sobriquets 'five per cent philanthropy' and 'capitalist philanthropy'. Model dwellings companies operated on a principle of private investment, but the experiment would have been impossible without preferential borrowing rates and significant government assistance.[2] In this sense, such companies combined capitalist enterprise with government support and in doing so were ideologically pitched between self-help and civic paternalism.

Yet for Harkness, who was consistently critical of economic motives, the model dwellings movement was an inadequate response to the social inequity created by capitalism. Worse still, the hypocritical model of capitalist philanthropy risked exploiting the very people it purported to help. In *A City Girl*, Harkness connects the model of economic paternalism that characterised the model dwellings movement with the familiar narrative of the fallen woman – which, as Sally Ledger notes, Harkness partly rewrites.[3] The novel follows the story of the young, working-class protagonist Nelly Ambrose, whose respectability and middle-class ambition do not lead to an improvement in social status. Instead, her vulnerability allows for her seduction by a bourgeois bohemian radical who – devastatingly – discards her without even the conventional melodrama of the fallen woman narrative. With a quality of emotional detachment and style that Ingrid Von Rosenberg describes as the 'cool accuracy' common to naturalist writers of the period, Nelly's seducer simply seems to forget her altogether until an infant corpse is deposited at his feet.[4] After the death of her child, Nelly is left with little choice other than to marry the caretaker of the model dwellings in which she lives.

Philanthropy and Passivity

A City Girl imaginatively interrogates the relationship between social and physical coercion, both in the built environment and in personal relationships. Upon the completion of *A City Girl* in 1887, Harkness sent a copy of the novel to Friedrich Engels and received what is now the well-known letter in which he challenges her representation of the working classes. Although he claims to have read the book 'with great pleasure and avidity', he suggests that Harkness portrays the working class as 'a passive mass, unable to help itself' and that '[a]ll attempts to drag it out of its torpid misery come from without, from above'.[5] The criticism is, in some ways, not unwarranted; the novel does not present the working classes as particularly politically engaged, let alone efficacious. In the preface to the second edition of *The Housing Question*, Engels criticises the 'petty utopias' proposed by 'bourgeois-socialist philanthropists' that only sought to yoke the working classes to capitalist interest through private property.[6] Although *A City Girl* stops short of representing the 'revolutionary hotbed' that Engels believed inevitable in working-class neighbourhoods, it does offer a potent criticism of private property. More specifically, the novel characterises the model dwellings movement as a concession by capitalism that is designed to pacify the working classes and forestall the development of revolutionary sympathy; the buildings, both in structure and management, purposely inculcate the inhabitants' passivity – and the political significance of the narrative inertia is an important point that Engels seems to have missed. This chapter focuses on the narrative associations between forms of coercion produced by philanthropic capitalism – and specifically the model dwellings movement – and those that characterise the fallen woman narrative in order to reveal the ways in which *A City Girl* offers a trenchant critique of both.

For three months in 1886 Harkness lived in a block of model dwellings in London's East End alongside her second cousin, Beatrice Potter (later Webb), who worked as a rent collector with Ella Pycroft, who was also estate manager alongside Maurice Eden Paul.[7] Her motivation for doing so seems to have been for the purpose of conducting social research for a literary purpose, as the rent books indicate her role as an 'observer' in Katharine Buildings.[8] This experience of living in one of the city's poorest districts provided the substance of her first novel, *A City Girl: A Realistic Story*. This decision seems to have been among the reasons why Harkness became estranged from her upper-middle-class and well-connected family. Despite her conservative upbringing, Harkness seems to have frustrated her family's expectation that she would enter society and eventually marry. When she instead enrolled in a nursing education programme at Westminster Hospital in 1877, one of the 'few acceptable positions for young women' as Terry Elkiss notes, her family was predictably dismayed.[9] While studying at Westminster in 1878, Harkness wrote to Potter to say that her 'people objected to the mixed society' of the house in which she was staying; in fact, she explains to Potter: 'You see they are conservatives [and] live in a small country set, [and] they think a place where all classes are received [and] no differences made, unfit for a lady to be in.'[10] By the time of her father's death in 1886, Harkness seems to have become estranged from her immediate family and probably gave their prejudices little consideration when she elected to live in another situation that they would have thought 'unfit for a lady': a block of model dwellings in East Smithfield, intended for the poorest casual labourers in London's East End.

Built on a slum clearance site by the East End Dwellings Company, Katharine Buildings (Fig. 2.1) has been the focus of several historical studies, largely made possible by the records and diaries kept by

Figure 2.1 Katharine Buildings, Cartwright Street, front elevation. Designed by Davis & Emmanuel for the East End Dwellings Company (built 1884; photograph 1970)

Potter and Pycroft.[11] Ruth Livesey has examined the dynamic spatial and social practices in Katharine Buildings, and specifically the ways in which the 'tenants' levelling gaze' challenged the methods of control presumed by middle-class forms of surveillance.[12] Livesey's examination is important for its interpretation of Katharine Buildings not only as place, but as historical actor. Certainly *A City Girl* foregrounds the ways in which Katharine Buildings, which becomes Charlotte's Buildings in Harkness's novel, is a formative force in the lives of the novel's characters.

In *A City Girl*, Charlotte's Buildings is regularly associated with physical passivity. The passivity that the building seems to induce in its residents is initially attributed to the weather, but upon closer examination is closely associated with its structural components and furnishings: '[T]he maternal voices were drowsy, and the maternal strokes were languid, owing to the sultry weather', while '[i]n the buildings from six to eight hundred people stewed and panted, at doors and windows, upon beds, chairs and sofas'.[13] When introduced, the inhabitants expand upon the narrator's observations by explaining that the building is 'cheap and nasty' (9), and an old woman shrewdly remarks, 'rich people think they'll keep us from coming nigh 'em by packing us close like this' (11). Such testimony quite precisely aligns the tenants' physical immobility – they are so constrained as to be barely able to breathe – with their social immobility. This is a correlation that evidently occurred to Harkness, who in a rare interview with the *Evening News and Post* commented on having lived in one of the 'poorest and densest' districts in London and gives some indication of her motivation for doing so:

> A great deal was then being talked and written about the East-end and about its misery and suffering. An opportunity offered itself of seeing and studying the life there. I therefore went and lived in one of the poorest and densest districts for several months. Just before then Walter Besant had brought out his first book on the East-end and I was so disgusted with its untruthfulness that I conceived the idea of writing a story which should picture the lives of the East-enders in their true colours. I commenced 'A City [Girl],' half of which was written whilst I was living in the slums.[14]

According to Harkness, much of the philanthropic and literary interest in London's East End was not derived from a desire to improve the lives of the inhabitants, but instead to capitalise on the sensationalism of poverty and deprivation. The extraordinary popularity of Walter Besant's novels *Children of Gibeon* (1886) and *All Sorts and Conditions of Men* (1882), which he famously defined in the novel's preface as an 'impossible' story, were to Harkness flagrant forms of 'untruthfulness'. In *All Sorts and Conditions of Men*, two young philanthropists determine that the problems of the East End might be solved by the construction of a 'Palace of Delight' that would offer local inhabitants various forms of education and entertainment.[15] Besant's 'pretty stories', as Harkness would describe them in her later novel *Captain Lobe* (1889), concealed the extent of poverty in London's East End. Worse still, in doing so it mollified the very audience who might instead have been urged to campaign for meaningful reform.

Novels such as *All Sorts and Conditions of Men* that featured elaborate philanthropic projects were not so distant, in Harkness's mind, from the buildings that they so often represented. While Katharine Buildings provided relatively inexpensive housing to residents of East Smithfield, its poor construction and design were a sign of middle-class contempt for those whom the building was meant to house. The East End Dwellings Company had purchased the awkwardly shaped site on which Katharine Buildings was built in 1883, which was made available after the clearances initiated by the Metropolitan Board of Works' Whitechapel and Limehouse Improvement Scheme (1879–81). The fact that the site was narrowly sandwiched between the Royal Mint and another site purchased by the Peabody Trust, and that the company was legally obliged to rehouse an unrealistic number of people evicted during the clearance, resulted in a structure hardly more comfortable than the buildings it replaced.[16]

As Harkness explains in the *Evening News and Post*, one half of *A City Girl* was written while she was 'living in the slums', and it is therefore not surprising that the building and its situation are described with precision, as according to architects' plans and elevations, even if the names are altered slightly: Cartwright Street becomes Wright Street, for instance, and Cable Street becomes Abel Street. The novel's omniscient narrator, who introduces the reader to Charlotte's Buildings on the first page, describes not the building's front elevation but its rear. This is significant, as this was the perspective familiar to inhabitants but largely unseen by the general public. Architects Davis & Emmanuel designed the structure so that traffic into and out of the building was restricted from the dominant perspective, that is, its position on Cartwright Street. Instead, for tenants to enter the building there was a narrow passage between the north facade and an adjacent building that provided access into a yard that faced the back of the Royal Mint (Fig. 2.2).

Unlike other model dwelling companies such as the Improved Industrial Dwellings Corporation or the Peabody Trust, which provided housing mostly for the artisan classes, Katharine Buildings was intended to house the lowest classes of casual workers in the East End. In response to the architects' plans, Octavia Hill commented that 'the fittings should be of the simplest in view of the destructive habits of the tenants, the buildings airy and wholesome, and the rents low'.[17] Whether deliberately or not, Katharine Buildings was designed in such a way as to ensure that tenants were hidden from people passing by in Cartwright Street and Cable Street. In addition to restricting passage into and out of the building, such a design would have ensured that tenants would socialise in the rear yard out of public view. Not only, therefore, were the inhabitants of Katharine Buildings physically restricted by the cramped

'Out of its torpid misery' 25

Figure 2.2 Katharine Buildings, Cartwright Street, rear elevation. Designed by Davis & Emmanuel for the East End Dwellings Company (built 1884; photograph 1970)

site and internal overcrowding, but its very design enforced their social invisibility.

Whereas the front elevation looked not unlike the regulated brick facades and stacked chimneys of accommodation provided by other model dwelling companies, from the rear one discovered that:

> [t]he buildings were not beautiful to look upon; they might have even been termed ugly. Their long yellow walls were lined with small windows; upon the rails of their stiff iron balconies hung shirts, blankets and other articles fresh from the wash-tub. Inside their walls brown doors opened into dark stone passages; and narrow winding staircases led from passage to passage up to the roof. (10)

The perspective that the narrator of *A City Girl* describes is precisely the one that the architects of the building wished to conceal from public view, but it is one that Harkness was compelled to expose to counter the untruthfulness of novels such as Besant's *All Sorts and Conditions of Men*. Harkness implicitly criticises Octavia Hill's insistence that sanitary improvements in working-class housing would only succeed alongside the inhabitants' commitment to moral respectability: in Katharine Buildings, 'articles fresh from the wash-tub' hang on stiff iron rails framed by yellow walls and dark passages. In this contaminated environment, the novel suggests, it is impossible to maintain standards of cleanliness and respectability; and yet to fail at this task rendered one undeserving of charity and sympathy by the standards of philanthropists such as Hill.

The novel's attentive consideration of life in Charlotte's Buildings calls the reader's attention to the ways in which the organisation's model dwellings, informed as they were by the moralising programme of philanthropy, were a form of social design. Such descriptions suggest that while model dwellings companies wished to provide charitable housing for the working classes, this practice was underpinned by a desire to obscure rather than solve the problems of capitalism. The substandard design of Charlotte's Buildings, the text suggests, worked to placate middle-class concerns about insanitary housing at the same time as it sought to physically and socially pacify its working-class inhabitants; as the narrator explains, '[t]he company wished to put money in their pockets; and, so long as the rents were forthcoming, did not care what went on in Charlotte's Buildings' (55).

Aspiration and Futility

The model dwellings movement's moral crusade often sought to conform working-class behaviour to middle-class expectations of propriety. In addition to questioning the motivations of capitalist philanthropy and the model dwellings movement, *A City Girl* also interrogates the philosophy of self-help by aligning philanthropic paternalism with what Deborah Epstein Nord describes as the 'ideological hypocrisies and the personal callousness of the politically committed bourgeoisie'.[18] Although *A City Girl* follows the conventional narrative of the fallen woman, there are important differences that attest to what Sally Ledger refers to as Harkness's 'feminist credentials'.[19] For instance, while the working-class seamstress Nelly Ambrose is seduced by a middle-class dilettante who leaves her with an illegitimate child, Ledger points out that she avoids the classic descent into prostitution.[20] Equally important is that, four years before the controversy roused by Thomas Hardy's *Tess of the d'Urbervilles* (1891), Harkness identifies social inequity as the principal villain in the fallen woman narrative: her novel emphasises circumstance over character. Even the philandering, self-styled radical by whom Nelly is seduced, Arthur Grant, is exonerated, and neither the narrator nor Nelly herself hold him to account for his behaviour. Instead, when the reader is eager for retribution at the novel's conclusion, all that is offered is Nelly's admission that her pregnancy 'wasn't all his fault' (162). The representation of Arthur Grant as egotistical and asinine is in many ways a more powerful critique of male sexuality than the conventional nefariousness that characterises Alec d'Urberville. In *A City Girl*, Grant's self-interest is associated with motivations of philanthropic capitalism, and specifically model dwellings companies that design housing such as Katharine Buildings. Both character and setting in this novel seem to promise Nelly a path to middle-class respectability, but instead both place her in a position of physical and (at least by nineteenth-century standards) moral insecurity.

Yet Nelly is not a passive nor guiltless victim, and Harkness avoids the regular assertions of the heroine's purity that characterise *Tess of the d'Urbervilles*. While Nelly's motivations are governed by self-interest, Harkness represents the structural origins of such behaviour rather than suggesting that it is the result of moral failing. Where capitalist structures of self-interest determine that Charlotte's Buildings exists, ultimately, to produce dividends for shareholders and Grant's motivation is most often his own physical gratification, Nelly's materialism is predetermined. For instance, Nelly is not captivated by Grant's personal charisma – of which, the narrator implies, he has very little – but rather his social status and financial resources. The period of their time together is characterised by outings to the park and the theatre, and any interest that Nelly betrays in Grant personally is generated by his middle-class mannerisms and attire, which she contrasts favourably with those of the building's caretaker, George. While Nelly's preoccupation with choosing the right feather for her hat, or her dream of spending all day reading novels, might seem trivial to middle-class audiences, her interest in these objects and activities is aspirational as well as material. Nelly's desire to achieve middle-class respectability – once again precisely the ambition Octavia Hill thought model dwellings could engender – is itself the cause of her degradation.

Unlike the conventional aristocratic rogue of the fallen woman narrative, Arthur Grant's interest in Nelly seems almost incidental. There is no malicious plotting; rather it simply fails to occur to him that '[factory] "hands" have hearts' (77). In fact, much like the philanthropic capitalists of the model dwellings movement, he congratulates himself for having any interest in the working classes at all and believes his very presence should be ennobling: '[Grant] felt very satisfied with himself that evening. He had cause, he thought, for contentment. Not only was he giving a little East End girl great pleasure, but he had just run away from the charms of a married lady, with whom he had been greatly tempted to flirt' (74).

Grant's self-interest, obliviousness to the realities of working-class life and propensity for energetically celebrating his own generosity correspond to the motivations and behaviour of model dwellings companies such as the East End Dwellings Company. The company, like many others, was happy to design buildings for the working classes without any input from – or indeed, any consideration of – the lifestyles of those for whom they were designed. For instance, Octavia Hill insisted that one communal lavatory per floor was sufficient for Katharine Buildings, although she and others were scandalised when the residents used this space for socialising, although no other area for this purpose had been provided.[21] Most model dwellings companies also remained indifferent to inhabitants' lives after the buildings were completed. In *A City Girl*, the simple but good-natured caretaker George is not only charged with maintaining order in the building, but also helps correct narrative disorder by offering to marry Nelly once she is abandoned by Arthur Grant. Not coincidentally, it is George who expresses the clearest criticism of the East End Dwellings Company. He comments that such corporations care little about the lives of inhabitants, and are concerned only to 'pocket the rents and until there's a murder they'll make no difference' to the lives of tenants (124). The response that follows George's assertion – 'And they call themselves philanthropists!' (125) – is not only a charge levelled at the corporation, but also a personal remark directed at disingenuous radicals such as Arthur Grant.

A City Girl develops the association between romantic paternalism and philanthropic capitalism by demonstrating the futility of moralising initiatives such as Samuel Smiles's *Self-Help* (1859) in the nineteenth-century free market. Sally Ledger correctly observes that Nelly is 'emphatically unexceptional' insofar as representations of nineteenth-century working-class women go; however, she is exceptional in the context of Charlotte's Buildings.[22] Unlike the other residents, Nelly is preoccupied by her own middle-class aspirations, which involve an ambition '[t]o sit on a sofa, to read a novelette, to sip coffee with a teaspoon, to have someone to put on and take off her boots' (16–17). Nelly is described by the narrator as hard-working, favoured by her employer for her skill at sewing trousers, and is contrasted at home with her brother, the 'loafer' (23). As has been suggested, her fascination with Arthur Grant owes as much to social status as to any genuine romantic interest, and in this sense, Nelly's social aspiration is the cause of her moral fall.

If Charlotte's Buildings is representative of the social and physical coercion of the working classes, Arthur Grant's suburban home in West Kensington equally illustrates the futility of middle-class material ambition. At Christmas, long after Grant has grown tired of and forgotten his affair with the 'little East End Girl' (74), Nelly travels across the city by Underground from Mansion House to his home in order to inform him of her pregnancy. In addition to drawing on the conventions of the fallen woman narrative, this scene is also a modern retelling of the Holy Family's search for shelter on the night of Christ's birth. Recast as the figure of Mary (and therefore absolved from personal blame), Nelly emerges from the Underground into the heavy snow and walks slowly along the pavement, peering into the uncovered windows, where she 'stops short in front of a bow window' (97) to see Grant ensconced in idealised domesticity, sitting with his wife and young child by the fire. The residential suburb of West Kensington was itself consciously aspirational: it had been developed alongside the construction of the Metropolitan District Railway station of Fulham (North End), which opened in 1874. The station was renamed West Kensington in 1877 in an effort to associate the growing neighbourhood with the more centrally located area of Kensington proper, and soon became a popular area for authors and artists (William Butler Yeats, Edward Burne-Jones and Henry Rider Haggard all lived in the neighbourhood in the latter half of the nineteenth century).[23]

It is significant that Nelly stops in front of the bow window, or curved bay window, which was a defining feature of much of the terraced housing built in middle-class suburbs during the nineteenth century. In a thirteen-page article that appeared in *British Architect* in 1898, 'The Morality of the Bay Window', the author notes that the extravagance of the bay window means that it is 'bound to be either the glory or the shame of a building to which [it is] applied'.[24] In the novel the bow window, at least from Nelly's perspective, provides both interior glory and exterior shame. The window, which projects beyond the structural wall of the building, is designed to provide a broader view of the building's exterior (generally, in residential architecture, the garden). However, in this scene, the window becomes a form of thrust stage which grants Nelly sight of but no access to the domestic picture of the house's interior. Nelly is again physically constrained, and socially fenced out of her middle-class ambitions. Standing alone in the cold, her 'arms shook on the railings; [and] she could hear her teeth chattering' (98). Yet she soon finds 'the shutters closed and the picture she had been watching vanished into darkness' (99). The symbolism is clear: Nelly is denied even the image of her own delusion. Grant lived in a 'different world than the one she had imagined', and it was not one to which he would grant her access; it was instead 'a world shut in by the golden gates of domestic peace and happiness' (99–100).

The chapter, appropriately titled 'East and West', demonstrates by way of Nelly's journey 'how far, how very far, the East is from the West [. . .] [and] that Whitechapel may talk to Kensington, and Kensington may shake hands with Whitechapel, but between them there is a great gulf fixed' (100–1). Although this scene focuses on the consequences of social and sexual inequality from Nelly's perspective, the chapter more broadly reveals that one continuity between east and west is an economic system built on the false promises of material ambition. The novel focuses on the ways in which Nelly is particularly vulnerable in the context of her relationship with Arthur Grant – she is at this moment a pregnant woman abandoned to a snowstorm – but so does the novel imply that the 'golden gates' of domestic bliss were their own form of unpleasant confinement. The narrator confronts the reader with the reality of middle-class domesticity:

> Had [Nelly] seen him there, looking out at the night, thinking whether he would go to his club or see what his wife had at home for dinner, saying to himself that it was a nuisance to be poor and forced to live in the suburbs, yawning, and putting up his eye-glass, she would have been astonished. (99)

In *The Housing Question,* Engels determined that private property is not a system in which equality is ever possible because it merely 'chain[s a person] in semi-feudal fashion' to capitalism.²⁵ Grant's pathetic complaint about being 'poor' and 'forced' to live anywhere – even an unfashionable suburb – of course expresses his wilful ignorance and his betrayal of Nelly and of the radical socialist ideals to which he claims to be committed. While this scene dramatically reveals the callous indifference of middle-class philanthropy, Grant's weary complaint about the inadequacy of his own home also corresponds to Engels's argument that any form of private property merely yokes a person to capitalism. The novel does not criticise Nelly for her desire to have access to the domestic happiness that she only glimpses through the window, but it does imply that middle-class domesticity is equally an illusion driven by an aspirational economy. Unlike Nelly, the reader is permitted into the interior of the middle-class home, but only to discover that its inhabitants are bored, unhappy and perceive themselves to be 'poor'.

A City Girl is structured around the material differences between middle-class suburbs and the poorer neighbourhoods of the city's East End – but in this particular scene the novel calls attention to similarities rather than differences: all social groups, the novel suggests, are bound by the oppressive chains of material ambition. Even as Nelly walks through the West End neighbourhood she notices that the 'roads looked all alike; the rows of houses showed no difference' (101). Much like the experiences of middle-class novelists and journalists investigating East End slums, Nelly is 'bewildered' (96) by her experience of the West End. Using the language of the investigative literature that bolstered public interest in the work of the model dwellings movement, the text describes the bewildering sameness of urban space not as a characteristic of economically deprived areas, but instead as a result of estrangement produced by social difference. Although a 'great gulf' may be fixed between the material experiences of the working classes and the middle classes, *A City Girl* proposes that all classes, at the very least, are united by the futility of their ambitions under capitalism.

Stasis and Circularity

Contemporary reviewers of *A City Girl* were pleased to find that 'the story ends happily enough', with its capitulation to two conventions of the romance genre: a proposal of marriage and a move to the country.²⁶ *The Athenaeum* expressed grateful surprise that the author had 'contrived so happy an ending for what threatened to be a tragedy'.²⁷ More recently, scholars have also read the novel's ending as filtered through nineteenth-century romantic conventions. This is, of course, true to an extent because, as Ingrid Von Rosenberg acknowledges, it was necessary that the characters or story not be overly objectionable if it were to disseminate its socialist message to the desired audience.²⁸ Yet Harkness's method is strategic in that she introduces the conventions of the romance genre, but does not fully espouse them. Although the caretaker George proposes to Nelly after the death of her child, she does not agree to the marriage within the space of the narrative, and instead responds with a plaintive cry that suggests that any union would be one of defeatism rather than affection. Although George also proposes a move to the country, the novel ultimately ends where it began, in Charlotte's Buildings, and denies narrative progress in favour of a form of static circularity.

While the narrative may seem to offer a conventional form of closure through marriage, another form of resolution is a provided in a description of housing that is alternative to both the model dwellings movement and private property ownership. George explains to Nelly that, when they marry, he would like to move

> [i]nto the country. There's a society, or a club, just started, I don't know quite what they call it, but it is made up of people who write books. They've got a lot of little cottages, about an hour out of London; and they want someone to look after the gardens [. . .] It's a very nice place [. . .] and a lot cleaner than the buildings. (188)

The novel may allude here to cooperative housing societies, a few of which were developing on the fringes of London at the end of the century. The meals are to be cooked and carried to the cottages by two servants, a position George implies would be suitable for Nelly. Yet Nelly's response to this proposal ('Oh, I ain't worth it!'), and George's pronouncement of his familiar incantation throughout the novel ('I wish I'd never left the service') (190), clearly contradict any notion of conclusion or even contentment.

The cooperative society that George refers to might have been one of the communities planned by the Tenant Co-operators Ltd, a housing cooperative established in 1887 with the ambition of constructing houses around London that would be let at nominal rents to local working-class groups that would receive a dividend credited to the share account; the houses, although initially supported by outside shareholders, would eventually be owned collectively by tenants.²⁹

More likely, Harkness is mocking 'communistic societies' such as the Fellowship of New Life, which aimed to expunge social divisions in part by uniting physical and intellectual labour.[30] As Livesey remarks, the Fellowship was 'an easy target for satire', and was perceived by many contemporaries as a 'band of sentimental Luddites' with the thoroughly middle-class ambition of 'resigning from lucrative professions to become market gardeners'.[31] While the housing cooperative and its middle-class artists' colony is presented as an attractive alternative to life in Charlotte's Buildings, both Nelly and George would remain in service to people much like Arthur Grant. Furthermore, the new cooperative model of housing does not offer a solution to, nor does it even address, the particular forms of gender exploitation that capitalism makes possible and which the narrative unearths. As George explains about the housing cooperative, he asks Nelly to make him tea, fill his pipe and 'take her old place' at his knee (187).

Sally Ledger has identified the tensions in *A City Girl* between socialism and feminism, and suggests that Harkness refuses to 'conform unequivocally to either paradigm'.[32] Yet in *A City Girl*, Harkness identifies the projects of model dwellings corporations as misguided in their attempt to address social problems through the very economic system that created them, and offers a clear criticism of the interest of private property. It is also no mistake that Harkness aligns this movement with the narrative conventions of the fallen woman; although Arthur Grant espouses socialist philosophy, lectures at East End radical clubs, and writes psychological novels, he is oblivious to women's different exploitation under capitalist patriarchy – so much so that he personally perpetuates this system out of his own self-interest. Engels's criticism that the novel offers no example of an effort by the working classes to lift themselves out of oppression overlooks the fact that this very activity is Nelly's chief desire throughout the novel. Denied political participation and economic opportunity, the chances for Nelly to 'drag [her]self out of torpid misery' are few. While *A City Girl* casts light on the relationship between working-class oppression and the nineteenth-century housing question, it also articulates that intrinsic to this question are further inequalities, particularly in view of gender, that must be separately addressed and differently solved.

Notes

1. While legislative changes such as the Torrens Act (Artisans and Labourers Dwelling Act 1868) and the Cross Act (Artisans and Labourers Dwelling Improvement Act 1875) were important in calling national

attention to housing policy, it was not until a series of amendments to both Acts were made that a coherent urban renewal policy was put in place. For a detailed analysis of changes in housing legislation between 1850 and 1880, see Wohl, 'The Weight of the Law', in *The Eternal Slum*, pp. 73–108. See also Balchin and Rhoden, *Housing*, pp. 3–5.
2. Wohl, *The Eternal Slum*, p. 144. See also Balchin and Rhoden, *Housing*, pp. 3–4.
3. Ledger, *The New Woman*, p. 49.
4. Von Rosenberg, 'French Naturalism and the English Socialist Novel', p. 155. In addition to Von Rosenberg, Ledger and Nord both comment on Harkness's use of literary naturalism. See Ledger, *The New Woman*, p. 49; Nord, *Walking the Victorian Streets*, p. 184.
5. Engels, 'Letter to Margaret Harkness, Beginning of April 1888 (draft)', in Baxandall and Morawski (eds), *Marx & Engels on Literature and Art*, p. 115.
6. Engels, *The Housing Question*, pp. 17–18.
7. Tooley, 'Domestic Economy and the L.C.C. an Interview with Miss Pycroft', *The Woman's Signal*, 4 February 1895. In this interview, Pycroft recounts some of her experiences intervening in violent disputes in Katharine Buildings.
8. British Library of Political and Economic Science, Coll Misc 0043: 99.
9. Elkiss, 'A Law Unto Herself', p. 19.
10. British Library of Political and Economic Science, Passfield Papers, PASSFIELD/2/1/2/2, ff. 40.
11. O'Day, 'How Families Lived Then', pp. 129–67. See also O'Day, 'Caring or Controlling?', pp. 149–66.
12. Livesey, 'Women Rent Collectors and the Rewriting of Space, Class and Gender in East London', p. 98. See also Livesey, 'Soundscapes of the City', pp. 111–29.
13. Law [Margaret Harkness], *A City Girl: A Realistic Story*, pp. 7–9, 11. Further references to this work are given in parentheses in the text.
14. 'A Slum-Story Writer', *The Evening News and Post*, 17 April 1890. The article erroneously refers to the title of Harkness's novel as *A City Evil*.
15. While Besant's 'Palace of Delight' has often been interpreted as the inspiration for the People's Palace at Mile End in East London, which began construction in 1886, Eliza Cubitt has discovered evidence that this presumption likely resulted from another one of Besant's 'untruths'. See Cubitt, *Arthur Morrison and the East End*, pp. 68–74.
16. Tarn, *Five Per Cent Philanthropy*, p. 82; Wohl, *The Eternal Slum*, p. 134.
17. Cited in Tarn, *Working-class Housing in Nineteenth-Century Britain*, p. 27.
18. Nord, *Walking the Victorian Streets*, p. 195.
19. Ledger, *The New Woman*, p. 44.

20. Ibid. p. 45.
21. O'Day, 'How Families Lived Then', pp. 146, 148.
22. Ledger, *The New Woman*, p. 45.
23. Swinnerton, *The London Companion*, p. 103. The district is also lightly ridiculed for similar reasons in George Bernard Shaw's novel *The Irrational Knot*.
24. Waterhouse, 'The Morality of the Bay Window', *British Architect*, 2 (1898), p. 398.
25. Engels, *The Housing Question*, p. 17.
26. 'A City Girl', *Time*, May 1887, p. 638.
27. 'Novels of the Week', *The Athenaeum*, 30 April 1887, p. 573.
28. Von Rosenberg, 'French Naturalism and the English Socialist Novel', p. 158.
29. Birchall, *Building Communities*, pp. 94–5.
30. Cited in Livesey, *Socialism, Sex and the Culture of Aestheticism in Britain*, p. 86.
31. Ibid. pp. 86, 88.
32. Ledger, *The New Woman*, p. 44.

Chapter 3

'More making the best of it': Living with Liberalism in Mary Ward's *Marcella*

After achieving extraordinary success with the best-selling *Robert Elsmere* (1888), a novel that follows a clergyman's crisis of faith, Mary Ward set out to write a story 'concerned not with theology, but social ethics'.[1] The novel that followed, *Marcella* (1894), shares with *Robert Elsmere* a structure that traces the protagonist's intellectual development in the context of late nineteenth-century social and political changes. While *Marcella* foregrounds the emergence of British socialism at the end of the nineteenth century, its impulse is intellectual more than ideological; it is not, as one reviewer claimed, 'a sugar-coated pamphlet', but instead examines the effect of political debate on the protagonist's emotional and intellectual development.[2]

The novel follows the political engagement and social commitment of the young heroine, Marcella Boyce, from her early interest in socialism, through to her engagement with legal lobbying and social support, a career in district nursing and, finally, marriage. Although Ward's reputation as a fusty Victorian persists, due in part to her association with the anti-suffrage movement – and certainly not helped by Lytton Strachey's rather uncomfortable characterisation of her as 'that shapeless mass of meaningless flesh' – recent scholarship has contested this designation through careful readings of her work and a reconsideration of her personal politics.[3] *Marcella* is certainly a form of *bildungsroman*, as these studies point out, but it is also a narrative exercise in nineteenth-century political liberalism in its sustained examination of the patterns of its protagonist's ideological deliberation.[4] By the mid-Victorian period liberalism was, as Elaine Hadley explains, the 'fashionable form of opinion'.[5] Contemplative thought was, in fact, the principal form of political activity for the liberal subject. To engage in the processes of reflection, deliberation and abstraction produced liberal ideas, which then entered the public domain of political opinion.⁶

This process of reflection and deliberation, or 'liberal cognition' as Hadley describes it, is one that provides *Marcella* with both its subject and its structure. Ward's novel gives substance to the processes of liberal cognition by following the development of Marcella's political convictions. As Hadley remarks, nineteenth-century political liberalism was preoccupied with *how* one ought to think, but not precisely what to think.⁷ In *Marcella*, Ward is concerned with writing into fiction the process by which a reader might be coached into practising liberal cognition. The model dwellings in which Marcella lives while working as a district nurse materially represent the processes of private liberal cognition, and in so doing encourage in Ward's readership the practice of liberal habits of thought.

Architecture and Social Progress

While employed as a district nurse on the fringes of Bloomsbury, Marcella takes residence in a complex of recently completed model dwellings. Brown's Buildings, or Peabody Buildings as it is referred to in the original manuscript, plays an important role in the text both structurally and metaphorically.⁸ Marcella's temporary residence in a block of model dwellings, her experience in nursing, and her enthusiasm for socialism are likely what provoked one reviewer to propose that the portrait seemed 'a kind of cross between Miss Margaret Harkness, who, for some time, was the patron saint of the dockers, and guardian angel of the Labour elector [*sic*], and the Countess of Carlisle'.⁹ Marcella's flat in the model dwellings provides her with an independent space where she can engage in self-reflexive thought and political deliberation, a space away from the overbearing influence of others. That this novel, which engages with the processes of liberal free thought, features a determined and politically spirited young woman and not a young man is a crucial part of the text's project. Matthew Arnold's political essays in *Culture and Anarchy* (1867–68) engaged with the ways in which the nation's collective culture might change in response to increasing enfranchisement, and Ward's task in *Marcella* is related to this.¹⁰ Aware of women's demands for political rights and social freedoms, and concerned with the consequences of women's participation in politics without having been sufficiently educated or trained in the liberal qualities of reason and reflection, *Marcella* is Ward's effort to coach her readership into performing the acts of liberal cognition that would enable them to make (what Ward would have considered) sound judgements about political matters. Liberalism's 'trademark diversity of opinion', Hadley notes, was 'best brought under control by a formalised narrative of mental development'.[11] In *Marcella*, Ward represents the heroine's disinterested 'free play of the mind', but she also ensures that such deliberation returns at the novel's conclusion to the privileging of abstract liberal thought.[12]

Several scholars have interpreted *Marcella* as expressive of conflicting ideologies, which Ward epigrammatically described as 'the clash of old and new'.[13] While the novel does indeed explore the contention between conservatism and liberalism, tradition and transformation, and most palpably between the rich and the poor, criticism has been too eager to interpret this conflict as reconciled only through victory and defeat. Such a reading is no doubt inspired by the novel's romantic plot, which follows the division of Marcella's interest and affection between two men who are political antagonists. Although early in the novel Marcella accepts a marriage proposal from Aldous Raeburn, a dyed-in-the-wool Tory who is heir to the neighbouring estate, she rescinds out of uncertainty; this uncertainty, however, is in part motivated by her intimate friendship with the radical politician Harry Wharton. When, after considerable soul-searching, Marcella returns (on her knees, no less) to Raeburn, the novel certainly seems to trumpet the triumph of conservatism.

While this account is irrepressible, it is also reductive. Marcella's independence and experience are not necessarily subsumed by her return to Raeburn at the novel's conclusion; instead, the novel seems to suggest that it is these very qualities that make her decision possible (after all, it is she who proposes). The ancestral home where Marcella passes the first sections of the narrative, Mellor Park, is a symbol of an agrarian social model that is organised on a traditional and hierarchical structure. The model dwellings in which she lives while working in London, Brown's Buildings, symbolise the social complexities of nineteenth-century modern industrial society. Yet, like Marcella's return to Raeburn, her reinstatement at Mellor at the conclusion does not necessarily render the narrative regressive. Marcella's liberal intellectual development knits together the combined significance of both forms of housing – traditional and modern – and her experience of living in these different spaces provides a material exemplum of self-reflection and political deliberation that allows her to arrive at an informed conclusion. In this sense, the novel uses liberalism to achieve a progressive return to conservatism.

In 'The Virtues of Architecture' John Ruskin theorises the relationship between individual morality and the built environment, and suggests that 'in no art is there closer connection between our delight in the work, and our admiration of the workman's mind, than in architecture'.[14] While Ruskin's evaluation of delight in architectural virtue is firmly rooted in Christian morality, the connection is otherwise important because it foregrounds nineteenth-century thought concerning the relationship between architectural design and emotional affect. For Ruskin, architecture's affect forges emotional connections not only between the artist and viewer, but also among communities. This emotional affect is produced by two separate qualities of a building: action and aspect.[15] These dual qualities broadly refer to a building's formal construction, and its invention (or decoration), both of which are necessary in order for the structure to be virtuous. While these two qualities enable a building to 'act well' and to 'look well', a building must also 'speak well'.[16] Ruskin acknowledges that this final quality is not essential to a structure, but rather existential; that each conventional (as opposed to natural) expression 'has its own alphabet'.[17] In this sense, Ruskin imagines architecture's method of communication as linguistic: successful unity between these complementary contraries – action and aspect – give a building the capacity to communicate. In *Marcella*, too, it is the narrative's communication (rather than its conclusion or resolution) that is its purpose: communication between radical and conservative; rich and poor; tradition and transformation; the individual and the community. Like liberal opinion that enters the public domain after a period of reflection and deliberation, a building's capacity for communication is only possible after balancing action and aspect.

What is important about Ruskin's work for *Marcella* is not a question of influence, but of contemporary understandings of the relationship between architecture and social progress. Still, Ward was familiar with Ruskin's work. In fact, she wrote that until her family moved to Oxford in 1867 (the year her uncle, Matthew Arnold, was elected Professor of Poetry at Keble College), 'Ruskin – *The Stones of Venice* and certain chapters in *Modern Painters* – had been my chief intellectual passion'.[18] Although Ward wrote that while at school she had learned 'nothing thoroughly or accurately', she nevertheless recalled 'the haunting beauty of certain passages of Ruskin which I copied out and carried about with me'.[19] In *Robert Elsmere*, Ruskin's social theories are acknowledged to be outmoded (if not irrelevant) by a character who explains: '[I]n my youth people talked about Ruskin; now they talk about drains.'[20] The quip is charged with an awareness of the development of social reform in the latter half of the nineteenth century – from moral idealism to practical socialism – and reappears in the pages of *Marcella*. When describing Marcella, Raeburn writes:

> She may be twenty, or rather more. The mind has all sorts of ability; comes to the right conclusion by a divine instinct, ignoring the how and why. What does such a being want with the drudgery of learning? to such keenness life will be master enough. Yet she has evidently read a good deal – much poetry, some scattered political economy, some modern socialistic books, Matthew Arnold, Ruskin, Carlyle. (91)

Like the author herself, Marcella has read broadly (Ruskin included) if not thoroughly, but in the novel this owes less to a restricted education than to her 'ability' and 'keenness'.[21] The narrator comments that 'at twenty-one people who take interest in many things, and are in a hurry to have opinions, must skim and "turn over" books rather than read them, must use indeed as best they may a scattered and distracted mind' (41). More interesting, though, is Raeburn's assessment that Marcella reaches the conclusion while 'ignoring the how and the why', for over the course of the novel Marcella's intellect develops in such a way that her political affinities are swayed by practical considerations rather than idealism.

Architectural 'Action' and Brown's Buildings

The novel's opening initiates Marcella's relocation from a student boarding house in South Kensington to the family home of Mellor Park, an ancestral property unexpectedly inherited by her father upon her uncle's death. The initial move lays the foundations of Marcella's intellectual progress throughout the novel, and its close connection to the built environment. After this initial relocation to Mellor, Marcella begins to attend socialist meetings and organises campaigns, but eventually she returns to London where she becomes a district nurse. While John Sutherland suggests that Ward drew the political plot of *Marcella* partly from George Gissing's *Demos* (1886), it is possible that Gissing's rendering of working-class housing also influenced – or perhaps provoked – her consideration of model dwellings in the novel.[22] While Gissing's representation of working-class housing most often communicates the materially circumscribed lives of the inhabitants of such buildings, in *Marcella* Brown's Buildings figures differently: Marcella's experience living in model dwellings *enables* her intellectual and emotional development.

Such a reading unearths its own problems. There is, of course, a distinct social insensitivity in granting an upper-class woman access to temporary residence in working-class dwellings so that she might personally benefit from the placement. The people whose friendships she enjoys while living in the building do not have the resources to make the (personal or political) choices that are available to Marcella in this novel. Yet *Marcella* is more than a testament to the revitalising powers of what Seth Koven refers to as 'slumming', or the movement of a privileged individual across spatial and social boundaries.[23] The loose template of the *bildungsroman* that guides the novel positions the protagonist, and her development, at the centre of the narrative.

The novel's commitment to the positive effects of individual philanthropy and charitable projects such as model dwellings initiatives is perhaps not surprising, given that Ward herself was active in social improvement schemes throughout London during the late nineteenth and early twentieth centuries. The published version of the novel refers to the model dwellings in which Marcella lives as Brown's Buildings, but as noted previously, the original manuscript helpfully refers to them as the 'Peabody Buildings'.[24] The description of Brown's Buildings' geographical location in 'West Central London [. . .] within the same district' (341) as one character's lodgings on an 'old-fashioned street' (351) in Bloomsbury makes it identifiable as the Peabody dwellings on Little Coram Street (later Herbrand Street), which was completed in 1884. That Marcella becomes resident of these particular dwellings owes much to Ward's knowledge of the Herbrand Street dwellings and her familiarity with the inhabitants, for Ward had herself established a philanthropic settlement in the neighbourhood only four years before publishing *Marcella*. Bloomsbury's development during the nineteenth century was in part motivated by the sale of large portions of land that once belonged to the Duke of Bedford, but which had been sold to the Foundling Trust for the construction of the Foundling Hospital. Having purchased considerably more land than was necessary, the Trust was eager to sell the slum area on Little Coram Street to the Peabody Trust in 1882, on which the Herbrand Street buildings (Brown's Buildings in the novel) were constructed.[25]

Just around the corner from these buildings was a large site that the Duke of Bedford – keen to increase the value of his own property – agreed to long lease for £10 per annum for the establishment of a new philanthropic project: the University Hall Settlement.[26] Modelled on Toynbee Hall, which had been established in London's East End in 1884, the University Hall Settlement was first established by Ward in Bloomsbury in 1890 in order to offer lectures, classes and social events to local working-class residents. By the mid-1890s, the Settlement had grown to such a size that it required premises larger than its original site at Gordon Square. After raising finances for the construction of a new building, the largest portion of which came from the newspaper magnate John Passmore Edwards, the new building was eventually constructed on a corner at Tavistock Place, opposite the Peabody dwellings, and was opened by Ward in October 1897.[27] The University House Settlement attracted many residents of the nearby Peabody dwellings during its time at Gordon Square and after its move to Tavistock Place, and Ward was therefore familiar with the personal circumstances of the model dwellings' inhabitants. In fact, in 1881 Ward moved to 61 Russell Square, situated only slightly south-west of Little Coram Street, and would therefore have witnessed Bloomsbury's development during this period.[28]

The Peabody Trust has become in the twentieth century the name most associated with model housing for the working classes, largely due to its role as the company that 'excited the most interest and stimulated the most controversy'.[29] The Trust erected dwellings that were not for the poorest residents of the city, but for artisans and skilled labourers. Despite their barrack-like appearance, the building stock was of good quality and many of the Trust's buildings remain part of the architectural fabric of London today. Founded in 1862 by the American banker George Peabody, the Peabody Trust was soon one of the city's largest and fastest-growing contributors to the construction of model dwellings for the urban poor.[30] By 1907 the Trust had provided 5,469 tenements or flats for residents across London, from Whitechapel to Southwark and in many neighbourhoods in between.[31]

While the design of each Peabody block depended partly upon the area in which it was constructed, the majority of the buildings were designed by Henry Darbishire, who, in using certain consistent features, developed an architectural typology that is evident at Herbrand Street. Constructed on a slum-clearance site, the estate at Herbrand Street consists of a series of four, shallow, four-storey blocks arranged to form an internal courtyard. These buildings are of yellow brick (local stock brick and therefore less expensive), and each central range is bound by a crossing tower at each end. During the nineteenth century the buildings were often considered bulky and like army barracks (mostly, of course, by the middle classes), but the architect has skilfully balanced the vertical massing of the buildings by using a series of horizontal string courses of stone marked off by an entablature and a heavy cornice. The buildings at Herbrand Street attracted a diversity of residents, many of whom were financially secure enough to live alone in a two- or three-bedroom dwelling.[32]

In the novel, Marcella rents tenement 'number 10' (347) of the 'E. block' in 'Brown's Buildings' (349) while working in the area as a district nurse. Unlike the representation of model dwellings in most contemporary writing, the model dwellings in *Marcella* are austere but still an important social project. Brown's Buildings gives evidence of the ways in which model dwellings were purported to emancipate their residents from (what were understood as) characteristic working-class habits and behaviours, and to offer them a leg-up on to the ladder of social mobility by inculcating certain middle-class habits and aspirations. The novel makes clear that the action – or functionality – of these dwellings is in good order, both in the sense of their structural solidity and social effectiveness. It does not, however, shy away from the buildings' evident want of aspect: the degree to which they could be considered aesthetically pleasing. Brown's Buildings is therefore appropriately named; it is functional but uninspired, 'tall yet mean' (347).

In this sense, the novel follows the conventional characterisation of model dwellings in nineteenth-century literature. Perhaps most famous is George Gissing's description of Farringdon Road Buildings in *The Nether World* (1889) as 'those terrible barracks!' With the dramatic cynicism characteristic of Gissing's prose, the narrator describes the building as

> [v]ast, sheer walls, unbroken by even an attempt at ornament; row above row of windows in the mud-coloured surface, upwards, upwards, lifeless eyes, murky openings that tell of bareness, disorder, comfortlessness within. [. . .] An inner courtyard, asphalted, swept clean – looking up to the sky as from a prison. Acres of these edifices, the tinge of grime declaring the relative dates of their erection; millions of tons of brute brick and mortar, crushing the spirit as you gaze. Barracks, in truth; housing for the army of industrialism, an army fighting with itself, rank against rank, man against man, that the survivors may have whereon to feed. Pass by in the night, and strain imagination to picture the weltering mass of human weariness, of bestiality, of unmerited dolour, of hopeless hope, of crushed surrender, tumbled together within those forbidding walls.[33]

Although the reader may have a general sense of the architecture of the building based on this description, the narrative is clearly preoccupied with relating its visual oppressiveness through metaphor: the windows are 'lifeless eyes' and the central courtyard, although clean, is 'prison-like'. The description is, of course, exaggerated. The building did, in fact, present varying courses of brick, concrete sills and also an ornamented cornice. More remarkably, at a time when most model dwellings companies were building associated tenements that shared washroom facilities, Farringdon Road Buildings provided self-contained flats and even offered residents balconies on which they might grow flowers.

This impression, drawn from the perspective not of a resident but of someone who would 'pass by', reveals what Richard Dennis identifies as an aspect of Gissing's 'prejudice against flats': as a member of the middle class, Gissing was less able to appreciate the improvement to working-class housing made by many model dwellings companies.[34] Farringdon Road Buildings was built between 1872 and 1874 and financed by the Metropolitan Association for Improving the Dwellings of the Industrial Classes, one of the most established of the city's model dwellings companies. Although these buildings housed a class of residents somewhat less financially secure than those in the Peabody dwellings at Herbrand Street, the inhabitants were engaged in regular employment and were by no means as destitute as those housed in the model dwellings that feature in Margaret Harkness's *A City Girl*, Katharine Buildings in East Smithfield. In fact, the dwellings were 'highly appreciated' by the tenants.[35] The description of the buildings in *The Nether World* is hyperbolised for the purpose of illustrating the relationship between industrialisation and oppression; the inhabitants of Farringdon Road Buildings, in other words, were not only exploited as employees, but were also circumscribed by the very structures that industry made possible.

In *Marcella*, although the narrator reveals the bleak aspect of the new structures provided by model dwellings companies, the narrative itself endorses the improvements that these buildings were designed to enable. One of the ways the novel accomplishes this is by describing the cognitive stability, and in particular the sense of practical independence, that the buildings make possible for Marcella. On her way home after a night shift, as Marcella

> entered the iron gate of the dwellings, and saw before her the large asphalted court round which they ran – blazing heat on one side of it, and on the other some children playing cricket against the wall with

chalk-marks for wickets – she was seized with depression. The tall yet mean buildings, the smell of dust and heat, the general impression and packed and crowded humanity – these things, instead of offering her rest, only continued and accented the sense of strain, called for more endurance, more making the best of it. (347)

This description lacks the histrionic style of Gissing's prose, but the difference is that the struggle faced by the buildings' inhabitants in *The Nether World* is perceived to be 'man against man' whereas in *Marcella* it is a struggle of will and 'endurance' against oneself. For Marcella, this struggle contributes to the development of her character and judgement throughout the novel.

Architectural 'Aspect' and Brown's Buildings

Although living among a 'very respectable though poor class' (348), Marcella is determined to achieve certain domestic improvements in her situation. For instance, her patrician inclinations encourage her to invite a young widow and her children to live with her under the pretence of having the widow assist with household duties. With the permission of the trustees she makes 'a temporary communication' between the two flats 'so that she could either live her own solitary and independent life, or call for their companionship, as she pleased' (348). Marcella's relationship with the widow is clearly hierarchical: it is she who can 'call for their companionship' whenever she grows weary of her independence; and of course, the other residents of Brown's Buildings do not have the economic resources to simply 'endure' (347) their way out of personal difficulty. Although this novel is more complex in its treatment of women's intellectual development and political theory than has previously been assumed, it would be misleading to suggest that it is in any way progressive in its treatment of the working classes. As stated, Ward is concerned with her protagonist's development – a convention of the *bildungsroman* – and the way this development begins is in her willingness to entertain multiple perspectives and ideas. Marcella's often insensitive individualism is a consequence of her status as the novel's liberal subject.

Such individualism is expressed by Marcella's very presence in Brown's Buildings. For instance, in the extract quoted above, the building's exterior instils in Marcella a sense of strain and depression, but those aspects of the building that she can influence or alter provide her with a sense of accomplishment and contentment. There is evident satisfaction for Marcella in her isolation and self-determinacy that is absent from the heavily circumscribed characters of Gissing's work:

> As she shut her door behind her she found herself in a little passage or entry. To the left was her bedroom. Straight in front of her was the living room with a small close range in it, and behind it a little back kitchen.
> The living room was cheerful and even pretty. Her art-student's training showed itself. The cheap blue and white paper, the couple of oak flap tables from a broker's shop in Marchmont Street, the two or three cane chairs with their bright chintz cushions, the Indian rug or two on the varnished boards, the photographs and etchings on the walls, the books on the tables – there was not one of these things that was not in its degree a pleasure to her young sense, that did not help her to live her life. (348)

The room offers to Marcella the aspect that is absent from the building's exterior, and is enhanced due to her personal involvement in establishing and influencing its character. Beth Sutton-Ramspeck and Nicole Meller note that 'residents' alterations were strictly controlled' and for this reason 'Marcella's re-modelling seems implausible' (349, n. 1). Despite this inaccuracy, Marcella's renovations are significant, but not only because this 'temporary communication' implies that she has greater freedoms than the other tenants and in the space of Brown's Buildings is a privileged subject.

The time Marcella spends as resident of Brown's Buildings, which is structurally the novel's centre, is also the most pivotal point in her personal development. The modifications that Marcella makes to her flat are not merely superficial, but instead closer to Ruskin's ideas of 'aspect': they involve deliberation and compromise, and as such, 'help her to live her life' (348). Marcella's flat in Brown's Buildings is an architectural ideal that balances action, that is, the building's functionality and social purposiveness, with aspect, provided by Marcella's 'art-student's training'. This balance of commitments or interplay of ideas, the novel suggests, enables individual development and, correspondingly, the transition of private free thought into public opinion. The novel therefore pays particular attention to the ways in which Brown's Buildings enables Marcella's emotional maturity and intellectual development through its presentation of action and aspect, which together enable forms of communication.

This interplay of ideas, given further substance by the variety of opinions and ideas Marcella encounters while living in the building, becomes a method by which the novel proposes that social and political change can be achieved. Marcella's intellectual development would not be possible without the residential improvements, not only in the sense that it makes her environment more aesthetically pleasing, but because it changes the dwelling's function and permits communication: her flat becomes a space that allows for the coexistence of the domestic, the social and the political. For instance, the novel offers a reconceptualisation of the conventional nineteenth-century 'at home', a gathering that Marcella hosts and to which she invites groups of people from various social and economic backgrounds, and of differing political sympathies. These meetings stimulate Marcella's critical judgement, and provide a forum for her to communicate these ideas with her neighbours. She remarks to a friend:

> I am full of perplexities; and the Cravens, I see, will soon be for turning me out. You understand – I *know* some working folk now! [. . .] [N]ow I am in their world – I live with them – and they talk to me. One evening in the week I am 'at home' for all the people I know in our Buildings – men and women [. . .] The men smoke – when we can have the windows open! – and I believe I shall soon smoke too – it makes them talk better. We get all sorts – Socialists, Conservatives, Radicals – [. . .] (399)

As the social and political nucleus of Brown's Buildings, Marcella's flat epitomises the ideological diversity that matches the variegated aesthetic character created by the Indian rug, chintz cushions and old oak table. The two-room dwelling is a space that enables Marcella's self-determination – the will and 'endurance' to '[make] the best of it' (347) – as well as a venue for intellectual 'talk' that all contributes to the development of what Peter Collister defines as her 'conscience, judgement and discrimination'.[36] The experience of living independently at Brown's Buildings therefore does not 'correct [Marcella's] radicalism', but instead allows her to test the limitations of her ideological convictions.[37]

Brown's Buildings, the novel suggests, provides the structural framework that allows for the expression of individual character. It is in the context of these public 'at home[s]' that Marcella, having been given space for self-reflection and deliberation, can express her own thoughtful and informed opinions. These processes of continuing intellectual and emotional exchange, first the liberal individual's private cognition and, later, the communication of these ideas into public opinion, strike closer at the novel's ideological heart than does a simple exchange of socialism for conservatism. When Marcella begins to question socialism's effectiveness at the novel's conclusion, it is partly because she believes its emphasis on circumstance denies individual agency and in this sense does not allow for meaningful change. After a socialist friend reproaches her for her inconsistent political affinities, she retorts:

> [S]o far as Socialism means a political system – the trampling out of private enterprise and competition, and all the rest of it – I find myself slipping away from it more and more. No! – as I go about among these wage-earners, the emphasis – do what I will – comes to lie less and less on possession – more and more on character. I go to two tenements in the same building. One is Hell – the other Heaven. Why? Both belong to well-paid artisans with equal opportunities. (377)

Marcella's argument at this stage recalls the familiar nineteenth-century doctrine of self-help, that is, the notion that social position depends less on what one *has* and rather on what one *does*; after all, she does not question the material circumstances that might result in the development of different kinds of character. Marcella's use of the word 'character' is significant in the context of nineteenth-century liberalism, because it was this abstract quality that was seen to define the liberal individual. As Lauren Goodlad explains, in the nineteenth century, 'character' ceased to be a trait only available to gentlemen. Instead, character and its 'moral content' was often pitted against the 'levelling and materialism [. . .] of economic independence'.[38] Character soon came to define political individuality and thereby became a central component of liberal subjecthood.[39] By the late nineteenth century, as Ruth Livesey notes, character had become 'the causal factor in social explanation': it was 'a selfhood constructed from ideal moral dispositions rather than material physicality'.[40]

Before Marcella leaves Brown's Buildings to return home to Mellor in order to nurse her dying father, she experiences a 'dangerous significant moment' (387). This moment is one that indicates to the reader Marcella's intellectual maturation: after having had access to a space that allows her to develop her individuality, she also comes to appreciate what she defines as the 'character' of others. After 'shut[ting] herself up' in the solitude of her flat she

> hung at the window a long time, watching the stars come out, as the summer light died from the sky and even the walls and roofs, and chimneys of this interminable London spread out before her, to a certain dim beauty. And then, slipping down on the floor, with her head against a

chair – an attitude of her stormy childhood – she wept with an abandonment and passion she had not known for years [. . .] '[W]hat are opinions – what is influence, beauty, cleverness? – what is anything worth but *character* – but *soul?*'

And character – soul – can only be got by self-surrender; and self-surrender comes not of knowledge but of love. (386)

Marcella interprets character not as an inherent quality but as a responsive process: character is the consequence of self-surrender to liberalism's diversity of opinion rather than the self-assertion of a particular ideology. In this scene, the city is laid out before her: an assemblage of walls, roofs and chimneys that expresses an 'interminable' process of continuous responsive building and rebuilding that gives to London a 'certain dim beauty' of character. The scene makes a direct connection between the representation of the built environment and the process of Marcella's intellectual development. This perspective of the city, looking out over London, gives evidence to the social and structural interdependency of individual and cumulative processes. It is a similar process of exchange and interdependence that Marcella eventually realises is necessary for the development of individual character. For Ruskin, to contemplate a building was 'not simply to look at something beautiful, it was also to contemplate a way of living, an ordering of human communities'.[41] *Marcella* engages with one example of the model dwellings movement to ask the reader to consider the 'ordering of human communities', and how such social projects might serve to suggest a model for political debate more generally.

Yet the novel, which uses the materialism of domestic architecture to give substance to its demonstration of the processes of liberal cognition, returns at its conclusion to an unsatisfying abstraction: character. While it espouses the importance of materiality in shaping the patterns of liberal ideology, it ultimately fails to take account of how this materialism might enable or disable an individual's capacity for these forms of self-reflection, deliberation and reason.

Building Character

The building designed for the University Hall Settlement, which was named the Passmore Edwards Settlement (Fig. 3.1) when it was opened by Ward in 1897, offers a less abstract conclusion to the novel's engagement with themes of ideological deliberation and

Figure 3.1 Passmore Edwards Settlement, C. C. Brewer and A. Dunbar-Smith (1895). Illustration from *Academy Architecture and Architectural Review*, 9 (1896), p. 29

reconciliation. Designed by Arnold Dunbar Smith and Cecil Claude Brewer and constructed from 1895 to 1897, the Passmore Edwards Settlement has been described as one of London's finest Arts and Crafts buildings.[42] What is particularly notable is that Smith and Brewer were best known for their work in domestic architecture, and the building at Tavistock Place offers an example of an original and unprecedented use of residential style in public building. Yet the building is also an illustration of what an article in the *British Architect* describes as a 'problem of architectural design', because it is necessarily 'a combination of domestic and public uses: a home for residents and a recreative and educational institution for the public'.[43] It was important that the Passmore Edwards Settlement allow for a range of activities – dining, debating, public lectures – and its design reflects these purposes in both action and aspect, to return once again to Ruskin's terms. The building's front elevation uses predominantly red brick, a material associated with domestic architecture during the nineteenth century, but the unusual projecting wings that flank this central section, the use of white plaster above the cornice and the low-hipped roof all offset the residential design. The entrances to the building are designed differently depending on purpose: from each wing projects a symmetrical portico with a curved balustrade that allows access to the public spaces of the building, and an off-centre projecting stone vestibule punctuated by a four-point arched entranceway provides access to the residential area. An article published in the *British Architect* also points out that the building's interior exhibits a similar combination of styles, a 'real homeliness' but also a 'simplicity of general effect'.⁴⁴ Despite this 'simplicity' – a statement made clearer when one considers the more elaborate Toynbee Hall (1884) – it had clearly been designed with 'every care as to [its] purpose' and for this reason it marked a departure from most nineteenth-century buildings; it looks ahead to the twentieth century's emphasis on design over decoration. This combination of residential and civic purpose, and the resulting marriage of styles, marks a radical departure from conventional ways of thinking about buildings.

In both design and purpose, then, the building designed for Ward's University Hall Settlement expands upon the ideological complexity that is rather disappointingly flattened into abstraction at *Marcella*'s conclusion. In its deliberation between and unification of styles, the design of the Passmore Edwards Settlement brings together the political and ethical programme that Ward explores in *Marcella*. Like Brown's Buildings, the Passmore Edwards Settlement provided a broader structure of organisational support for the seventeen residents who lived there as social workers, and also for the members of the community who subscribed to the Settlement's classes, debates, lectures and facilities, which included men's and women's gyms, a library, common rooms and a drawing room.⁴⁵ The building's dual purpose as both a residential and civic structure is articulated in its design, which at once distinguishes between uses but also unifies these differences. Although a design for the building had been submitted by well-known architect A. H. Mackmurdo, the committee decided that the plans were too costly and too fussy and instead, under the adjudication of Norman Shaw, settled on a modern design that Adrian Forty believes embodies 'an inspired moment in British architecture'.⁴⁶ It was a time when, architect Owen Fleming recollects, 'we believed that earnest and true thought expressed in buildings would awaken some response in the popular mind'.⁴⁷

Although 'tall and mean' in aspect, Brown's Buildings in *Marcella* works through many of the same ideals that the Passmore Edwards Settlement would animate socially and architecturally: in particular, the relationship between individual and community, and the methods of exchange that structure this relationship. Although Ruskin's moral imperative is dampened in *Marcella*, Ward asks her reader to consider the interplay between action and aspect in the relationships represented in the novel – those between individuals and communities, and also between social groups and the built environment. The novel's ambition is, therefore, not to correct political persuasions but instead to engage the minds and morals of its readership. In so doing, Ward gives the reader a similar task to the protagonist in the novel: to develop their own individuality, or 'character', within the broader theories and ideas present in the novel, and in social discourse more generally.

Notes

1. Gwynn, *Mrs Humphrey Ward*, p. 42.
2. 'Novel Notes', *Bookman*, November 1896, p. 49.
3. Holroyd, *Lytton Strachey: A Critical Biography*, vol. 1, p. 443. For such reconsiderations, see in particular Sutton-Ramspeck, 'Mary Ward and the Claims of Conflicting Feminism', pp. 204–22, and Coit, 'Mary Augusta Ward's "Perfect Economist"', pp. 1213–38.
4. Anne Bindslev points out that the novel is an unconventional *bildungsroman* given its treatment of a woman's reconciliation of the self with society in a genre that was 'almost exclusively a male prerogative'. See Bindslev, *Mrs Humphry Ward*, p. 55. See also Argyle, 'Mrs Humphry Ward's Experiments in the Woman Question', pp. 939–57, and Collister, 'Portraits of "Audacious Youth"', pp. 296–317.
5. Hadley, *Living Liberalism*, p. 1.
6. Ibid. pp. 8–9.
7. Ibid. p. 10.
8. Ward, *Marcella*, ed. Sutton-Ramspeck and Meller, p. 349, n. 1. Further references to this edition are given in parentheses in the text.
9. 'Editorial Notes', *Women's Penny Paper*, 5 April 1894, p. 226. The Countess of Carlisle, Rosalind Frances Howard, was a temperance and women's rights activist and was known in the period as the 'radical countess'.
10. Arnold, *Culture and Anarchy*, ed. Wilson, pp. xxiii–xxiv.
11. Hadley, *Living Liberalism*, p. 27.
12. Arnold, 'The Function of Criticism at the Present Time', in *Culture and Anarchy and Other Writings*, ed. Collini, p. 35.
13. See Collister, 'Portraits of "Audacious Youth"', pp. 306–7, and Sutton-Ramspeck, 'Mary Ward and the Claims of Conflicting Feminism', p. 220. For Ward's evaluation, see 'Introduction to the Westmoreland edition', in *Marcella* (1910), p. v.
14. Ruskin, *The Stones of Venice*, vol. 1, p. 42.
15. Ibid. p. 41.
16. Ibid.

17. Ibid. p. 40.
18. Ward, *A Writer's Recollections*, vol. 1, p. 77.
19. Ibid. p. 133.
20. Ward, *Robert Elsmere*, p. 170.
21. For a discussion of the similarities between Marcella's childhood and Ward's own, see Ward, *Marcella*, ed. Sutton-Ramspeck and Meller, 'Introduction', p. 12.
22. Sutherland, *Mrs. Humphrey Ward*, Appendix B.
23. Koven, *Slumming*, p. 9.
24. Ward, *Marcella*, ed. Sutton-Ramspeck and Meller, p. 349, n. 1.
25. Ashton, *Victorian Bloomsbury*, pp. 293–300.
26. Baynes, *John Passmore Edwards and Mary Ward*, p. 17. See also Ashton, *Victorian Bloomsbury*, pp. 295–7.
27. Although the building was officially opened in February 1898, it was in use as of October 1897. See Ashton, *Victorian Bloomsbury*, p. 299.
28. Baynes, *John Passmore Edwards and Mary Ward*, p. 5.
29. Wohl, *The Eternal Slum*, p. 153.
30. This was largely a consequence of the funds received in interest and profits on rents being paid back into the trust rather than being fully divided among shareholders, as was common in other philanthropic housing schemes. Thompson, *Housing Up-to-Date*, p. 147.
31. Wohl, *The Eternal Slum*, p. 149.
32. Dennis, *Cities in Modernity*, p. 250.
33. Gissing, *The Nether World*, p. 274.
34. Dennis, 'Buildings, Residences and Mansions', pp. 41–62.
35. As Dennis points out, the residents of Farringdon Road Buildings have considerably less hostility to these model dwellings than does the narrator. Despite their contentment, they are nonetheless characters who are, according to the narrator's descriptions, severely limited by their complacency regarding their own living conditions. See Dennis, 'Buildings, Residences and Mansions', p. 53. See also 'Farringdon Road', *Survey of London: Volume 46 South and East Clerkenwell* (2008), pp. 358–84, <https://www.british-history.ac.uk/survey-london/vol46/pp358-384> (last accessed 1 June 2019).
36. Collister, 'Portraits of "Audacious Youth"', p. 307.
37. Argyle, 'Mrs Humphry Ward's Experiments in the Woman Question', p. 947.
38. Goodlad, *Victorian Literature and the Victorian State*, p. 26.
39. Hadley, *Living Liberalism*, p. 7, n. 11; Goodlad, *Victorian Literature and the Victorian State*, pp. 26–7.
40. Livesey, 'Reading for Character', pp. 45–6.
41. Johnson, *English Houses*, p. 4.
42. The architects were in fact residents of the University Settlement during its time at Gordon Square, and moved into the building they designed upon its completion in 1898. According to Peter Davey, 'many of the

[Settlement's] inhabitants were young architects'. See Davey, *Arts and Crafts Architecture*, p. 144.
43. 'The Passmore Edwards Settlement', *British Architect*, 25 February 1898, p. 125.
44. Ibid.
45. Baynes, *John Passmore Edwards and Mary Ward*, p. 16.
46. Forty, 'The Mary Ward Settlement', p. 28.
47. Cited in ibid. p. 48.

Chapter 4

Labour Leaders and Socialist Saviours: Individualism and Collectivism in Margaret Harkness's *George Eastmont, Wanderer*

In 1891 the author and activist Margaret Harkness contributed a series of four articles to the *Pall Mall Gazette* on London's most prominent 'labour leaders': John Burns, Tom Mann, Henry Hyde Champion and R. B. Cunninghame Graham. During the London dockworkers' strike of 1889, Harkness worked closely with all the labour leaders, and her character sketches reveal a thorough knowledge of the strike itself and also the personal qualities of its leaders and what she viewed as their strengths and weaknesses. Writing of Champion, she acknowledges that his upper-class background bequeathed to him a patrician quality that made him 'a soldier, brave and tender-hearted, [and] a proud and very reticent man'.[1] Yet his efforts to 'declass' himself, she explains, could only ever fail:

> [I]t is one thing to become a Socialist because your class is oppressed, and another to throw in your lot with the oppressed because your class is the oppressor. In the latter case you may preach that all class is wrong, and spend your time and strength in trying to break down social barriers; but you will merely find yourself declassed in a world of classes. Your own class will treat you as a renegade, and the oppressed class will be suspicious.[2]

The particular dynamics of Champion's attempt to live 'declassed in a world of classes' is a theme that Harkness would revisit in her novel *George Eastmont, Wanderer* (1905). The novel, 'which contains the writer's experiences in the labour movement, and thoughts about it', traces the growth of the British socialist movement during the 1880s through to its apex at the 1889 London dockworkers' strike by way of the experiences of its eponymous protagonist.[3] In a way, the novel is a *roman à clef* of the early socialist movement in Britain, but one that privileges the personal history of an 'aristocratic socialist' who John Barnes identifies as Henry Hyde Champion.[4] Despite certain similarities between Champion's life and Eastmont's experiences in the novel, *George Eastmont, Wanderer* is in no sense a straightforward biographical history.[5] In fact, one formal technique of Harkness's novel is to confound biography – and thereby challenge socialist forms of heroes and hero-worship – by deliberately conflating her own experiences with those of Champion.

George Eastmont, Wanderer is structured in two divergent parts: the novel's first half begins with Eastmont's socialist conversion and political activism in London's East End up to the climactic moment of the dockworkers' strike of 1889; the latter half traces Eastmont's disengagement from this community and his emigration to Australia, where he investigates political questions around land and labour. In this sense, the novel seems to examine the failures of the early socialist movement more than it celebrates its successes. While it is tempting to read Eastmont's eventual disengagement from collective politics as the failure of the late nineteenth-century socialist movement itself, such a comparison fails to take account of the ideological complexity and protean nature of political commitment at this point in history. In fact, David Glover suggests that the socialist themes that characterise the novel's first half become more radical in its second half, where they are replaced by a consideration of the 'co-operative ideal' and even forms of anarchism that might offer some promise for the future.[6] The novel does not offer readers a celebratory or official history of a political movement, but rather interprets the emotional cost of ideological commitment: is it even possible, the novel asks, to reconcile individual political commitment with collective goals and priorities.[7] In 1889 Harkness spoke to her cousin Beatrice Potter of her dispiriting experience working with the Social Democratic Federation and implied certain personal grievances that she was reluctant to share, but she explained, 'I shall get out of the whole thing some day – and then I can tell you all.'[8] *George Eastmont, Wanderer* is, it seems, an attempt to better explain this disappointment; by the point of its publication sixteen years later, Harkness's personal objections were subdued by an evaluation of the possibility of ideological commitment in a period of political turmoil.

Central to the novel's examination of late nineteenth-century socialism is its representation of the conflict between individualism and collectivism. To be sure, Harkness was not unique in her identification of this ideological opposition, which was in many ways an important debate within the late nineteenth-century socialist community. Stephen Yeo explains that the tension between individualism and collectivism was a central socialist problematic, and that Sidney Webb was forced to coax himself into '"self-deadness" in order to subordinate the individual self to the collectivist social whole'.[9] In writing to Beatrice Potter (later Webb) in 1888, Olive Schreiner comments: 'I was [. . .] working out what seems to me the reconciliation of Socialism & Individualism. Then I thought you had probably worked it out much more completely yourself.'[10] An examination of this tension also helps to shed light on what has often been interpreted as Harkness's waning commitment to socialism during the last decade of the nineteenth century. Scholars such as Seth Koven have suggested that Harkness was 'forever trying on and taking off new religious and political beliefs', in a way (particularly given the sartorial metaphor of this phrase) that seems to attribute her inconsistency to feminine capriciousness rather than serious opposition to certain principles of the socialist movement.[11] One of the greatest consistencies in Harkness's work, in fact, is her dedication to documenting women's marginalisation within social and political communities.

George Eastmont, Wanderer offers an opportunity to interrogate the relationship between individualism and collectivism in two communities – socialist and religious – where women's engagement was routinely sidelined. By engaging with religion, specifically Christianity, the novel participates in a broader cultural discourse during the last two decades of the nineteenth century that associated socialism with religion, particularly the ways it 'presented itself as a certain ground for hope, a convincing analysis of what had gone before, a morally impeccable challenge, and as an organised movement demanding commitment, sacrifice and missionary activity by the newly converted'.[12] If socialism adopted the religious community's commitment and compassion, however, so too did it inherit a social hierarchy that produced internal conflict. Deborah Mutch has examined how British socialist discourses were developed through a rearticulation of established political discourses, especially Tory paternalism, which were constructed and disseminated in serialised fiction such as Champion's *Labour Elector*.[13] Where the discursive paradigms of the early socialist movement were inflected by a religious precedent, so too did socialism build upon models of religious paternalism in order to construct what Mutch describes as the 'role of the guiding hand'.[14] *George Eastmont, Wanderer* interrogates the contradictions that socialism inherits from its religious precedent: specifically, those forged by a theology in which individuals might advocate socialist egalitarianism, but which must also rely upon the authority warranted by its hierarchical organisation. The novel grapples with this contradiction and determines that for the Church to earnestly support egalitarian socialism would ultimately render Christianity's power impotent.

Although *George Eastmont, Wanderer* was published by the religious press Burns & Oates, its representation of religion – like its representation of socialism – is neither plainly advocative nor condemnatory.[15] Rather, the novel questions whether organised commitment necessarily relies on unequal power relationships, and whether egalitarianism necessarily produces conflict. The conflict between individualism and collectivism is given expression in the novel's representation of Eastmont's time living among 'the people' in an 'Artizan's Block' (5).[16] In the novel, Eastmont is an intercessory figure who thematically unites both religion and socialism, but his moral and political authority are undermined by his presence among 'the people'. *George Eastmont, Wanderer* rearticulates Christianity's spiritual paternalism in the material and secular paradigm of the Artizan's Block, and in so doing reveals the inadequacies of both religious and socialist philosophy.

Political and Religious Paternalism

The internal schisms of the early socialist movement in Britain have been well documented by scholars who helpfully examine the origins and legacies of these divisions, and also their continual repositioning.[17] Although Harkness had lived alongside her cousin Beatrice Potter during Potter's tenure as a rent collector at Katharine Buildings, from this early point she dismissed Potter's commitment to the gradualist and reformist methods of Fabian socialism as merely her 'phantom theory'.[18] It is an opinion that Harkness seems to have maintained into the twentieth century, one that she shared with Champion, and one that Eastmont echoes in *George Eastmont, Wanderer*.

Early in the novel, when Eastmont is seeking guidance on how best to enact his socialist enthusiasm, he consults two figures of religious authority: Cardinal Lorraine, an Archbishop of the Church of Rome, and the Revd Edgar Podmore, a parish priest of the Church of England. Described by Easmont as an 'arm-chair socialist' (41) on account of his commitment to Fabian socialism, Podmore is nevertheless a sympathetic character – albeit one who is invested in his own authority.[19] The novel clearly aligns Podmore's religious authority with the paternal ideology that underpins the Fabian belief in the superiority of liberal middle-class culture. Podmore warns Eastmont that his ambition to live among the working classes in order to raise their awareness of their own exploitation is useless: '[Y]ou have no idea how ignorant they are. I've lived amongst them for many years, and I know them, you don't. If you did you would be a Fabian' (41–2). Although Podmore shares many of Eastmont's socialist concerns, his spiritual guidance and material generosity are both predicated on demanding recognition of his own authority.

Perhaps the novel's most important figure of paternalism, however, is Archbishop Cardinal Lorraine, who is modelled on Cardinal Henry Edward Manning, and with whom the novel begins and concludes. Lytton Strachey archly recalls Manning's participation in 'philanthropic gatherings in Exeter Hall, from strike committees at the docks to Mayfair drawing-rooms', and marvels at his ability to become 'one of the leaders of the procession less through merit rather than through a superior faculty for gliding adroitly through to front ranks'.[20] *George Eastmont, Wanderer* is similarly critical of the cult of personality that surrounded Manning, even while its effects are central to the narrative development. Lorraine shares Podmore's belief in Christian charity, but is firm that radical activism will only 'inflame the masses, [and] lead to nothing'. He asserts proleptically that '[t]here is much hardship and distress [. . .] but English working men will never join Socialists' (8).

Podmore and Lorraine discourage Eastmont's egalitarianism, but his political conviction inspires him to cast off both models of religious authority and live among 'the People' (5). While the process of political awakening to socialism was often rendered through religious discourse in the late nineteenth century, particularly as a form of conversion narrative, in Eastmont's case it is doubly significant: it establishes the novel's connection between religious and political conviction, but also allows Eastmont to adopt a Christ-like role as socialist saviour to the masses. However, Eastmont's experience living in the Artizan's Block reveals the fallacy of his presumed moral authority.

The increasing tendency towards paternalist intervention from the state during the nineteenth century, according to David Roberts, 'formed a parallel to the paternalism of property and the church'.[21] This trinity – property, religion and government – weaves a complex web throughout *George Eastmont, Wanderer* that makes apparent the ways in which each one of these three aspects contends with conflicts between individualism and collectivism. When Eastmont renounces his own position of privilege in favour of living in the Artizan's Block with members of the skilled working class, he believes that he resigns individual ambition for the purpose of collective political goals. In doing so, however, he also aggrandises his own position. After spending a night sleeping in a doss-house, Eastmont decides to 'cut [himself] off for ever from the classes that fatten on the miseries of the poor' (7). However, his proposed sacrifice on behalf of the poor is diminished by his sense of self-importance: 'A Saviour of the masses was wanted, someone who would go amongst them and show them how to help themselves, rouse them out of their apathy and ignorance, and give them hope. Where was the man?' (15). A representational conflict emerges in the novel at this point, one that is characterised by dramatic irony, as the narrator is quietly conscious of Eastmont's hubris in appointing himself political 'saviour of the masses' (15) and the contradiction between the authority of such a role and an allegedly egalitarian purpose. When finally 'the day of reckoning is at hand' (17), Eastmont decides to sacrifice himself and 'go down among the People', for as his friend Charleston (a figure who Glover suggests is a 'hybrid' of Tom Mann and Ben Tillett) explains, 'they would listen [to him] as they will not listen to one of themselves' (19).[22] Eastmont's motivations and ambitions embody the conflict between individualism and collectivism, and both become increasingly legible during his time living among those he proposes to save in the Artizan's Block.

Authority and the Artizan's Block

The related agendas of religion, government and property under nineteenth-century paternalist ideology, as Roberts explains, involved methods of 'defending and disciplining its subjects'.[23] *George Eastmont, Wanderer* combines the paternalism of both government and property in its representation of one of London's earliest housing schemes to be initiated by a public authority. Unlike many of Harkness's other novels, which provide detail enough for residences to be easily matched with their historic counterparts, *George Eastmont, Wanderer* does not specify either the full name or the location of the Artizan's Block, other than to mention that it is in 'the City' (26), and that Eastmont's route home one evening takes him past St Paul's Cathedral. From this limited information, it is very likely that the building is modelled on the Artizans' Buildings at Golden

Figure 4.1 Architect's drawing of the Artizans' Buildings (or Corporation Buildings), Petticoat Square. Designed by William Haywood for the City of London Corporation (1885). Illustration from *The Builder*, 26 September 1865, pp. 425–6

Lane and Petticoat Square (Fig. 4.1), financed by the City of London Corporation. Only three schemes were constructed in the City during the 1880s and they were built by the Corporation itself, ostensibly in order to rehouse residents displaced by slum clearance earlier in the century: Tower Bridge Buildings, Viaduct Buildings, and the buildings at Middlesex Street (Petticoat Square and Golden Lane).[24] Both the location and the formal detail of the building described in the novel most closely match the five blocks constructed at Middlesex Street, which were referred to during the period as simply the 'Artizans' Buildings' or the 'Corporation Buildings', which partly explains Harkness's uncharacteristic imprecision.[25]

Originally on the site at Stoney Lane off Middlesex Street stood the notorious slum Angel Court, 'housing a population so bad no policeman could go alone among them at night, on an area so unhealthy as to be a disgrace'.[26] When the site was cleared between 1877 and 1879 by the City Corporation under the Artisans' and Labourers' Act, the improvement scheme displaced 1,783 people. The Select Committee required that new dwellings house at least the same number of people as had been evicted from the site, a nearly impossible task given the overcrowding in most slums.[27] This difficulty was further complicated by the high value of the land, which left the Corporation unable to secure a tender for the site except at a tremendous loss.[28] Eventually the City was able to amend the bill so that half the number of people could be rehoused on the site, and the remainder could be rehoused at 'some reasonable and suitable distance'.[29] In 1884 the City of London Artizans' Dwellings Corporation constructed five separate parallel blocks with accommodation for 937 persons – roughly half the number evicted, supposing, as the *British Architect* points out, that 'one person slept on the ground-floor of the tradesmen's premises'.[30] In this sense the Boundary Estate, the LCC's first social housing development, which was opened in 1900, was preceded by social housing constructed by the City of London (which predated the creation of London's local councils).

In his book cataloguing the reforms and improvements to the late nineteenth-century metropolis, *The London Programme* (1891), Sidney Webb notes that by 1888 the majority of flats in the Corporation Buildings had been let and 923 persons were in occupation, but '[n]o other public authority in London has yet erected any dwellings'.[31] Like the model dwellings built by philanthropic corporations such as the Peabody Trust or the Guinness Trust, those built by the City of London Corporation were for the 'aristocracy' of London's working classes.[32] In Harkness's novel, Eastmont decides that it is necessary to live among the working people whom he intends to save, and selects one such 'aristocratic' building – yet he finds even the high-standard accommodation of the Artizan's Block utterly unendurable. Eastmont's time living in the building exposes his deeply rooted class prejudice, and reveals his inability to sacrifice his individuality on behalf of the community. In *The London Programme* Webb points out that the 'ideal three rooms and a scullery [. . .] should be [the] goal' in providing accommodation.[33] Eastmont is privileged to have such ideal accommodation in the Artizan's Block, to the degree that 'the other men [think] his home too luxurious' (30). Yet he finds the 'dreary little room[s]' (32) in the Artizan's Block unbearable:

> [H]e reached the Artizan's Block in which he lived. He paid seven shillings and sixpence a week for three rooms in it, sitting-room, bedroom, and kitchen. It was a tall, ungainly structure, built of red brick; and round it was an asphalt path. (26)

Despite his relentless socialist rhetoric, Eastmont's prejudices are intractable. Expressing the kind of abhorrence towards model dwellings typical of many of George Gissing's middle-class characters, Eastmont regularly describes the way his environment fills him with 'disgust and annoyance' (39). Although he consoles himself by turning his imagination to the '[o]ne who had been meek and lowly, sitting on an ass [...] and the common people followed him' (39), Eastmont's revulsion is apparent to the people among whom he lives – the very people he hopes might 'follow him'.

During his time living in the Artizan's Block, Eastmont attempts to gain the trust of the residents by appointing himself the moral authority of the building. To his disappointment, the building's inhabitants refuse to be influenced by his presence, or even by his constant exhortations. Particular admonishment is reserved for his wife, Julia, who herself is described as one of Eastmont's socialist 'experiment[s]' (16). The 'disgust and annoyance' (39) that Eastmont feels for the Artizan's Block also characterises his response to his wife's company. At one point, he soliloquises:

> Having lived all his life amongst people who make eating a fine art, he found Julia's gymnastics with her knife and fork rather a trial to his appetite [...] [H]e had hoped that Julia would drop the peculiarities she shared with the People, and copy him when they were married. (25)

Much like the Artizan's Block's other residents, Julia is conscious of her husband's contempt but she is also isolated from the rural community in which she was raised on account of her marriage. While Eastmont is in prison, having sacrificed himself for 'the People' (5) while participating in the Trafalgar Square riots, Julia dies of a drug overdose, a habit she develops partly on account of his hostility, which gradually becomes a form of emotional abuse. Eastmont's bitterness towards Julia is partly the result of his inability to compromise his authority over their shared domestic environment. The narrator, focalised through Eastmont, explains: '"What's thine is mine, and what's mine is my own", is the creed of most husbands; but he had carried communism into his domestic life, with the result that only his writing-table and letters remained his private property; nothing else was safe from his wife's encroachments' (33). Although the religious language of this sentence differentiates Eastmont from 'most husbands' in his domestic 'communism', his resentment at having done so is apparent, betrayed by the implication that Julia's very presence is a kind of hazardous intrusion.

The model dwellings movement, which emerged in the middle of the nineteenth century, was motivated by philanthropic initiatives to provide the skilled working classes with improved accommodation. Yet the moral project of this movement was governed by, and sought to reinforce, middle-class behaviour and values. The improvement schemes enacted and the residential buildings constructed in response to London's slum clearance had, according to Martin Gaskell, 'a dimension beyond architectural creativity, patronage and philanthropic endeavour: that dimension was didactic'.[34] Model dwellings were, as Gaskell explains, designed to influence behaviour and effect moral improvement through design. The Artizans' Block at Petticoat Square operated on the principle of 'associated flats' with shared communal facilities. For the other inhabitants of the Artizan's Block in *George Eastmont, Wanderer* the associated facilities are no terrible compromise, but Eastmont resents 'liv[ing] without a bathroom' (29). Eastmont feels that he is unable to establish authority in his own domestic space, and comparatively, he is also unable to gain the authority to which he feels entitled among the residents of the Artizan's Block owing to his supercilious behaviour. He scoffs at the 'dirty children [. . .] on the staircase, rolling over one another and talking cockney gibberish', and recoils from an 'untidy woman on her way back from the market' (26). The man who claims that his 'heart is full of sorrow for the People' (31) looks upon those same people as 'dirty' and 'untidy', and derides their dialect as meaningless and unintelligible.

Although 'bitter complaints' had been made across the social spectrum about the ways in which model dwellings were not designed to give relief to the poor, but rather to reward the upwardly mobile working classes who had regular employment as '[g]overnment employe[es] – policemen, postmen', Eastmont conflates the Artizan's Block in which he lives with the dingy quarters of the 'Doss-House' (7).[35] On several occasions he refers to the Artizan's Block as 'the great beehive' (60). The phrase is significant both architecturally and socially. The term 'beehive house' referred to Britain's 'ancient dwellings' used by agricultural labourers in Ireland and Scotland, and therefore in the novel it alludes obliquely to notions of uncivilised poverty.[36] During the late nineteenth century the phrase 'beehive' – beyond its more general associations with industry – was also connected architecturally with Rowton Houses.[37] Although the first Rowton House was not completed until 1892 (and therefore after the period represented in the novel), by the time of the publication of *George Eastmont, Wanderer* in 1905 the Rowton House had been memorably described as the 'Monster Doss-House' in Jack London's *People of the Abyss* (1902).[38] Initiated by the philanthropist Lord Rowton, the houses were designed to provide temporary, low-cost accommodation for working-class men. Rowton Houses were notably safer and cleaner than London's other lodging houses, and the residents were given clean sheets, the use of tiled washrooms with hot water and a splash bath, and access to a dining room and library for 6d a night.[39] However, sleeping accommodation was arranged in rows of cubicles, for which reason the buildings received the appellation 'the beehive'.[40] While Rowton Houses would have provided many working-class men with comfortable, safe and clean accommodation, the status of these buildings was well below that of the respectable artisans' dwellings provided by the City.

The connection between the beehive and society, which was styled in the seventeenth century as a 'great Bee-hive of Christendom [. . .] [which] swarmes foure times in a yeare, with people of al Ages, Natures, Sexes, Callings', had by the nineteenth century become recognised as a well-regulated and efficient social structure.[41] George Cruikshank's popular satirical etching 'The British Beehive' structures the country's social classes into a consolidated hierarchical order, with the unskilled trades at its base (above the foundation of institutions such as the Bank and the Navy) and the Queen appropriately at its crown. The Artizan's Block paradoxically embodies both representations of the beehive: the hierarchical and the chaotic. The prescriptive design of the building architecturally represents the social hierarchy of broader society. It privileges those middle-class morals and behaviours that it hopes to effect, and in doing so attempts to coax its inhabitants towards middle-class lifestyles and family homes in the suburbs (to which many of the urban artisan classes would eventually move after the turn of the century). In practice, however, the novel suggests that the building is chaotic and refuses to order itself along the principles imposed by the 'moral tradition' that inspired the model dwellings movement.[42] Unable to assert his moral authority and personal gravitas over the inhabitants of the Artizan's Block, Eastmont questions the effectiveness of the building's design:

> Who can live by rule in a place to which tradesmen pay slovenly visits, where they drop milk and eggs on the staircase, leave the wrong meat, and say: 'You can get the things yourself, if you're not satisfied!' The water-taps were constantly out of order, the gas burnt badly, and the former inhabitants of the tenement had left behind them a legacy in the cracks of the walls and floors. To Eastmont's surprise his wife accepted these things with indifference, and smiled when he talked of fumigation, fresh plaster and new wall paper.
> 'It would be all the same in a fortnight,' she told him. (34)

Eastmont means to govern by the 'rule' of his own moral authority and that of those whose philanthropic project gave rise to the construction of model dwellings; however, this 'rule' is born of the same prejudices that produce his total loathing of the building and its inhabitants. Eastmont's efforts to improve the Artizan's Block and the behaviour of the people who live in it only demonstrate the flaws central to his hierarchical system: imbued with the authority of one who presumes to know better, Eastmont is unwilling – and unable – to compromise. Although he suggests that new facilities such as gas and water (a reference to the municipal 'gas and water' socialism that H. M. Hyndman so criticised) would allow for rule and order, augmented by 'fresh plaster and new wallpaper' (a satirical reference to Octavia Hill's housing management), neither Eastmont himself nor the building have proved to be effective models of influencing behaviour. After his wife's death and his growing inability to tolerate 'the discomfort of the life to which he had pledged himself' (30), Eastmont decides to abandon his residential experiment. His experience of the Artizan's Block illustrates the difficulty of reconciling a belief in individual authority with socialist commitment.

(Men's) 'Ignorance of Women'

Although Eastmont identifies the paradox between individualism and collectivism when he reflects, 'Did he not aspire to be saviour of the masses? And was not that a form of ambition?' (32), he is unable to achieve – at least materially – the 'temporary denial of the divide between structure and personal life in socialist consciousness' that Yeo suggests was characteristic of socialist commitment during this period.[43] Eastmont's experiment of living in the Artizan's Block is important because his inability to materially overcome this divide anticipates his discouraging experience of political action during the London dockworkers' strike. While the strike provided a 'cathartic release from the social tension of the mid 1880s', it also produced social divisions among the working classes and between members of the socialist movement. Gareth Stedman Jones notes that the dockworkers' strike was a 'means toward decasualization which would enforce the separation of the "respectable" working class from the residuum, the fit from the unfit'.[44] In an article written for the *New Review* in 1891, Harkness also commented that the dockworkers' strike elevated the status of dockworkers to respectable labourers – but that important status divisions remained between the workers who were represented by trade unions and the 'scum of our population that haunts the slums of our great cities'.[45] In *George Eastmont, Wanderer*, the dockworkers' strike fragments the 'little band of socialists' (162) and creates division between those who unreservedly support trades unionism, and those who believe that unionism ignores the poorest of society and compromises the more immediate necessity of securing representation in parliament.

If historically the dockworkers' strike was politically cathartic, as Stedman Jones suggests, in the novel it is the notional climax of the conversion narrative (what Edmund Morgan would refer to in his morphology of conversion as the 'combat' phase) – but it is one that delivers not assurance, but intense doubt.[46] The divisions among the socialist movement discourage Eastmont's commitment to collective politics; equally, he interprets the strike as not having been won by his own command or the will of the people, but by spiritual authority: Cardinal Lorraine descends in the manner of a *deus ex machina* in order to resolve the conflict. Although the Cardinal 'stood before them a citizen like themselves' (149), his apostolic authority influences the strikers and the directors, '[t]he greater number of [whom] were Catholics [...] [and who] told their wives afterwards, that while he talked they saw a halo of light round his head, and his face seemed to shine like the face of an angel' (150). In an article in which Harkness reflects on the strike, she suggests that the greatest lesson she learned from the experience was that 'it is almost useless and sometimes dangerous to represent people whose demands have not been made clear by themselves'.[47] While the novel does not pretend to resolve the conflict between individualism and collectivism – nor indeed does it suggest that it is a problem in need of solving – it does indicate that a freedom from dogmatic ideological commitment is the only way in which to avoid traps that render social change impotent. In this sense, Eastmont's decision to abandon the British socialist movement in favour of independently investigating the Land Question in Australia should not be interpreted as defeat, but instead as his realisation that his engagement in socialism relied too heavily on ideological coercion. Eastmont's 'mental history had been one of continual development' (21), and as such, he resolves to match this development physically by committing himself to geographical wandering.

Yet an important aspect that remains to be addressed is how the novel's representation of the conflict between individual identity and political commitment sheds some light on the obscure but important ways that gender operates in *George Eastmont, Wanderer*. While the text, as Lynne Hapgood suggests, 'demonstrates the collapse of collectivity into individualism', it places the revaluation of ideological commitment within a broader repositioning of geographical experience: Eastmont's 'wander[ing]'.[48] The novel acknowledges that an individual's intellectual experience is continually formed (and reformed) by responses to other individuals, social groups and material environments, and is therefore by definition variable. Yet the novel also indicates, as Hapgood observes, that while 'pursuing the ideological struggle for social justice with the socialist self' – or indeed in any ideological foundation – Harkness struggled 'to find a role within that framework for the female self'.[49] For Harkness, socialism seemed to be predicated on women's marginalisation. Although Beatrice Potter claims that Harkness was personally 'mad with vanity' about her participation in political communities, Terry Elkiss points out that in her diaries Potter was regularly disparaging towards her second cousin; and the fact that Harkness seems to have largely written herself out of *George Eastmont, Wanderer*, despite her pivotal role in the London dockworkers' strike, is evidence of some humility.[50]

In the novel, Eastmont asks Cardinal Lorraine to intervene on behalf of the dockworkers and to help negotiate a resolution to the ongoing strike. Yet it was Harkness, who was a close personal friend of Cardinal Manning, and not Champion who played this important role in actual the strike. When Manning died January 1892, in fact, Harkness contributed an article to the *Pall Mall Gazette* in which she discussed the Cardinal's interest in labour questions and socialist politics and – while disavowing her religious commitment – also described him as her 'best friend'.[51] In this article, Harkness recounts the moment she decided to ask Manning to intervene in the strike:

> At the time of the dock strike I happened to be at the Wade Arms when a general strike was suggested. That night I could not sleep; for I thought if the gas-stokers were called out, and London was left in darkness, there might be bloodshed. Before eight o'clock the next morning I went to Cardinal Manning's house. He was in bed.
> 'Religion?' asked old Newman, pointing to the chapel – 'No,' I replied, 'politics.' (2)

Harkness had witnessed the violence and bloodshed of the Trafalgar Square riots only two years earlier in 1887, and while she no doubt wished to avoid unnecessary violence, she also understood that any perception of unruly behaviour would compromise public sympathy for the dockworkers.

If Harkness writes candidly of her participation in the London dockworkers' strike in her journalism, why does she attribute this act in *George Eastmont, Wanderer* to a figure who so often draws the narrator's criticism? This decision is not one of mere modesty; instead Harkness sought in writing the novel to achieve what Eastmont cannot: the surrender of individual ambition for the purpose of something greater. Although Eastmont is quite clearly modelled on Champion, there are aspects of his character – specifically his efforts to 'declass' himself, as well as his 'pride and reticence' – that might equally be attributed to Harkness, who herself was from an upper-middle-class family.[52] However, this decision also inscribes women's marginality into the text: despite Harkness's determining role in the outcome of the London dockworkers' strike, she would never be celebrated alongside the foremost 'labour leaders' who were championed for their contributions to this cause.

While it is tempting to read the novel's only portrait of a woman activist, the socialist Mary Cameron, as Harkness's self-portrait, it is clear that she intended to extricate her own identity from the narrative. While Cameron is a woman of independent means who lives alone in lodgings and demonstrates compassion for working-class characters, including Eastmont's estranged wife Julia, this character's habitual despondency, her poor background, her physical characteristics, as well as her romantic interest in Eastmont, are not traits that defined Harkness.[53] What Harkness does share with Cameron, however, is this character's evident marginality in the text. Cameron provides a method by which Harkness could express the ways in which women's political contributions were regularly diminished or unrecognised. She also dramatises the incompatibilities between socialist ideologies and women's experience: for instance, Cameron's friendship with Eastmont does not evolve into a romance plot due to his belief that the wife of a socialist should be 'a simple, guileless woman, clever about a house, and domestic' (24).[54] Eastmont, of course, does not indicate the characteristics required of a socialist's husband.

The marginal role of women in this novel, both as characters and as author, helps, then, to illuminate the relationship between gender and politics in the text beyond the protagonist's infrequent reflections on 'the Woman Question' (219–20). While Eastmont is unable to abandon his personal vanity, or his prejudices, for the sake of his political ambitions, Harkness reveals that personal surrender and self-sacrifice is an experience that is eternally familiar to and expected of women. At the novel's conclusion Eastmont receives a letter from Podmore in which he explains: 'the Woman Question I no longer look upon as a side issue, for I have learnt how fatal the ignorance of women is to the Labour Movement' (219–20). Yet Podmore misses the point: it is not women's ignorance that is fatal to the labour movement, but rather men's ignorance of women. In *George Eastmont, Wanderer*, Harkness reveals that closer attention to 'the Woman Question' and in particular to women's experience could provide the socialist community with resources not made available by conventional ideology.

Notes

1. J.L. [Margaret Harkness], 'Labour Leaders II – H.H. Champion', *Pall Mall Gazette*, 7 February 1891, p. 1.
2. Ibid.
3. Law [Margaret Harkness], *George Eastmont, Wanderer*, dedication. Further references to this work are given in parentheses in the text.
4. Barnes, 'Gentleman Crusader', p. 119.
5. John Barnes has examined the degree to which Eastmont's life and experiences correspond to those of Champion. For instance, Barnes explains that 'one of the strangest episodes in Champion's life' was his marriage in 1883 to 'twenty-eight-year-old Juliet Bennett, of whom nothing is known except that she died after less than three years of marriage, one of the few causes being alcoholism from which she had suffered for a "few years"'. In Harkness's novel, Eastmont's wife Julia dies shortly after their marriage as a result of a drug overdose that, although accidental, is at least partly the consequence of her husband's negligence. Like his fictional counterpart, Champion 'conceived of leadership more in terms of officers and other ranks than the democratic ideal of power coming "from below", and unconsciously assumed that his own role would be that of a "commander"'; his inability and unwillingness to compromise his authority 'partly explains his failure as a politician'. See Barnes, 'Gentleman Crusader', p. 119. See also Barnes, *Socialist Champion*, pp. 31–2.
6. Glover, 'The Vicissitudes of Victory', pp. 104–6.
7. For a discussion of the immediate historicisation of the dockworkers' strike by the labour movement, see Janssen, 'What You Write is Going to the Press', pp. 162–74.
8. British Library of Political and Economic Science, Passfield Papers, PASSFIELD /1/1/13.
9. Yeo, 'A New Life: The Religion of Socialism in Britain', p. 13.

10. Olive Schreiner to Beatrice Webb (née Potter), April 1888, Olive Schreiner Letters Project, <https://www.oliveschreiner.org/vre?view=collections&colid=125&letterid=1> (last accessed 2 June 2019).
11. Koven, *Slumming*, p. 167.
12. Yeo, 'A New Life: The Religion of Socialism in Britain', p. 10.
13. Mutch, 'Socialist Paternalism: Fathers, Father-Figures and Guidance in Serialised Fiction, 1885–1895', paper given at conference, 'Father Figures: Gender and Paternity in the Modern Age', Liverpool John Moores University, 2003.
14. Ibid.
15. Burns & Oates was best known in the nineteenth century for publishing the work of John Henry Newman and other Tractarians. See Wilberforce, *The House of Burns & Oates*.
16. The building is referred to throughout the novel as the 'Artizan's Block', rather than the 'Artizans' Block' as would be expected, and this usage has been retained.
17. See Laybourn, *The Rise of Socialism in Britain*; Pierson, *British Socialists*.
18. Webb, *The Diary of Beatrice Webb*, p. 80.
19. The character may be based partly on Frank Podmore, who was a founding member of the Fabian Society. In the novel, his interest in Spiritualism and Mesmerism seems to be translated into a more conventional devotion to the Established Church.
20. Strachey, *Eminent Victorians*, p. 4.
21. Roberts, *Paternalism in Early Victorian England*, p. 188.
22. Glover, 'The Vicissitudes of Victory', p. 101.
23. Ibid.
24. The City of London Corporation had also constructed one building 'voluntarily' (meaning not out of the necessity to rehouse local populations) at Farringdon Road in 1865. See Thompson, *Housing Up-to-Date*, p. 81.
25. Thompson, *Housing Up-to-Date*, p. 81.
26. Broderick, 'The Homes of the Poor', *Fortnightly Review*, October 1882, p. 426.
27. Cassan, 'London Evictions', *Macmillan's Magazine*, October 1882, p. 502.
28. Ibid.
29. The amendment suggested that this reasonable distance included 'facilities for transit by railway, boat, or tramway be taken into consideration in determining reasonable and suitable distance'. This amendment allowed for the rehousing of large portions of the working classes in London's suburbs, not always successfully, during the late nineteenth and throughout the twentieth century. See Cassan, 'London Evictions', pp. 502–3.
30. 'Petticoat Square', *British Architect*, 23 November 1883, p. 242. See also Thompson, *Housing Up-to-Date*, p. 81.
31. Webb, *The London Programme*, p. 128.
32. Wohl, *The Eternal Slum*, p. 156.

33. Webb, *The London Programme*, p. 128.
34. Gaskell, *Model Housing*, p. 3.
35. Webb, *The London Programme*, p. 129.
36. 'Beehive Houses', *The Leisure Hour*, 22 May 1880, p. 328.
37. The 'beehive of industry' was also a regular part of the nineteenth-century iconography of trades union banners, and *The Bee-hive* was the title of a weekly trades unionist journal established by George Potter that ran from 1861 until 1878. See Ravenhill-Johnson, *The Art and Ideology of the Trade Union Emblem*, pp. 189, 195.
38. London, *People of the Abyss*, p. 245. The Macmillan edition of 1903 contains an image of the Rowton House; opposite is an image of the 'Working-Men's Homes Near Middlesex Street'. The Rowton House would later be written about somewhat more favourably by George Orwell in *Down and Out in Paris and London* (1933).
39. Sheridan, *Rowton Houses 1892–1954*, pp. 9–28. For a discussion of Rowton Houses and domestic ideology, see Hamlett, 'Model Lodging Houses', in *At Home in the Institution*, pp. 135–59, and Hamlett and Preston, 'A Veritable Place for a Hardworking Labourer?', pp. 93–107.
40. Sheridan, *Rowton Houses 1892–1954*, p. 26.
41. Lupton, *London and the Countrey Carbonadoed*, p. 267.
42. Gaskell, *Model Housing*, p. 4.
43. Yeo, 'A New Life: The Religion of Socialism in Britain', p. 14.
44. Stedman Jones, *Outcast London*, p. 317.
45. Law, 'A Year of My Life', p. 377.
46. Morgan, *Visible Saints*, p. 72.
47. Law, 'A Year of My Life', p. 377.
48. Hapgood, '"Is this Friendship?"', p. 141.
49. Ibid. p. 135.
50. Elkiss, 'A Law Unto Herself', p. 18.
51. Law, 'The Cardinal as I Knew Him', *The Pall Mall Gazette*, 18 January 1892, p. 2.
52. J.L., 'Labour Leaders II – H.H. Champion', p. 1.
53. Nord comments that the character Mary Cameron is semi-autobiographical, particularly because, like Harkness, she is '[b]orn in a country rectory' (49). See Nord, *Walking the Victorian Streets*, pp. 196–7. It is more likely that this character is based on the Mary Cameron who was a journalist who contributed to *Christian Socialist* and who was also on the executive committee of the Fabian Society in the 1890s. John Barnes also suggests that the character Mary Cameron (who he mistakenly refers to as Margaret Cameron) 'reads like a self-portrait', but does not offer any further evidence for or analysis of this claim. See Barnes, *Socialist Champion*, pp. 31–2; Barnes, 'Gentleman Crusader', pp. 120–2.
54. Webb, *The Diary of Beatrice Webb*, p. 302.

Part II

Chambers, Lodgings and Flats: Purpose-built Housing for Working Women

Chapter 5

Irritating Rules and Oppressive Officials: Convention and Innovation in Evelyn Sharp's *The Making of a Prig*

In an article written for *London Society* in 1888, an anonymous author who uses the pseudonym 'a Frenchwoman in London' chronicles her attempt to find suitable lodgings in London. The task is nearly impossible. Although the streets are lined with houses, and there are spare rooms to be let, each is rendered unsuitable – or she herself is ineligible – due to a failure to comply with social expectations. Boarding houses that are tolerably clean enough for consideration 'don't take in ladies' on account of the suspicion that such tenants might 'go out late in the evening'.[1] The alternative, the less respectable lodging houses, are patrolled by dishevelled women reeking of spirits and offer second-hand furnishings that are 'really too disgusting to think about'.[2] Although the Frenchwoman eventually finds a draughty garret with an unremarkable landlady, the flame once fanned by the chimera of independence has been snuffed out. Her disillusion comes not from an inability to evince or maintain a spirit of independence, for that is what motivates her to seek employment and accommodation in London, but rather from the disappointing realisation that there exists no social or material infrastructure to support women's self-determination. The author remarks that if a woman is lucky enough to find respectable and affordable lodgings, unlike a man she suffers from (among other unpleasant experiences) isolation:

> [A] man more often works in the company of his fellows, and can always spend his evenings at his club or with his companions; he can frequent his pet restaurant, his favourite theatres and music halls, or any place his fancy selects where he can meet friends and acquaintances. How different must be the woman's life.[3]

The author makes an important point: women were living and working independently in the city, but social convention and architectural practice had not developed at the same rate as their autonomy. One important consequence was the scarcity of appropriate accommodation. The author notes that 'there are many thousands of women working for their daily bread' living in poor conditions, and suggests

> how great a boon it would be if some nice places could be built containing suitable apartments, in which large numbers could live under one roof and have suitable attendance provided. There is a set of buildings in Oakley Street, Chelsea which answers to this description – but it is like a drop in the ocean. Many more such places are wanted, for there are thousands of women living in London who would gladly avail themselves of such advantages [. . .][4]

During the late 1880s, a series of articles on women's housing appeared in journals and newspapers. These ranged from personal accounts of the city's unsuitable accommodation to polemical essays accusing the government of insufficiently confronting the dearth of housing available to women. It was in the pages of publications such as the *Englishwoman's Review*, the *Englishwoman's Year Book* and *Work and Leisure* that women campaigned for suitable homes for a demographic described as 'Educated' – that is, middle-class – 'Working Women'.[5] The development of purpose-built accommodation for middle-class women in London during the last two decades of the nineteenth century was given its impetus by changes to the labour market, which drew many women from homes in rural areas to the growing metropolis. Middle-class women's residences, often referred to as 'ladies' chambers' during the period, provided safe and respectable accommodation – and as Lynne Walker and Martha Vicinus note, they also offered an important opportunity for women to establish feminist networks.[6] Yet these spaces struggled to interpret and respond to rapidly shifting beliefs about gender and sexuality, and as such, many representations of life in women's residences complicate the romanticised pictures of shared domestic space established in school fiction of the period.

Evelyn Sharp's *The Making of a Prig* (1897) is one novel that foregrounds such complexity by engaging with the representational conflict produced by buildings that were designed to address changing social roles, but which also insisted upon retaining many conventions associated with middle-class femininity. This representational conflict, Sharp's novel suggests, is exasperating for those individuals who must live with such contradiction – but it is also the natural product of social progress. *The Making of a Prig*, a novel that features one such example of ladies' chambers, offers an opportunity to examine the representational conflicts that emerge from a building that was at once designed to safeguard middle-class women's social status but also accommodate the changing conventions of women's domestic lives.

Conventional Forms and New Practices

By the last decade of the nineteenth century, the single woman living independently in the metropolis was a familiar figure both in the pages of novels and on the city's streets. Once equally the subject of derision and the recipient of pity for her unmarried status, the middle-class woman who earned a living under her own steam gradually emerged from under the caricatures of her independence to attest to the advantages of these new social freedoms. She was no longer an old maid, but neither was she a New Woman. According to Emma Liggins, this new figure was the 'bachelor girl' who was 'a permutation of the figure of the Glorified Spinster christened in the *Macmillan's* article of 1888 [and who] indicated the new associations of singleness with Bohemianism, professional work, access to higher education, ladies' clubs, and new living space for women in the city'.[7] Access to advantages such as higher education and ladies' clubs suggests that, like the New Woman, the bachelor girl was a chiefly a middle-class phenomenon. That is not to say, however, that in the literature in which she is represented her status is secure; certainly many bachelor girl novels use the misfortunes associated with the difficult social position of the independent woman as an important force in the narrative action.

Evelyn Sharp, who is best remembered for her active participation with the militant suffrage organisation the Women's Social and Political Union, drew upon her own experiences of the difficulties of living independently in London as a young woman in *The Making of a Prig*. Although the novel was not her first – she wrote *At the Relton Arms* (1895) and contributed six short stories to the *Yellow Book* while living with her family in Dulwich – it did establish certain progressive themes in view of gender and class that Sharp would return to throughout her career as a novelist and journalist.[8] *The Making of a Prig* follows the emotional and intellectual development of Katharine Austen, a 'bachelor girl' who moves from rural south-west England to London in search of employment. During her time in London, Katherine resides in one of the city's new, purpose-built homes for working women: the fictional Queens Crescent, Marylebone. Although *The Making of a Prig* was reviewed widely upon its publication – including in the *Academy*, the *Spectator*, *Literature* and the *Standard* – most reviewers were puzzled by the presentation of its protagonist who, as the reviewer for the *Academy* put it, 'despite her good looks, her sincerity, her gaiety, her intelligence [. . .] proves a failure all round'.[9] Meanwhile, the reviewer for the *Spectator* bemoaned the protagonist's willingness to 'be led into a compromising situation'.[10] Although the particular situation the reviewer had in mind was probably a romantic one, Sharp's protagonist is otherwise compromised in the novel – yet not necessarily on account of her 'ignorance of the code of society'.[11] Instead, Katharine is compromised by the environment in which she finds herself at the ladies' chambers at Queens Crescent. Sharp's novel creatively reimagines women's housing in order to comment on the conflicts that emerged during this period between conventional domestic forms and new social practices.

In *The Making of a Prig* Katharine's initial spirit of independence is compromised by the experience of independence. At the novel's opening, she is relentlessly self-assured; but living out this self-determination unfurls the mythology around women's social freedoms. Both Emma Liggins and Wendy Parkins suggest that many novels that pivot on women's experience of the city, in Liggins's words, 'use much more depressing descriptions of urban living than the supposed "reality" to underwrite their heroines' struggles for independence and the new forms of subjectivity this will entail'.[12] These 'depressing descriptions' are a central aspect of *The Making of a Prig*, yet their inclusion does not romanticise the struggle for independence nor does it generalise women's experience in order to present its protagonist as heroic or triumphant. At the novel's centre is a concern with what Liggins refers to as the development of 'new forms of subjectivity'; more precisely, new subjectivities that cannot be reconciled to conventional forms.[13] In many instances in this novel, these new subjectivities remain half-formed on account of the persistence of social expectations concerning appropriate behaviour for middle-class women. In a consideration of Sharp's *Yellow Book* short fiction, Kate Krueger makes the related comment that her narratives investigate 'the personal challenges women face when they transform themselves into career women'.[14] In *The Making of a Prig*, the protagonist's self-assured independence is compromised, and a new subjectivity evinced, by the failure of broader social systems to support her self-determination.

Women's Residences and Ladies' Chambers

Changes to the city's labour market in the latter decades of the nineteenth century make possible Katharine's relocation to London, which, as stated, was also the case for many of her historical counterparts. Emily Gee, who has produced the only extended study of women's housing during this period, notes that the number of women engaged in work was comparable to statistics from a century earlier, but the *kinds* of work women were doing changed.[15] As a number of scholars have indicated, more women were involved in clerical and professional positions; however, Gee makes the important point that this 'burgeoning community of women workers' created 'a major spatial and moral challenge', which was addressed by the construction of housing for middle-class working women.[16] Oakley Street Chambers in Chelsea, the building that the author refers to in 'A Frenchwoman in London', was the first purpose-built accommodation for working women in London. The project was financed by the Working Ladies' Guild, an organisation established by Lady Mary Feilding in 1876, which was dedicated to improving the lives of 'unmarried and widowed gentlewomen' by facilitating personal and institutional connections.[17] Members of the Guild were 'associates' who were asked to contribute personally and financially to its operations, and those who received such assistance were expected eventually to become associates themselves. The emphasis on cooperation and mutual support between associates also served to differentiate the Guild from a traditional charitable organisation, which was an important distinction that would enable the middle-class women who were its beneficiaries to retain their social status.

The Guild also recognised the need for affordable accommodation, and in 1879 it purchased a block of artisans' dwellings in Kensington that was converted into accommodation for professional women. Campden Hill Chambers, as the building was named, offered affordable housing for women at a rate between 2s. 6d. and 4s. per week.[18] This building provided a 'few free rooms, where ladies [were] welcomed for a short time, when it [was] necessary', while the remainder of the rooms were rented at higher though affordable rates to 'families or single ladies having the highest references', which allowed the entire project to be self-supporting.[19] The affordability of these rooms, Gee points out, ensured that they were constantly oversubscribed.[20] The popularity of Campden Hill Chambers inspired the Guild to propose a purpose-built structure designed to house professional women exclusively, to be built at Oakley Street in Chelsea.[21] This project was eventually completed in 1882, and the Working Ladies' Guild developed a financial scheme comparable to those used by model dwellings corporations. The model dwellings movement, which began roughly at mid-century, saw private companies build subsidised housing with a promise of a small dividend for investors. This financial model permitted the flats at Oakley Street to be let at the lower end of the market, but ultimately remain self-supporting.[22]

While the Working Ladies' Guild operated with a purpose analogous to an organisation such as the Improved Industrial Dwellings Company, which sought to improve housing for the city's artisan classes, it was anxious to engineer its public image as a one of a self-sustaining enterprise and not a charity. Much like its programme of cooperation among associates as opposed to direct relief, the Working Ladies' Guild implemented a financial model that encouraged ethical investment rather than charitable donation.[23] At this early stage of women's increasing social and professional opportunities it was crucial that women and their organisations be seen as self-sufficient in order to offset criticism of their unsuitability for these new roles. As Gee notes, these women wished to distance themselves from 'the urban poor who needed philanthropic or municipal assistance in housing themselves and their families'.[24] This was a class of women who were defined in part by the bestowal of charity, not its receipt.

Another way in which organisations such as the Working Ladies' Guild sought to disassociate their efforts from those of model dwellings companies, which focused on housing for the city's working and artisan classes, was in the designation of their buildings. Housing for middle-class and upper-middle-class women was most often described as 'ladies' chambers' – or these words were integrated into longer titles such as Oakley Street Chambers (1882) or New Brabazon House, Home for Ladies (1900) – whereas homes for working-class women were usually referred to as women's hostels, lodging houses or girls' homes. While there was some interest in financing housing projects for independent working-class women during this period, the trajectory of its development was different. There existed from mid-century a number of hostels for working-class women operated by charitable Christian organisations such as the YWCA or the Girls' Friendly Society; however, these were not residences but rescue homes, and accommodation was to be let temporarily during a period of crisis or emergency. There were a small number of homes for working-class women that developed at the same time as residences for middle-class women, such as Maude Stanley's Soho Club and Home for Working Girls (1880), but it would not be until after the turn of the century that large-scale hostels – free from moral constraint and religious obligation – would be established for single, working-class women.

The emergence of purpose-built accommodation for middle-class women was therefore complicated by the obligation to protect the social status of its residents. In the principles of its social organisation, its financial scheme, as well as the titles of its projects, the Working Ladies' Guild devised a public image that was clearly distinct from charitable organisations and models of working-class philanthropy. Oakley Street Chambers provided housing for women whose social position was already made difficult by the fact they were both unmarried (or on occasion widowed) and employed, and as such it was necessary that certain aspects of middle-class femininity were secured by their domestic arrangements. Sharp's *The Making of a Prig* offers an opportunity to examine the representational conflicts that emerge from a building that was at once designed to safeguard middle-class women's social status but also accommodate the changing conventions of women's domestic lives.

Representation and Experience

In Sharp's novel, before Katharine leaves the fictional village of Ivingdon, she arranges to rent a room at 'a certain home for working gentlewomen, near Edgware Road' (86). Writing to a childhood friend, she explains that the residence 'seems respectable, and it is certainly cheap' and in striking out on her own she feels that she is doing something 'splendid and heroic' (86). However, her enthusiasm is subdued when she arrives at the 'well-worn doorstep' of 10 Queens Crescent, Marylebone, where the east wind blows 'dirty pieces of paper against the iron railings' (90). The dismal and uninviting nature of the building falls into a long tradition of gloomy representations of women's housing that reaches from the construction of the single woman's home as 'a brick and mortar funeral', as is the case of Miss Wade in Charles Dickens's *Little Dorrit* (1857), to a depiction of the gritty reality of the independent woman's struggle as experienced by Mary Erle in Ella Hepworth Dixon's *The Story of a Modern Woman* (1894), who contends with a 'grimy back yard'.[25]

The representation of Queens Crescent's cheerlessness makes use of this convention, but for a different purpose than to simply comment on the unhappy lives of the city's single women. In Sharp's novel the building's bleak character throws into relief the incongruity between representation and reality. Both the architecture of the building and its description in advertisements and prospectuses rely on the symbolism of conventional domesticity. In Katharine's experience, however, these buildings do not exhibit the usual comforts of conventional middle-class homes. Katharine suspects that even the maid's role is not custodial; she functions instead to 'support the advertisement that [Queens Crescent] was a home' (90). At Queens Crescent, the forms of traditional domesticity aim to conceal the unconventional lives of the building's inhabitants – yet these conventional forms also frustrate the residents, whose lives would be much easier without constant recourse to the expectations of traditional domesticity. As the narrative unfolds, it becomes clear that this impulse to rehearse these conventions in new spaces produces the restlessness that characterises both Queens Crescent and its inhabitants in this novel.

The 'advertisement that this was a home' (90) to which Katharine refers appears in the prospectus she consults before moving to London, and it is one that evidently misrepresents the establishment. When Katharine finds herself 'alone with her two boxes in a curtained corner of a dingy room' (95) a shorthand clerk in the neighbouring compartment comments, 'Well, it is not much like the prospectus, is it?', at which point 'Katharine remembered the plausible statements of the prospectus, and broke into a laugh' (96). The residents' repeated references to this deceptive document call the reader's attention to the disparity between representation and experience. For the purpose of attracting residents and generating revenue, Queens Crescent must advertise itself as an environment comparable to a middle-class home, not unlike the ones from which its occupants were drawn. For instance, when Katharine asks, 'Where are the newspapers?', another resident replies with a laugh: 'In the prospectus; never saw them anywhere else!' (98). The conversation continues among several of the residents:

> 'It's like the baths, and the boots, and everything else.'
> 'Surely, the bath-room is not a fallacy?' exclaimed Katharine in dismay.
> 'Oh, there is one down in the basement; but all the water has to be boiled for it, so only three people can have a bath every evening. You have to put your name down in a book; and your turn comes in about a fortnight.'

'And the boots?' said Katharine, suppressing a sigh.

'You have to clean your own, that's all. They're supposed to provide the blacking and brushes; but, my eye, what brushes! Of course you get used to it after a bit. When you get to your worst, you will probably wear them dirty.' (99)

The prospectus represents Queens Crescent as an establishment that provides all of the comforts and conveniences of a middle-class home. In this scene, the residents' unfulfilled expectations underscore the discordance between representation and experience.

Crucially, though, their disappointment is not merely a response to the lack of middle-class comfort, but is rather a consequence of the frustration they experience in attempting to carve out new social roles while contending with the expectations of conventional femininity. Their overwhelming dissatisfaction is not a consequence of having to perform certain domestic tasks or provide for themselves; after all, the women 'get used to it after a bit' (99). *The Making of a Prig* paints a bleak representation of women's housing in order to contest the popular belief that single, middle-class working women were miserable simply on account of having eschewed the domestic conventions of cosy coupledom. While many of these women would no doubt have been discouraged by the change of economic and social position that accompanied their independence, the novel communicates that their agitation is not merely a bourgeois reaction to changed circumstances. Their cynicism is born of the paradox of their independence, one that was highlighted earlier in this chapter: for women's self-determination to carry beyond individual freedoms, social and material systems of support – or what I have referred to as infrastructure – would need to be in place.

Although Queens Crescent is an unconventional domestic space, its capacity to support its inhabitants' independence is compromised by its relentless capitulation to the image of the conventional middle-class home. This important observation, that independent working women were continually being offered the very superannuated domestic conventions that they sought to eschew, departs significantly from contemporaneous novels on related subjects. Although George Gissing's *The Odd Women* (1893) is attentive to the ways in which women's lives were circumscribed by the economic necessity of marriage, and correspondingly their adherence to domestic convention, this novel is preoccupied with the ways in which women suffer when they reject the security of either economic or romantic stability. Simply stated, while independent women populate the pages of Gissing's novel, not one of them seems to enjoy her independence. Conversely, in Sharp's novel the women who live at Queens Crescent value their independence and also fare well emotionally (if not always economically), despite their struggle against conventionality.

As social practices began to change, conventional domestic arrangements revealed themselves to be insufficient in fostering the development of these new practices. While sitting in the common room on the evening of her arrival at Queens Crescent, Katharine

> looked round the silent occupants of the room, – some of them too tired to do anything but lounge about, some of them reading novelettes, some of them mending stockings. She wondered if her existence would become like theirs, – a daily routine, with just enough money to support life, and not enough to enjoy its pleasures; enough energy to get through its toil, and not enough to enjoy its leisure. (100)

Like the earlier scene that referred to the domestic dreariness of the single woman's experience, here the problems of finance and labour are depicted in a way not dissimilar to the representation of the working classes in the mid-century 'Condition of England' novel. This description, for instance, brings to mind Elizabeth Gaskell's representation of the urban poor half a century earlier. Yet in novels such as *Mary Barton* (1848), working-class characters are even refused these evenings of exhaustion, forced to '[take] to their sewing' in order 'earn a few pence by working over hours'; and in *Ruth* (1853) it is not the protagonist's lament but rather her ambition 'to lodge very cheaply, and earn [her] livelihood by taking in plain sewing, and perhaps a little dressmaking' after she gives birth to an illegitimate child.[26] Despite the significant difference in social status, such scenes indicate a form of ambivalence that is attendant on the women's position as residents of this dwelling: they are given enough economic freedom to live independently, but they are socially isolated on account of this freedom. Their social marginalisation and the lack of 'leisure' time are impediments to developing networks that would help to challenge restrictive conventionalities.

The disparity between representation and experience, made apparent by the prospectus with its emphasis on conventional domesticity, corresponds to a similar preoccupation with domesticity in the design and organisation of most middle-class women's residences built during the late nineteenth and early twentieth centuries. The Ladies' Associated Dwellings Company was formed in 1888, and like the Working Ladies' Guild, it sought to address the 'need for comfortable and cheap homes, securing privacy and respectability, and suitable for a gentlewoman'.²⁷ Their first project was Sloane Gardens House, which was opened that year (also the year that 'A Frenchwoman in London' was published) at 52 Lower Sloane Street, with fees set at roughly 2s. 6d. a week.²⁸ The building was constructed using the standard domestic material of red brick, and was accented by rubbed brick and terracotta dressings. Its rich ornamentation, Gee argues, aligned it with 'the wealthy mansion blocks in the area'.²⁹ Internally the building could accommodate 150 women in either bed-sitting rooms or cubicles, and also offered communal areas such as a library, music room and dining room. The red brick and heavy ornamentation was clearly an effort to visually associate this large-scale home for women with the vernacular conventions of single-family dwellings; as was, no doubt, the inclusion of the library and music room. However, the high spec of this design combined with its location in the affluent neighbourhood of Sloane Square (chosen for its convenient location for women who worked in the West End) pushed the rents to a rate nearly three times that of Oakley Street Chambers.³⁰ Thus, in an effort to align the building's design with conventional domestic patterns, the Ladies' Associated Dwellings Company failed to provide accommodation for those who needed it most: working women with no guaranteed income. As stated, these companies operated as businesses and therefore relied on the appeal of their product – including features such as a library and music room – to attract residents; it is unlikely that Queens Crescent would have secured so much interest had it advertised that baths were only available once a fortnight. While this relentless appeal to domestic convention complicated the emergence of new social practices, it also produced the 'new forms of subjectivity' and 'personal challenges' to which Emma Liggins and Kate Krueger refer.

Cubicles and Cockatoos

The representation of Queens Crescent in *The Making of a Prig* was no doubt informed by Sharp's own experience of living in a similar building after first moving to London in 1894 out of an obligation to earn her own living. The author remembered being introduced to the artist James Whistler at a dinner party, who laughed when he was told that she 'was a writer and lived in a flat of [her] own', then derisively remarked: 'Not understood at home, I suppose? [...] No scope for the development of your own personality?'³¹ Although it was nearly a decade before her engagement with the radical politics of the WSPU, and later the United Suffragists which she helped to establish, these early experiences exposed her to the contradictions of women's independence which she later sought to repair through political engagement. Although Sharp was surprised at Whistler's 'old-fashioned attitude towards women', given his radicalism in other respects, she noted that his reaction was born of a 'very common prejudice when [she] first threw down her challenge to convention'.[32]

A daily pupil in Bedford Square who was the daughter of the architect J. D. Sedding provided Sharp with income enough to obtain a room at Brabazon House, Home for Ladies, at 8–9 South Crescent, just off Store Street in Bloomsbury.[33] In addition to private tutoring, Sharp lectured in schools during the day and remembered: 'in the evenings I wrote in my curtained cubicle, with the bed for a table and the candle for a lamp after the gas was turned off at eleven'.[34] Although Brabazon House was a retrofit of two houses rather than a purpose-built structure, it offered a series of different styles of rooms including cubicles, single rooms and double rooms, all with either full or partial board.[35] Sharp's autobiography *Unfinished Adventure* (1933) provides few details of the interior of Brabazon House, and if it serves as the basis of the building in *The Making of a Prig* it is moved from Bloomsbury to Marylebone. Given that Queens Crescent in *The Making of a Prig* is (at least ostensibly) a home for 'gentlewomen', and that the novel's protagonist occupies a slightly higher social position than did Sharp herself, it is fitting that the building was moved to the more respectable West End address.

Having stayed at Brabazon House in Bloomsbury, Sharp would have been aware of the more up-market Chenies Street Chambers (Fig. 5.1), which had been built in 1889 and which was located only a block away from her own residence. Chenies Street Chambers was the first project of the Ladies' Residential Chambers Company, which had been formed by the designer Agnes Garrett (the sister of Millicent Garrett Fawcett) in February 1888 – only one month after the Ladies' Residential Dwelling Association was established. Like Sloane Gardens House, Chenies Street Chambers makes use of standard red brick in order to underscore the building's association with vernacular domestic architecture. The composite Queen Anne style was considered suitably feminine by architect J. M. Brydon, as it allowed large-scale structures to retain the character of small-scale buildings by way of features such as sash windows, gables and a hooded shell doorcase.[36] The Ladies' Residential Chambers Company followed this

Figure 5.1 North-west elevation, Chenies Street Chambers. Designed by J. M. Brydon for the Ladies' Residential Dwellings Corporation (1887). Illustration from *Scribner's*, 2 (July–December 1887), p. 601

successful scheme with a similar building at York Street in Marylebone which was completed in 1892.[37] Both Chenies Street Chambers and York Street Chambers were arranged in a series of two-, three- and four-room flats, each one self-contained (meaning the provision of a WC). These buildings were perhaps the city's best appointed and most comfortable women's residences (Fig. 5.2), and were therefore also the most exclusive; residents were professionals who were drawn mostly from the upper middle classes.

Figure 5.2 Interior entranceway, Chenies Street Chambers. Designed by J. M. Brydon for the Ladies' Residential Dwellings Corporation (1887). Illustration from *Scribner's*, 2 (July–December 1887), p. 601

It is clear that the women's dwellings at Queens Crescent in *The Making of a Prig* were not intended for the established professionals or upper-middle-class women who found homes at Chenies Street and York Street. Yet the prestige of these buildings and the relative luxury in which their residents found themselves did not necessarily make it any easier to reconcile domestic conventions with new social practices. Elizabeth Crawford notes, based on the records of Chenies Street Chambers, that residents complained about everything: 'the staffing, the food, the charges, the provision for their bicycles, [and] the maintenance of the fabric in their room'.[38] It seems that at both York Street and Chenies Street it was not only the quality and cost of meals to which residents objected, but also the dining charge. Residents were required to spend 'at least 5s in the house on food per week' and furthermore were required to give notification by 11 a.m. each morning if they intended to dine out that day.[39] Nevertheless, such practices only thinly disguised the expectation that residents would dine together each evening in the communal dining room, in the understanding that this would foster a level of domestic sociability that was expected of women. While articles such as 'A Chat About Ladies' Flats with the Secretary of the York Street Chambers' aimed to dispel the suspicion that these buildings were highly controlled environments – in this case by offering the example that Olive Schreiner kept her sister's cockatoo in the top flat she occupied at York Street – both novels and journalism offer an indication that many women who lived in such buildings felt constrained by their furtive methods of regulating behaviour.[40] Three years after the publication of Sharp's novel, the housing campaigner Emily Hobhouse published in *Nineteenth Century* a survey of women's experiences of living in ladies' chambers. Hobhouse's survey indicates that many women left these establishments on account of the oppressive rules and interfering officials; one woman in particular responded: 'I am leaving because of the irritating rules. They should avoid treating tenants as a cross between a pauper lunatic and a rebellious schoolgirl.'[41] Although Hobhouse applauds the efforts of organisations such as the Ladies' Residential Chambers Company to solve the problem of women's housing, she concludes that such residences 'do not adjust and re-adjust themselves to keep pace with modern requirements'.[42]

The Making of a Prig foregrounds the communal dining arrangement as an experience that was especially at variance with conventions of domesticity. As stated, at many women's residences, particularly the more upmarket establishments, communal dining was enforced by charging women an obligatory subscription fee, which meant that residents were unlikely to dine elsewhere unless they had substantial funds at their disposal. Management thought the arrangement of communal meals was important, as it was expected that women would form social groups to fill the void of the family relationships they had left behind. Yet the novel's representation of these communal meals reveals the fallacy of this theory; indeed, many women were uninterested in socialising with other residents, and resented the enforced charade of companionability. Contemporary articles designed to promote women's residences regularly feature images of brightly decorated communal dining rooms with circular tables – often located in the basement of these buildings – that represent the experience as a cheerful and lively occasion.

In the *Making of a Prig*, Katharine finds the dining room of Queens Crescent rather different:

> The room she had entered was a bare-looking one, though clean enough, and better lighted than the hall outside. Long tables were placed across it, and around these, on wooden chairs, sat some twenty or thirty girls of various ages some of whom were talking, and others reading, as they occupied themselves with their tea. (91)

The 'bare-looking' refectory tables in the novel suggest a community that is not entirely unsociable, but certainly less social than promotional descriptions of these spaces. It is also an environment in which independent acts, such as reading, occur in a traditionally communal space. Katharine's first meal at Queens Crescent follows a convention of social induction, most often found in school or college fiction, which introduces the protagonist (and thereby the reader) to the methods of the new community into which they are being integrated. While in most novels this convention initiates intimacy, here the building and the community retain their anonymity. Katharine enquires about a vacant seat and is told by another resident who was 'friendly in a raw sort of way' (92) that the chair '[i]sn't anybody's; none of them are, unless the plate is turned upside down' (91–2). The woman, who is reading *Pitman's Phonetic Journal* while finishing her dinner, notices Katharine's perplexed response to the unorthodox table setting and continues, 'You have to get your own tea from the urn over there, and collect your food from all the other tables' (92).

At Queens Crescent it is not only the custom by which the evening meal is served that is irregular, but also the time of day. Katharine asks the woman '[i]f it isn't rather late for tea', and has the arrangement explained to her in detail:

'It always goes on until seven; most of them don't get back from the office until this time, you see.'

'What office?' Asked Katharine, who did not see.

'Any office,' returned the girl staring round at her. 'Post office generally, or a place in the city, something like that. Some of them are shorthand clerks, like me, – it's shorter hours and better paid as a rule; but it is getting overcrowded, like everything else.'

'Do you like it?' Asked Katharine. The girl stared again. The possibility of liking one's work had never occurred to her before.

'Of course not, but we have to grin and bear it, like the food here and everything else.' (92–3)

The same set of conditions – specifically, changes to the city's system of labour – that motivated the construction of these buildings has also destabilised social conventions within these buildings. The working day has caused disruption to the daily schedule and, despite management's attempt to marshal its residents into a performance of domesticity, it has proved impossible in practice, and the dinner hour has been eclipsed altogether by the less formal meal of 'tea'. In Eliza Lynn Linton's *The Rebel of the Family* (1888) a similar phenomenon occurs when Perdita secures a job at the Post Office Savings Bank and is not only unable to return home in time for the family's evening meal, but is also unable to indicate what time she might be home, requiring her mother to readjust her notions of feminine propriety. Perdita's ambition is, however, simply the glory of self-sufficiency, whereas Katharine's interlocutor makes an important comment: professional work was for many not necessarily a reward in its own right.

And yet this revelation is unlike that found in a category of novels, popular at this time, which sought to dissuade young middle-class women away from work and urban life as a moral project. For instance, in Flora Klickmann's *The Ambitions of Jenny Ingram* (1907), the young and naive protagonist of the novel's title ventures into London to establish herself as a journalist and instead endures an unpleasant plunge into personal and professional atrophy, only to finally collapse at the entrance of an East End women's refuge (she is, however, mysteriously revivified by a marriage proposal). Even more forward-thinking authors such as Emily Symonds (who wrote under the pseudonym George Paston) included in her novel *A Modern Amazon* (1894) a cautionary tale about a woman who leaves her husband only to find that living alone in lodgings is terribly dull. In *The Making of a Prig*, Katharine and the other residents 'get used to it after a bit' (99) or 'grin and bear it' (93). Women's residences were bound by architectural and social forms of conventionality in order to prosper as business models, and yet this pretence jarred with the activity for which these buildings were designed. Notorious detractors such as Eliza Lynn Linton and Dora Greenwell argued that women were unable to live together because – in Linton's words – it perverted the course of 'natural destiny', but a number of residents perceptively identified that in certain ways segregation in 'hen communities' or 'pusseries' only further marginalised women.[43] Some residents suggested that men and women should form unmarried cooperatives and live 'on equal footing', a radical scheme that W. T. Stead had proposed in *Women's Herald* in 1893; others suggested that allowing male visitors or outsiders to dine in the buildings would, at the very least, improve the food.[44]

While *The Making of a Prig* expresses many grievances about women's residences and articulates ideas for their improvement, this discourse is not necessarily unified, nor does it identify a central problem that can be addressed for quick improvement. Instead, the novel's attention to housing reveals a curious vacancy, for the problem of women's housing – despite the efforts of companies such as the Ladies' Residential Chambers Company – still needed solving. Building practices struggled to keep pace with rapidly shifting behaviours and circumstances around gender and labour at the century's end. As a result, buildings such as Queens Crescent seemed to amplify, just as much as they sought to address, women's inequality. There is no doubt, as Annmarie Adams argues, that '[t]he construction of these buildings marked an enormous victory in the nineteenth-century women's movement', on account of their acknowledgement of the need to accommodate independent women, as well as their 'recognition that the design of the traditional middle-class family home did not suit the needs of single women'.[45] Yet Sharp's novel expresses the exasperatingly slow process of social and political reform in its pages by representing the friction between middle-class domestic conventions and the emergence of new practices. It is, consequently, a struggle that is palpable for the reader. Nonetheless, the novel steers clear of abject cynicism, and instead suggests that these outmoded customs can also be generative, particularly if they highlight the need for broader social and infrastructural reform.

Notes

1. 'A Frenchwoman in London', *London Society*, May 1888, p. 492.
2. Ibid. p. 493.

3. Ibid. p. 502.
4. Ibid.
5. Zimmern, 'Ladies Dwellings', *Contemporary Review*, 77 (1900), p. 97.
6. Walker, 'The Entry of Women into the Architectural Profession in Britain', pp. 13–18; Vicinus, *Independent Women*, pp. 295–9.
7. Liggins, 'Having a Good Time?', p. 99. See also 'The Glorified Spinster', *Macmillan's Magazine*, 58 (1888), pp. 371–6.
8. John, 'Sharp [married name Nevinson], Evelyn Jane (1869–1955)', *ODNB*.
9. 'Book Reviews Reviewed', *The Academy*, 5 March 1898, p. 269.
10. Ibid.
11. Ibid.
12. Liggins, 'Having a Good Time?', p. 99. Wendy Parkins makes a related point in *Mobility and Modernity in Women's Novels*, pp. 2–3.
13. On this subject, see also Liggins, '"The Life of a Bachelor Girl in the Big City"', pp. 216–38.
14. Krueger, 'Evelyn Sharp's Working Women and the Dilemma of Romance', p. 564.
15. Gee, '"Where Shall She Live?"', p. 89.
16. Ibid. p. 90.
17. Garnett, 'Feilding, Lady Mary (1823–96)', *ODNB*.
18. Gee, '"Where Shall She Live?"', unpublished thesis, p. 40.
19. 'Working Ladies' Guild', *Women's Gazette*, April 1879, pp. 56–7.
20. Gee, '"Where Shall She Live?"', unpublished thesis, p. 40.
21. Crawford, *Enterprising Women*, p. 207.
22. Gee, '"Where Shall She Live?"', unpublished thesis, p. 40.
23. For a discussion of the ways that working-class housing offered the middle classes a form of ethical investment, see Morris, 'Market Solutions for Social Problems', pp. 525–45. I am grateful to Richard Dennis for recommending this article.
24. Gee, '"Where Shall She Live?"', unpublished thesis, p. 45.
25. Dickens, *Little Dorrit*, pp. 330–1; Dixon, *The Story of a Modern Woman*, p. 108.
26. Gaskell, *Mary Barton*, pp. 221, 143; Gaskell, *Ruth*, vol. 2, p. 54.
27. Cited in Crawford, *Enterprising Women*, p. 207.
28. Crawford, *Enterprising Women*, p. 207. See also Gee '"Where Shall She Live?"', pp. 91–2.
29. Gee, '"Where Shall She Live?"', p. 92.
30. Ibid. See also Gee, '"Where Shall She Live?"', unpublished thesis, pp. 40–1.
31. Sharp, *Unfinished Adventure*, p. 53.
32. Ibid. p. 53.
33. Brabazon House, Home for Ladies, was the initial project of the Brabazon House Company Ltd, which was established by Lady Brabazon, Countess of Meath, in 1890. The company would later design and commission a larger, purpose-built residence for working women

(known formally as Lady Brabazon's Home for Gentlewomen, or more casually as New Brabazon House). This new building was designed by R. Stephen Ayling and opened on Moreton Street, Pimlico in 1902. Another more upscale residence, Hopkinson House, was opened on the other side of Vauxhall Bridge in 1905. See Countess of Meath, *The Diaries of Mary Countess of Meath*, p. 10. See also Gee, '"Where Shall She Live?"', unpublished thesis, p. 69, n. 154.

34. Sharp, *Unfinished Adventure*, p. 55.
35. Wolseley, *Gardening for Women*, pp. 288–9. This book also indicates that the rent for the kind of cubicle that Sharp inhabited would have been between 5s. and 7s. per week in 1908.
36. Crawford, *Enterprising Women*, pp. 209–10.
37. Gee, '"Where Shall She Live?"', unpublished thesis, p. 43.
38. Crawford, *Enterprising Women*, p. 210.
39. 'A Chat About Ladies' Flats with the Secretary of the York Street Chambers', *Women's Herald*, 29 June 1893, p. 293.
40. Ibid.
41. Hobhouse, 'Women Workers: How they Live and How They Wish to Live', *Nineteenth Century*, 47.277 (1900), p. 482.
42. Ibid.
43. This is a theme that runs throughout much of Linton's journalism; however, her fiction often contradicts this point. Linton [erroneously attributed in print to Charles Dickens], 'Rights and Wrongs of Women', *Household Words*, 1 April 1854, p. 159. See also Greenwell, 'Our Single Women', *North British Review*, February 1862, pp. 62–87. The expressions used to refer to women's communities are documented in Hobhouse, 'Women Workers: How they Live and How They Wish to Live', p. 481.
44. Hobhouse, 'Women Workers: How they Live and How They Wish to Live', p. 482; Stead, 'Cooperative Homes for the Unmarried', *Women's Herald*, 13 April 1893, pp. 113–14.
45. Adams, *Architecture in the Family Way*, p. 154.

Chapter 6

The Kailyard Comes to London: The Progressive Potential of Romantic Convention in Annie S. Swan's *A Victory Won*

In an article written for *Women's Herald* in 1893, a 'special commissioner' visits two buildings designed to house independent working women, Sloane Gardens House and Oakley Street Chambers, in order to investigate 'Where the Unmarried Live'. Oakley Street Chambers, constructed in 1876 under the initiative of Lady Mary Feilding's Working Ladies' Guild, was the first structure designed for the purpose of housing independent working women. Sloane Gardens House, built in 1888, was the first project of the Ladies' Associated Dwellings' Company and was, as Emily Gee notes, 'the first large-scale, quality, purpose-built lodgings for lower wage but still quite clearly middle-class women'.[1] By 1893 a handful of buildings designed to house independent working women existed in London and their diversity attests to the complexity of women's changing social status at this time. Although the author of 'Where the Unmarried Live' might have chosen one of the residences built by the Ladies' Residential Chambers Company, which were designed for more affluent middle-class and professional women, both Oakley Street Chambers and Sloane Gardens House were by this point well-established institutions. Sloane Gardens House, a 'typical example as regards convenience of situation, charges, and general arrangements', the correspondent comments, is 'always filled with residents, and numerous applications have to be refused for want of room'.[2] Nevertheless, the correspondent also finds that life at Sloane Gardens House could be surprisingly solitary. One resident explains to the author that her first experience of the residence was 'intense loneliness'. Although many women formed small coteries with whom to 'chat [. . .] merrily' over dinner, others were 'glum and exclusive' and took no notice of the newcomer.³ This resident soon discovered that the 'majority of the residents stay in their rooms in the evening' and claims that, on one occasion, her desperation led her to 'rebel [. . .] against the spirit of indifference'. The newcomer's rebellious behaviour is, however, comically reserved: 'One morning I noticed a girl at the breakfast table looking very ill. I asked if there was anything I could do for her. That was the breaking of the ice and we are now good friends.'⁴

The resident's emotive language, set alongside what seems to be an almost instinctual and certainly very restrained gesture, reminds readers of the anxiety that could attend these new social situations. The majority of women who moved into these new domestic spaces would probably not have had any experience of collective living, as girls' institutional schooling was at this time still developing.⁵ The social campaigner Alice Zimmern – who championed the cause of women's dwellings – explains that the experiment of 'co-flatting' or the sharing of a three- or four-room flat between two women 'does not seem to be a success'.⁶ Zimmern suggests that the system of sharing is 'apt to lead to disagreement on the question of service, the use of pantry, etc.', and that it simply 'introduces an unnecessary complication in life'.⁷ Provision for social privacy was, Zimmern notes, necessary for middle-class women to retain status and respectability.⁸ While journalists both in favour of and against housing defined along gendered principles often claimed this situation as evidence of women's congenital inability to live together, Zimmern suggests that these disagreements were 'common to model dwellings as well as to Ladies' Chambers'.⁹ She points out that the expectation that middle-class women should adapt to shared domestic facilities was not dissimilar to another social group that also might not have had experience of institutional living: the working and artisan classes. Both groups were also more likely to live in inadequate accommodation due to various social and financial pressures.

Given the large scale of Sloane Gardens House – it was designed to accommodate 150 women – it is perhaps not surprising that so many residents found the experience of living there alienating.¹⁰ Yet when the special commissioner of 'Where the Unmarried Live' asks a resident about the social situation at Oakley Street Chambers, she receives a response that is similar to what she heard at Sloane Gardens House: the tenants have 'numerous friends in London' but 'prefer not to know their neighbours'.¹¹ While some inhabitants of women's housing responded with hostility to the obligatory communities that were prescribed by many of these new residences, it is important to note that many women did establish elective communities and form close friendships with other residents. Yet the success of women's housing schemes was not ensured simply by their existence; their construction revealed the need for broader social changes that would recognise and accommodate individuals whose lives were not defined by conventional family structures. One of the ways that women were able to negotiate this ideology and 'define themselves in terms beyond those of the nuclear family', as Martha Vicinus notes, was by creating supportive communities and establishing close friendships.[12]

Annie Shepherd Swan, despite her reputation as an author who 'strongly support[ed] conventional notions of womanhood', expresses the importance of these close friendships for the development of new social practices in her novel *A Victory Won* (1895).[13] The novel's familiar narrative is centred on a rebellious young woman, the daughter of a wealthy country gentleman, who is compelled by her father's tyrannical behaviour to move to London, where she is required to earn her own living. In its representation of the picturesque Scottish countryside, *A Victory Won* falls into the tradition of the Kailyard school: a sentimental – and to some such as Beth Dickson, 'falsely sentimental' – style of writing about rural life in Scotland that emerged in last decade of the nineteenth century in response to realism.[14] Although Swan is mostly forgotten today, she was one of the nineteenth century's best-known novelists and, according to Edmund Gardiner, as far as her achievements in serial fiction were concerned, '[n]othing like it had been seen since Dickens or Trollope [. . .] her output was phenomenal'.[15] Dickson notes that during a career that began in 1883 and lasted until her death fifty years later, Swan wrote 162 novels under her own name, at least forty under the pseudonym David Lyall, and countless pieces of journalism, some of which appeared under the name 'Evelyn Orchard'. In 1893 she was invited to become the chief contributor and editor of *The Woman at Home*, and her popularity was such that the publication was subtitled 'Annie Swan's Magazine'.[16] In 1934 she released the best-selling autobiography *My Life*. In addition to her literary output, Gardiner notes, Swan was also at one point mayor of the English town of Hertford, served in France during the First World War, and worked with Herbert Hoover for two years while travelling in the United States.[17]

Swan was well aware of her standing as a popular novelist, for it was a position that she professionally cultivated, recognising that in the literary marketplace, as she put it, 'he who pays the piper calls the tune'.[18] Yet she was not beyond feeling hurt when Margaret Oliphant, a writer whose work Swan greatly admired, dismissed her representations of Scotland as 'silly' and even 'pernicious' in their naivety.[19] On one level, *A Victory Won* can most certainly be read as a mawkish tale of filial piety: the central character, Eleanor Kerr, inherits her father's hot temper and obstinacy and in her ambition to prove herself to him neglects her dying mother. Meanwhile Eleanor's brother develops alcoholism, and nearly kills their father – who is also an alcoholic – in a brawl at the novel's conclusion. In this revisionist version of the parable of the prodigal son, Eleanor returns home before her mother's death in time to promise that she will care for her father. This theme of women's sacrifice, as Dickson notes, is common to most of Swan's novels – and although Eleanor does not marry, she is effectively placed in the equivalent domestic role without its emotional and biological advantages.[20] However, Swan's novel is unique in the way it represents the protagonist's experience of middle-class women's housing. Unlike most journalistic accounts of these residences or the representations found in novels such as Evelyn Sharp's *The Making of a Prig*, which tend to concentrate on the failure of these buildings to live up to middle-class expectations of home, *A Victory Won* focuses on the supportive and enabling features of women's residences.

Establishing Intimacy

In *A Victory Won*, Eleanor Kerr leaves her family's farmhouse in the Howe of Fife in order to follow to London the man whom her father refuses to allow her to marry. Once she arrives and realises that he is only interested in her fortune, from which she has now been disinherited, she is obliged to establish herself as an independent woman and earn her own living. Eleanor has the good fortune of being introduced to Frances Sheldon, a woman who rents a three-room flat in the fictional 'Barker Street Chambers'.[21] In the serialised version of the novel, which appeared in the *British Weekly* in 1894, the residence is referred to as 'Chenies Street Chambers' – but Elizabeth Crawford explains that Adeline Sergeant, a 'rival novelist' who herself lived at Chenies Street Chambers (Figs 5.1 and 5.2), objected to the use of the name.[22] This reaction suggests Sergeant's eagerness to establish authority over the building's reputation and representation, although it would be several years before she included a representation of Chenies Street Chambers in her own novel, *Anthea's Way* (1903).[23]

It is somewhat perplexing to imagine on what grounds Sergeant might have otherwise objected, for 'Barker Street Chambers' and its residents are depicted favourably in Swan's novel. Unlike most representations of middle-class 'bachelor women' who live apart from men's company, Frances Sheldon is unconventional and independent, but also ebullient and attractive:

> Miss Frances Sheldon was not a conventional person. She was sitting at her bachelor breakfast when the knock came to the door. Having no domestic, she opened it herself. She was a young woman of seven-and-twenty; and though she looked her age, there was a certain girlishness in her appearance which would remain with her likely for several years to come. Even her slightly mannish attire was not unbecoming to her, the stiff, pink linen collar, the neat black tie, and the tailor cut of her double-breasted jacket being even fascinating in their way. She wore her hair short, and the crisp brown waves looked as if they were carefully attended to, as indeed they were, Frances Sheldon being very dainty and fastidious in her way. Her speech was a trifle free, as was inevitable, owing to the conditions of her life. (132)

Frances does not fall into the conventional 'before' and 'after' caricatures of the independent city woman: the dewy-eyed and overdetermined girl, or the cynical and careworn spinster. She is, instead, nearer the age that Emily Hobhouse found in her survey of women's lodgings to be the average for women living in such accommodation: 34 years old.[24] Frances also lives without a domestic servant, although there were provisions for such at Chenies Street Chambers, which is an indication of her self-reliance. As Sally Ledger and Susan Shapiro both explain, such independent or 'New' women were usually characterised, in Ledger's words, as 'mannish, over-educated, humourless bores' whose femininity was compromised as much by their rational dress as it was by their progressive opinions.[25] Most often characters who are represented as rebellious and deficient in femininity are rehabilitated by heterosexual romance, as is the case with Rhoda Nunn in George Gissing's *The Odd Women* (1893). The above sketch of Frances Sheldon bridges such oppositions: the adjective 'mannish' is used to suggest her attractiveness, and the combination of a 'stiff, pink linen collar' and 'neat black tie' is not out of place but is instead 'fascinating' (132). Even her short hair is indicative of fastidiousness and daintiness, rather than signifying a sort of reckless utilitarianism.

In examining Swan's later novels, many of which are concerned with women's suffrage, Jane Eldridge Miller explains that Swan 'carefully emphasises the beauty and "womanliness" of her suffragist heroines'.[26] This is also common in novels that feature 'rebel women', Eldridge Miller suggests, as writers were often at pains to make their heroines attractive to their readership despite their lack of conventionality. What is interesting about Frances's attractiveness is that she is not the novel's protagonist, but Eleanor's foil; such secondary characters are not typically represented sympathetically in late nineteenth-century fiction, and more often feature as cautionary figures who suggest the fate of the woman who allows her independence to usurp her femininity. Yet Frances, in addition to being physically attractive and plain-spoken, is light-hearted, quick-witted and charismatic: 'charming, womanly, and true-hearted' (137), as she is described by the friend who arranges for Eleanor to say at Barker Street.

Any enduring misconceptions about the bachelor woman's appearance are set aright after Eleanor moves into Barker Street. Surprised at Frances's attention to matters of appearance, Eleanor comments, 'I thought girls who live like this, so independently, I mean, didn't care how they looked', only to be swiftly repudiated: 'Oh, that's a frightful mistake. I believe when a woman grows careless of her appearance there is something sapping the springs of her welfare' (139). Although this statement implies that it is a woman's responsibility to be mindful of her appearance, it also situates this responsibility alongside broader questions of health and social security. Frances suggests that women who are characterised as visual aberrations to conventional femininity are not degenerate, but are instead victims of social welfare. This argument emerges once more when Eleanor comments glibly that '[c]lothes are not everything', and Frances must remind her that, particularly for women who cannot afford the right garments but equally cannot abide the wrong ones, '[clothes] are a good deal' (139). Whereas Katharine Austen, the protagonist of Evelyn Sharp's *The Making of a Prig*, is rejected from work for the fault of being 'too young' and 'too attractive', Eleanor's attractiveness helps to secure her a position in journalism.[27] However, it soon becomes clear that rejection may have been preferable: she is regularly subject to the subtle harassment of her seedy employer, who demonstrates a level of 'personal interest' that makes Eleanor's work 'vaguely miserable' (228). This situation occurs at a point in the narrative when Eleanor is staying at Barker Street on her own, and she finds that '[e]xistence in London without that bright, unfailing spirit was a burden rather heavy to be borne, and the evenings in the little flat, which seemed so empty without [Frances], were intolerably long' (228). This intimacy and companionship, inspired by the 'feeling of trust' (141) that Frances engenders, is important to the development of their friendship. Without it, Eleanor confesses: 'I hate London. It ought to be sunk to the bottom of the sea' (232).

Barker Street Chambers

The narrative develops the quality of companionship between Eleanor and Frances through thoughtful and intimate conversation, which helps to make the unconventional lodgings at Barker Street into a comfortable home. In Margaret Harkness's *George Eastmont, Wanderer*, the ladies' chambers where Mary Cameron resides are 'dull and solitary' (264) and in Evelyn Sharp's *The Making of a Prig*, the comfort of home is only an 'advertisement' (90); however, *A Victory Won* represents these buildings as both suitable and desirable. Chenies Street Chambers was marketed to professional women who were also often supported by independent means and could afford a self-contained flat with multiple rooms; Frances Sheldon, for instance, lives in a three-room self-contained flat. Other ladies' chambers such as Sloane Gardens House offered, as Alice Zimmern notes, single 'bed-sitting rooms' that were for some women an economic necessity – although most hoped 'to work their way out of it to the two-room stage of existence'.[28] The flat represented in *A Victory Won* therefore has the advantage of floorspace and discrete rooms for different social purposes, all of which helps to advocate for its suitability as a home. Although there is no conventional dining area (the two rooms apart from the scullery being used, it seems, as a bedroom and a study), the friend who visits on behalf of Eleanor in order to ask whether she might share accommodation with Frances remarks: 'I had no idea a scullery could be such a cosy place' (133). Similarly, the narrator comments on '[t]he warmth and comfort of the odd little place', and notes that even the 'gas stove glowed cheerily' (133).

If the point that Zimmern makes, that having two rooms was seen to be an altogether different stage of existence for women living independently, is valid, then Eleanor's presence should threaten to disrupt the 'warmth and comfort' of the 'odd little place' (133). When asked whether she could accommodate another person in her flat, Frances responds:

> Here, in this very house, do you mean? Do you know the size of it? [...] I have two places beside this, and they are like boxes – big enough for me and my things; but where could I put another? Still, under pressure it could be done. (133–4)

As it turns out, the arrangement improves rather than diminishes the domesticity of the 'odd little place'. Eleanor's first evening at Barker Street establishes the sense of comfort and security that the flat and her friendship with Frances will provide:

> Frances Sheldon and her guest sat talking over the fire in the cosy little sitting-room at Barker Street, and it was evident that they had found plenty to talk about. The place was tiny, and the furniture was not substantial, but it had a certain airy prettiness about it, and the basket chairs were comfortable enough lounges after a hard day's work [...] Their meeting had been a curious experience, but after a cup of tea and a little talk on commonplace subjects, they were beginning to feel at home with each other. (139)

The scene that develops over the cup of tea as the two characters begin 'to feel at home with each other' enlists the two women as members of a household rather than independent residents of ladies' chambers. The description is symbolically loaded: the tea, the comfortable chairs and the fire all define this space as one that fits into patterns of conventional domesticity.

Zimmern explains the centrality of a fire as a determining factor in private space when she refers to a new, large-scale residential scheme developed for 400 women who earned between £50 and £120 per annum. The building, she explains, will 'bear some resemblance to Sloane Gardens House, but [is to] be larger and cheaper, and therefore necessarily more barrack-like'.[29] The scale was not the objectionable aspect of this scheme as far as Zimmern was concerned; after all she campaigned for the development of a 'Rowton House for Women'. It was rather that the design would 'abolish that Englishwoman's palladium, the individual hearth' as one of its labour-saving measure.[30] Zimmern explains:

> Can a room without a fireplace be a regarded as a home? Abolish the fireplace, and the room is no longer a sanctum [...] Surely it was Emerson who said that the chief good a man got from going to College was that he had a room and fire of his own. And it means even more to a woman.[31]

Exactly why such home comforts mean more to women is not made explicit, but Zimmern acknowledges that, unlike men, women have an 'overmastering tendency [. . .] to make a home out of the meanest attic lodging'.³² In ladies' chambers, Zimmern explains, 'the centre of gravity shifts itself naturally from the dining room and other public rooms to the private room. These are the individual centres: if these are right nothing can be very wrong.'³³ Such rhetoric constructs the individual fire – at least for middle-class women – as an important defining feature of private space. If women were therefore to feel at home in an unconventional or institutional building, the individual hearth and its association with women's domestic work and the centre of the household was necessary to set things 'right'.

While the symbolic value of features such as the hearth cannot be overlooked, the most significant quality that turns the Barker Street hearth into a home is the companionship that develops between Frances and Eleanor. The two women find 'plenty to talk about' after only just meeting, and feel entirely 'at home with each other' (139). On this first night, the three-room flat is represented as a more comfortable and familiar home to Eleanor than is her family's farmhouse in Fife. When Eleanor's brother Claud and his wife Mary visit Barker Street, the rather guileless Claud cannot help but articulate the perceived difference between the two houses: 'So this is where Eleanor hangs out [. . .] Rather a change from Haugh, eh, Mary?' (174). Mary, who is herself dissatisfied with domestic conventionality, dismisses Claud's doltish banter by replying, 'It is very nice, I think [. . .] I shouldn't mind it myself' (174). Her cutting remark gathers significance as the novel unfolds and the newlyweds' ambition of domestic bliss is undermined by Claud's alcoholism, which ruins Mary's hopes of making a family home of their own house, Annfield. Their situation worsens when Claud nearly kills his father in an alcohol-induced violent rage, and is then threatened with eviction from the family property. Eleanor disregards Claud's boyish raillery and insists that she prefers London's 'free and easy life', and so long as her mother does not send for her, she 'mean[s] to stay' (178).

Whereas Eleanor's initial motivation for staying in London originates in her sense of pride – or more specifically the desire to prove herself to her family, which is so often the reason for the independent woman's presence in the city in fiction – she eventually comes to appreciate the emancipatory possibilities of her new residential arrangements. These possibilities not only come from living at Barker Street Chambers, but from the social opportunities it provides. Sharing a small flat at Barker Street does not infringe upon that privacy that was assumed to be so necessary for bourgeois femininity and safeguarding the definition of a middle-class home. Instead, in Swan's novel, this spatial compromise provokes the personal development of both characters and is in this sense central to the way that the narrative progresses.

Co-flatting and Cooperation

A Victory Won implies that there is a connection between a woman's relationship with her mother and her capacity for forming friendships with other women. Having lost her mother at an early age, Frances is surprised to learn of Eleanor's disregard for her own mother and confesses that she 'would give ten, aye twenty years of my life to have a mother – good, bad, or indifferent [. . .] The first real desolation of life comes home to a girl, I can tell you, when she is made motherless' (142). It is Frances's loss of her own mother that seems to bestow upon her a desire to establish a support network in the city that she calls her home. Unlike Eleanor's father, Frances's father does not impetuously deny her support, but is not in a position to support her financially and seems unwilling to support her emotionally. The often uncharitable, and almost always incompetent, behaviour of both women's fathers in this novel is, interestingly enough, shared by Katharine Austen's father in *The Making of a Prig*. Apart from providing the impetus for these women to venture to the city to live independently, the behaviour of these men also serves to question the presumed stability of the conventional family by weakening the role of its paternal figurehead. Eleanor's mother is a mostly sympathetic character, although the narrator makes clear that her unfaltering deference to her husband's unreasonable behaviour and her efforts to whitewash his alcoholism do more harm than good.

Eleanor's friendship with Frances does not so much inculcate in her a sense of filial duty as launch an appeal for generosity and forgiveness towards her family more broadly. Frances feels that she is given a task, and that is 'to awaken the soul of Eleanor Kerr' (145), and her success in doing so is the 'victory' that is won through the course of the narrative. The method by which Frances achieves this victory is by imparting her own generosity and thereby enabling the development of a domestic or 'private' relationship with Eleanor. When a family friend travels to London to visit Eleanor (and to report back to Eleanor's mother), she is reassured by the supportive relationship that the women's domestic situation has allowed. Standing outside the door of the flat

Mrs. Allardyce heard a peal of girlish laughter – so genuine, so spontaneous, and so infectious, that it provoked a smile on her own lips, and brought a satisfied look into her eyes. Such laughter does not come with a heavy heart. If times were hard with the two working women within, care sat lightly upon them. (154)

Such representations of women's friendships are not uncommon in literature of the period, and as Sally Mitchell documents, they feature prominently in schoolgirls' stories.[34] What is interesting about this particular novel is that this friendship is its central relationship, and it is defined not only by their gleeful girlish naivety but also by their ability to mitigate each other's material and emotional difficulties. Most novels about women's dwellings represent these spaces and the (often superficial) relationships that develop within them as a temporary stopgap in the interim before marriage. Emily Hobhouse acknowledged that this not only occurred in the genre of romantic fiction that framed its conclusion with a marriage, but was a common misconception that informed the ways in which women's dwellings were designed and managed.[35] Residences for schoolgirls operated on very different principles than dwellings for professional women, Hobhouse explains, for 'students need only temporary, not permanent accommodation; and many rubs can be endured when they are known to be temporary'.[36] Although the novel's conclusion implies that neither Eleanor nor Frances will return to their shared flat at Barker Street, it is made clear that their friendship will endure.

The significance of this relationship is brought into greater relief when one considers the representation of women's friendship in novels such as Sharp's *The Making of a Prig* or Harkness's *George Eastmont, Wanderer*. An unrequited love interest is the only close friend of Mary Cameron, the journalist and political activist who lives in the ladies' chambers in *George Eastmont, Wanderer*. And while Sharp's protagonist, Katharine Austen, makes the acquaintance of a number of women living in her building, she regards them with suspicion on account of their inclination for gossip and conjecture. The only person with whom Katharine has any extended conversation, Phyllis Hyam, has a 'bluntness that estranged all her friends in time' (158), and is never really a friend to Katharine but a sounding board for her romantic dilemmas. When Katharine, for instance, decides to break off her relationship with an older man, she feels that without his companionship she will be 'left entirely friendless' (163). Katharine's closest ally is in fact her childhood friend from the country, Ted, whose good nature and devotion to her she unconscionably exploits.

The laughter that Mrs Allardyce understands to reveal the women's supportive and cheerful friendship is corroborated by her time spent in the flat as a guest. When she arrives, 'Eleanor was toasting muffins before the little gas stove in the scullery'; as a consequence of her newly developed sense of generosity, Eleanor offers Mrs Allardyce 'the most comfortable basket-chair in the sitting room', while 'Frances took her cloak, and untied her bonnet strings, and got her a footstool' (155). While the mawkish descriptions of the hearth, the 'little gas stove' and the 'comfortable basket-chair' appear in order to align this space with the comforts of a conventional home, the cooperation and companionship that Mrs Allardyce observes also convince her of the flat's domestic suitability. Watching Eleanor prepare tea and Frances act as hostess, Mrs Allardyce comments in the rather awkward dialect that Margaret Oliphant understandably spurned, 'You two are very comfortable here [. . .] [a]n' very sib-like for two that never saw other a week syne' (155). In the expression 'sib-like' she implies that the women have established a relationship akin to that of siblings in the short time that they have lived together.

It is easy to interpret this scene as an overly sentimental articulation of the way that these women, despite their compromised circumstances, adhere to domestic convention. It can also be interpreted in the tradition of schoolgirls' stories in which young and often rebellious girls are inculcated into traditional gender frameworks in homosocial environments that prepare them for an ineluctable heterosexual union at the narrative's conclusion. However, Eleanor and Frances do not only play at hostesses in order to entertain guests or behave in a way that designates their friendship as an ancillary relationship. Frances later reveals that they have been keeping a common purse that enables them to better negotiate expenses. She suggests that if Eleanor is unable to maintain a steady position that they will simply 'go on short commons', and adds: 'It isn't the first time I've only had a meat dinner once a week' (175). When Frances is invited to stay with Mrs Allardyce in Scotland after the two develop an affinity, Frances explains to Eleanor's father who sceptically inquires about his daughter's ability to live independently: 'We share and share alike. When times are hard, we fast together' (212). While the familiar trope of women's compulsion for self-sacrifice is used here, that it is a sacrifice for a life that is both independent and collaborative is significant: simply put, these women establish an egalitarian relationship and as a result its emotional landscape sits outside the conventions of either schoolgirl fiction or the Kailyard school.

This cooperative relationship allows each individual to benefit materially from the shared space of the flat and their united financial resources, but it also addresses emotional necessity. The clearest and most predictable character development is that of Eleanor, to whom Frances 'give[s] [. . .] the benefit of [her] experience' (156). Such experience does not speak only to practical lessons for the independent urban woman, but the development of what is referred to in the text rather vaguely as 'common sense' (213). This phrase, in the context of the novel, connotes generosity and consideration as much as it does sound judgement and self-sufficiency. After spending only a short time with Frances, Eleanor

> for the first time in her existence [. . .] found herself face to face with the reality of life as embodied in the experience of Frances Sheldon. Here was a girl not so much older than herself, and endowed with equal or perhaps deeper capacity for the enjoyment of all the prizes of life, cheerfully toiling to keep herself independent and respectable and denying herself to give a little enjoyment to those she loved, and to help others in greater need than herself. (144–5)

The passage suggests that the supportive relationship that has developed between the women while living at Barker Street is unique to that environment, Eleanor having experienced this intimacy 'for the first time in her existence' (145). Once again, the emphasis on self-denial and respectability fits into the nineteenth-century paradigm of behaviour appropriate for middle-class women. Yet this interpretation must take into account the intimacy and mutuality of their relationship, which is made possible by their common household. While Frances does manage to 'awaken' Eleanor's 'soul' (145), Eleanor equally encourages Frances to value her own experience more highly – and also brings her into contact with Mrs Allardyce, who will become to her a mother figure. The relationship between Frances and Mrs Allardyce is not one of substitution or surrogacy, but exists alongside Frances's own familial ties. The only instance of the narrator's direct address emphasises the significance of this relationship to the reader: 'These two women had been happier together than it is possible for me to express in words [. . .] and could have lived a lifetime together without jarring upon each other in the smallest degree' (248). Their relationship is suitably sentimentalised for the Kailyard tradition, but it also makes use of the novel's broader pattern of rearranging the conventional or biological family and articulating the emotionally fulfilling possibilities of elective relationships and households, particularly those between women.

In line with her earlier characterisation as a bachelor woman, but one who resists parody or predictable representation, Frances does not 'affect a cheap scorn of love and marriage' (247), as did many of her fictional contemporaries. The narrator explains that '[a]s for love, while not denying its existence, [Frances] regarded it from the standpoint of an audience who are pleased to be amused' (205). Notwithstanding Frances's position on marriage, the novel adheres to Kailyard convention in supplying Mrs Allardyce with an eligible and attractive son, Robert, who finds Frances's 'self-reliance [. . .] rather refreshing' (206). Although the novel concludes with a proposal and the suggestion of a marriage between Robert and Frances, she initially refuses the proposal and insists that they spend one year apart – her returning to Barker Street – after which point both 'will know [their] own minds' (206). It is tempting to interpret this conclusion as the rehabilitation of the independent woman, since the opportunity for marriage falls to the very character who disassociates herself from the possibility of such a union. Yet Frances is not exactly rehabilitated by one romantic relationship as much as she is enriched by a series of relationships that include Eleanor, Mrs Allardyce and Robert. The reader is given the sense that Frances has developed beyond the narrator's initial evaluation that she 'she did not belong to the Emancipated' (247), for before she agrees to marry Robert she asks him directly: 'I've sometimes called myself one of the emancipated. Are you prepared to have an emancipated wife?' (284).

Although *A Victory Won* closely follows the sentimental tradition of the Kailyard in many ways, it also makes number of important remarks about the degree to which new forms of urban housing allowed residents to form intimate and egalitarian relationships that would contribute to the development of what Vicinus describes as networks of independent women who would form important 'new communities'.[37] *A Victory Won* stops short of representing a broader network of support for independent single women in the city. In fact, there is very little detail about the urban environment and no description of Barker Street Chambers – its appearance or its management – beyond the flat that Frances and Eleanor share. In this sense the novel is restricted in the ways that it conceptualises these new homes: despite the important and enabling relationships that occur within this space, the flat at Barker Street is described very much like a traditional middle-class home, with the exception of its size. Evelyn Sharp's *The Making of a Prig* is concerned with the ways in which daily life in these new residences was markedly inferior to the traditional home. The reasons for this are no mystery; having herself lived in a cubicle-sized room at Brabazon House on South Crescent in Bloomsbury, which was below the high standards of Chenies Street Chambers, Sharp was working through her own experience of living in such accommodation. From Sharp's descriptions of life at Brabazon House, and journalistic accounts that suggest that women's residences exaggerated 'the British failing of exclusiveness and indifference to others, which is such a marked feature of London life', it seems that Swan's irrepressibly buoyant depiction of life in a shared flat in *A Victory Won* might be rather too rosy.[38] Perhaps, after all, it was this inaccuracy to which Adeline Sergeant objected in her response to Swan's earlier version of the story.[39] Yet Swan reworks the sentimental schoolgirl novel and places women's adult friendships at the centre of this narrative, and it is no surprise that ladies' chambers created an environment in which this relationship could thrive. While Swan's novel might seem hopelessly naive and utopian in its representation of women's dwellings when set alongside much contemporaneous journalism, or the work of authors such as Sharp and Sergeant who actually lived in these buildings, Swan's inexperience in this case allows her to focus on what these new domestic situations enabled, rather than what they compromised.

Notes

1. Gee, '"Where Shall She Live?"', unpublished thesis, p. 40.
2. 'Where the Unmarried Live', *Woman's Herald*, 20 April 1893, p. 131.
3. Ibid.
4. Ibid.
5. Hamlett, *Material Relations*, pp. 147–53. Alison Ravetz makes a similar point about the decanting of elderly tenants from council housing in the post-war period. See Ravetz, *The Place of Home*, p. 45.
6. Zimmern, 'Ladies Dwellings', *Contemporary Review*, 77 (1900), pp. 98–9.
7. Ibid.
8. Ibid. p. 97.
9. Ibid. p. 98.
10. Adams, *Architecture in the Family Way*, p. 154.
11. Ibid.
12. Vicinus, *Independent Women*, p. 5.
13. Dickson, 'Annie S. Swan and O. Douglas', p. 329.
14. Cuddon, 'Kailyard School', pp. 441–2; Dickson, 'Annie S. Swan and O. Douglas', p. 329.

15. Gardiner, 'Annie S. Swan – Forerunner of Modern Popular Fiction', p. 252.
16. Ibid.
17. Ibid. p. 254.
18. Ibid. p. 253; Dickson, 'Annie S. Swan and O. Douglas', p. 230.
19. Cited in Dickson, 'Annie S. Swan and O. Douglas', p. 241.
20. Ibid. p. 336.
21. Swan, *A Victory Won*, p. 148. Further references to this work are given in parentheses in the text.
22. Crawford, *Enterprising Women*, p. 214.
23. Sergeant, *Anthea's Way* (1903). Sergeant published several novels about wage-earning, independent young women, including the partially autobiographical novel *Esther Denison* (1889). She also included discussion of model dwellings in the novel *Caspar Brooke's Daughter* (1891).
24. Hobhouse, 'Women Workers: How they Live and How They Wish to Live', p. 480.
25. Ledger, *The New Woman*, p. 96. See also Shapiro, 'The Mannish New Woman: Punch and its Precursors', pp. 510–22. The Rational Dress Movement was committed to making clothing 'more comfortable and hygienic'. Women's undergarments, such as the corset, were given particular attention. See Bayles Kortsch, *Dress in Late Victorian Women's Fiction*, p. 92.
26. Miller, *Rebel Women*, p. 139.
27. Sharp, *The Making of a Prig*, p. 104.
28. Zimmern, 'Ladies Dwellings', p. 99.
29. Ibid. p. 101.
30. Ibid. Adams notes that this 'influential project', designed by Gilbert Parker, was never constructed. See Adams, *Architecture in the Family Way*, p. 158.
31. Ibid.
32. Zimmern, 'Ladies Dwellings', p. 97.
33. Ibid.
34. Mitchell, *The New Girl*, pp. 74–102.
35. Hobhouse, 'Women Workers: How they Live and How They Wish to Live', p. 480.
36. Ibid.
37. Vicinus, *Independent Women*, p. 31.
38. 'Where the Unmarried Live', p. 131.
39. Crawford, *Enterprising Women*, p. 214.

Chapter 7

Fugitive Living: Social Mobility and Domestic Space in Julia Frankau's *The Heart of a Child*

Although her earliest novel was most famous for its scandalous impropriety, Julia Frankau's writing was admired by critics and popular on both sides of the Atlantic in the decades around the turn of the twentieth century. Frankau's first novel, *Dr. Phillips: A Maida Vale Idyll* (1887), published, like all her novels, under the pseudonym 'Frank Danby', stoked significant controversy for its caustic portrayal of the affluent West End Anglo-Jewish community in which she was raised.[1] While Frankau's two subsequent novels met with some critical success and popular interest, it was not until the publication of *Pigs in Clover* (1903) – her first after a twelve-year hiatus during which she contributed regularly to the *Saturday Review* and published several historical and art historical texts – that her literary reputation was firmly established. Sarah Gracombe suggests that *Pigs in Clover* redresses the prejudice presented in *Dr. Phillips* in its 'far more complex, sympathetic look at Jewishness'.[2] Frankau's later novels relinquish the naturalism and melodrama that are characteristic of her earliest work and treat social and political questions with greater nuance; yet subjects such as colonialism, race, sexuality and gender all remain strong themes.

The popular success of her novel *The Heart of a Child* (1908) – there were at least two film versions of the story made, one an early Hollywood film – owes something to its basis on the Cinderella story popularised in the nineteenth century by the Brothers Grimm.[3] However, the sentimentality that results from this theme is kept in check by the satirical tone that characterises Frankau's fiction. *The Heart of a Child* traces the 'meteoric' career of a woman who begins life as Sally Snape and who, at the novel's conclusion, is Lady Kidderminster.[4] One reviewer described the familiar story, which is also the plot of Elinor Glyn's *The Career of Katharine Bush* (1916) and W. B. Maxwell's *Vivien* (1905), as one of the 'female climber to fame' by way of the route of 'social success'.[5] Yet to focus on the novel's representation of housing contradicts the heroine's ascent, for in her social climbing she experiences various restrictions that emerge from women's association with domesticity across classes. While Sally's access to housing improves and she is materially better off at the novel's conclusion, throughout the narrative she is limited and often imperilled by the social implications of the unconventional dwellings that she inhabits.

Angelhouse Gardens

Although Frankau's later novels relinquish the Juvenalian satire that characterises her early writing, in *The Heart of a Child* she parodies a variety of popular literary genres in order to rework conventions and undermine the reader's expectations.[6] *The Heart of a Child* draws upon different conventions at each stage of the protagonist's life, beginning with slum fiction in a scene that is a pastiche of Arthur Morrison's *A Child of the Jago* (1896). Born in the 'incredibly rotten and insanitary' slum of Angelhouse Gardens in Limehouse, Sally Snape is discovered by Ursula Rugeley, a Charity Organisation Society district visitor who feels compelled to support Sally on account of her moral integrity. The narrator explains, however, that in her work the district visitor 'was learning more than she was teaching, [and] receiving more than she was giving' (3). In fact the narrator's initial description of the 'foul gutters [. . .] tottering, low tenement houses, the front bulging, the broken windows filled in with rags of paper, the roofs rotting' is soon contradicted:

> Yet here, on that May day, ten years ago, the organ grinder turned his tune, and, with shoeless feet, or feet worse than shoeless, in men's boots, carpet slippers, gaping, ragged gear of every description, the draggle-tailed children danced. And they danced well, now a reel, now a polka, now a valse; not the latest fashionable variety perhaps, but always in strict time, with never a step missed, and a sense of gaiety and abandonment amazing to the district visitor. (1)

The opening sequence establishes a pattern that recurs throughout the novel, one that resituates the moral implications of generic conventions (here, those of slum fiction). Children who in *A Child of the Jago* are ineluctably immoral and devoted to 'coshing' are here engaged in a comparatively wholesome activity from which they draw pleasure, and their precision and determination in their practice implies a certain virtuousness. Whereas in the Jago 'children were born and reared in circumstances which gave them no reasonable chance of living decent lives', here the narrative resists the environmental determinism that had been especially popular with authors in the last two decades of the nineteenth century.[7]

There is another and more explicit clue that Frankau specifically had Morrison's text in mind: when the condemned Angelhouse Gardens is finally demolished by 'the men from the London County Council' (26), the district visitor reappears to offer assistance to the evicted tenants. At this point, the narrator suggests that 'the Reverend Mr. Jay, who had his hands very full indeed, was glad to [accept her help]' (28). The name would have been familiar to readers of Morrison's text, which was dedicated to the Revd Arthur Osborne Jay, who served as inspiration for the Jago's vicar Father Sturt, and who in the novel is served with the impossible task of rehabilitating the district.[8] Father Sturt recognises the story's protagonist, Dicky Perrott, as a child with potential and arranges for his employment at a local grocer. However, the young boy is 'fore-damned to a criminal or semi-criminal career' and the narrative follows his demise and eventual death.[9]

The Heart of a Child inverts this narrative, although not merely for corrective purposes; the novel suggests that an individual's material environment does not necessarily determine their moral stature nor correspond to their social status in any straightforward way. Like the Revd Jay, the district visitor in *The Heart of a Child* commits herself to improving Sally's circumstances after the destruction of Angelhouse Gardens. While Ursula Rugeley is a sympathetic character, she also serves to call into question the motivations and effectiveness of philanthropy. Ursula is, in fact, a character who would more conventionally have the role of the protagonist in such a narrative, and resembles the 'bachelor girl' figure from novels such as Evelyn Sharp's *The Making of a Prig* or Annie S. Swan's *A Victory Won*:

> Ursula Rugeley, who had rejected love and marriage, and turned her back on her relations, fighting through her adult years for some strange phantom of lately secured independence, failed, of course, to realize that here was her more robust prototype. (18)

This characterisation appears not only for the purpose of dramatic irony, but is also used to establish a thread of shared experience between the two women; it also, however, indicates their social difference. Whereas Ursula's rejection of love and marriage signifies a choice of independence, Sally's declaration, 'as for marryin', I 'ate the very name of it', is ambiguous on account of her class status. The only explanation that the narrator wryly volunteers at this stage is that 'Sally was never easy to understand' (30). Sally's rejection of romantic love cannot be so easily aligned with the motivations that a reader would presume of a middle-class woman, and instead it is hinted at that she is romantically naive, although 'quite definitely, and not ignorantly, virtuous' (29).

The parallel drawn between the two women, Sally and Ursula, causes the reader to modify simple characterisations of either figure in view of this more ambiguous description. For it is soon revealed that Ursula 'no more understood the sex question, as it appeared to the decent denizens of Limehouse, than Sally understood, later on, how the problem presented itself in Mayfair' (29). One of the novel's reviewers was perplexed by Sally's virtuousness, pointing out that it was unusual that her 'physical and moral fastidiousness' should endure throughout the novel, and that inconceivably 'she remains throughout her progress from gutter to factory, factory to hat-shop, hat-shop to stage, and stage to peerage the same person; there is no distortion of character, no sudden and incredible access of exterior refinement'.[10] The protagonist's immutability is another way in which the novel reworks a narrative that the *Saturday Review* derided as 'melodramatically commonplace', and is also an aspect that compromises its classification as a *bildungsroman*, for there is very little psychological development.[11] The plot's principal variable is not the protagonist but her environment, both her workplace and her residence. At every stage, however, Sally's 'meteoric' (6) career is compromised by the constancy of social prejudice – specifically that directed towards single women.

The Soho Club and Home for Working Girls

Several years after Sally's eviction from Angelhouse Gardens, the district visitor encourages her to apply for work in a factory, which will allow her to move from a flat in a Peabody buildings block that she shares with two male friends – a morally compromising arrangement, according to the district visitor. It is her eventual employment at Messrs Hall & Palmer, that 'celebrated jam and pickle warehouse' (30) on Shaftesbury Avenue, that allows her to move from

London's East End to Soho. Although it is not explicitly named, Maude Stanley's Soho Club and Home for Working Girls on Greek Street was a well-known residence and social club, which, according to *The Quiver*, began a 'movement' of residential clubs which 'brighten the lives of working girls in the principal cities of England and America'.[12] The Honourable Maude Althea Stanley was herself something of a philanthropic celebrity. Having begun her career as a Poor Law guardian in the parish of St Ann's, Soho, she later became a home visitor in the Five Dials.[13] In *Work About the Five Dials* (1878), Stanley writes of her experience establishing a night school, refuge and social club in the area. Stanley also established a Sunday School, but her approach was known to be 'broad minded': she recognised that proselytising would alienate the very people she intended to rally.[14] The Soho Club was similar in outlook, built as it was on 'the foundation of religion' but with the recognition that the establishment would not 'be [successful] by putting religion forward first, by severity, by exclusion of amusements, called by some worldly pleasures'.[15]

There were some for whom the liberalities of the Soho Club were too great. One journalist, writing for the *Wesleyan-Methodist Magazine* under the alias 'A Methodist Country Parson', is predictably opposed to the 'sanction of dancing for working girls' on account of the 'lamentable evils resulting from public and promiscuous dancing'; he suggests that girls' clubs should instead be 'an *auxiliary of the Sunday School*'.[16] Stanley herself expressed some hesitancy around matters of amusement, and she shared the country parson's concern that this new group of wage-earners would spend their money unwisely and in doing so develop debts, or worse, dishonest practices of acquiring money. It is partly for this reason that the Soho Club was intensely regulated – and much more so than even the most strait-laced of middle-class women's residences. Before her admission to the club, the potential resident was required to 'obtain from the Matron the rules and a paper to be filled up with references' and '[t]he Card of Membership [was] not given until a visit has been paid to the Candidate's home by one of the Council'.[17] The club's rules and management make clear that the purpose of the club was not only to provide accommodation but, in Stanley's words, to 'improve the lives of our working classes'.[18] She explained that club work 'raises and ennobles [. . .] by its wholesome pleasures, its varied interests, by its human sympathies between the ladies and the girls'.[19] Alongside the classes and activities offered by the club – which included gymnastics, mathematics, needlework, music and French – there was also a programme of moral training that was designed to be especially effective for those who were residents. An attendance register was 'ruled for every day' for all those who lived at the club, and a log book was kept of anyone who visited the club for a meal or the very popular glee club.[20] Seth Koven suggests that Stanley 'took a dim view of most women's motives for helping the poor', having recognised that charity was often as much a gift to the benefactor as the recipient.[21] This, however, did not preclude the club's paternalistic philanthropic model, which ensured – along with the rent and club fees – that residents were coached in 'culture and refinement' *de haute en bas*.[22] Stanley explains: 'We have not wished to take our girls out of their class, but we have wished to see them ennoble the class to which they belong.'[23] This, however, is the very rule that *The Heart of a Child* breaks.

Sally Snape's time living at the Soho Club on Greek Street is interrupted by several providential promotions that raise her from poverty to the peerage. She does not stay long enough to receive the white snowdrop brooch given to residents of the club after one year of membership, another of Stanley's incentives for physical and social stability.[24] Sally does attend the 'Continuation School for a year' (32) and has a 'sixpenny dinner [. . .] at the Girls' Club' (30), but there is scant mention in the text of the club's strict rules of propriety or its principles of management. In fact, like the Peabody dwellings, the Soho Club is largely left to the reader's imagination in this novel. This is unusual, given the level of detail that Frankau often devotes to the built environment in her fiction. The practical reason for the limited information about these buildings in the novel is probably that they were unfamiliar to the author – and unfamiliar in literature more generally. It is unlikely that Frankau would have had much personal knowledge of Limehouse slums or of working girls' clubs, given her affluence and membership of London's most fashionable literary and artistic circles. Yet there existed by the turn of the twentieth century a significant body of slum fiction that Frankau could draw upon, rework and satirise in her representation of areas such as Angelhouse Gardens.

The rendering of the Soho Club in *The Heart of the Child* is certainly one of the earliest depictions of a girls' club in popular fiction, and for its portrayal it is probable that Frankau made use of contemporary journalism and advertisements.[25] Together with Stanley's regular appearance in the pages of women's magazines – as Koven notes, she was the 'doyenne of aristocratic slum philanthropy' – the club was often featured in periodicals that reported on its 'success' and gave basic information about provisions and activities.²⁶ Middle-class readers were not appealed to as potential residents, but rather encouraged to visit and 'subscribe something towards clearing off the debt which has been incurred by the promoters in their anxiety to benefit the working girls'.²⁷ An advertisement included in *The Story of Old Soho* (1893), a promotional pamphlet for a fundraising bazaar in Soho Square, seems a likely example of the kind of source from which Frankau may have gleaned information about the Soho Club. The half-page advertisement, titled 'Soho Home & Club for Working Girls' (Fig. 7.1), offers details of payments, classes and facilities such as the library. It also enumerates the cost of 'a bedroom, with sitting room and Gas, Fire, washing of Bed Linen and Towels, 3s. And 4s. a week, paid in advance' although there were also available '[s]ome Rooms at 5s., 6s. And 7s. 6d. each'.²⁸ The advertisement states that breakfast, tea and supper were available at 2½d and dinner at a cost of 6d.²⁹ In *The Heart of a Child*, Sally shares 'a furnished room, at six shillings a week, in Greek Street' (30) with another young woman employed by that 'liberal and intelligent firm' (30), Hall & Palmer. The advertisement confirms that while single rooms were available for those who had the means, 'some [girls] are two or three in a room'.³⁰ Sally is pleased with the convenience of 'a sixpenny dinner [that] was to be had at the Girls' Club, and tea for twopence' (30). An appendix included in *Clubs for Working Girls* reveals that a number of Soho Club residents were employed at the nearby Crosse & Blackwell's jam factory, which is clearly the model for the Hall & Palmer warehouse in the novel.³¹

While it is difficult to discern the precise source from which Frankau drew her information about the Soho Club, it is evident that she did have knowledge of its basic operations. Although her unfamiliarity with this new form of housing can be cited as one reason for its restricted appearance in the novel, its textual marginality reveals important information about the relationship between working-class women's dwellings and conventional domesticity. The Soho Club was a new model of accommodation when it was built, and one that was – like the middle-class women's residences discussed in Chapters 5 and 6 – made necessary partly as a result of changes in the labour market. Descriptions of middle-class women's residences such as Chenies Street Chambers in Bloomsbury fit more comfortably with the conventions of the nineteenth-century novel, associated as it was with bourgeois domesticity. Relatedly, it is perhaps to be expected that residences for working-class women are not represented in fiction to the same degree nor in the same ways.³²

118 Home and Identity in Nineteenth-Century Literary London

Figure 7.1 'Soho Club & Home for Working Girls', advertisement from *The Story of Old Soho* (London: T. Pettit & Co., 1893), p. 26

During the period that Sally lives at Greek Street the majority of her time is spent not at home, but at work – even though '[o]nly ten hours a day was expected of her, and time from that was allowed for dinner in the middle of the day, and tea in the afternoon' (30), as opposed to the fourteen or fifteen she would have spent in her previous occupation sewing trousers. Of all the forms of housing represented in the novel – and indeed every conceivable option is cycled through – the Soho Club is the most supportive of Sally's independence but also the most structured. While living at Greek Street, she benefits from 'having practically a common purse' with her friend Mary and access to the club's 'community of goods and interests' (31). Where her employment is concerned, Sally had 'not been used to such luxury' (30) as lunch breaks and ten-hour days. Angelhouse Gardens is condemned and demolished by the London County Council, and the district visitor discourages her habitation in the Peabody dwellings with two men who were not family members, but Sally's accommodation in Greek Street meets with social approval on account of the clear moral project associated with girls' clubs. Like most middle-class women's housing, residential girls' clubs were understood to be temporary accommodation, even if this was not the case in practice. Where women's new communities and opportunities for housing were concerned, Lynn Walker explains that 'ideologically, the stakes were high; social stability, the good order of society, and even human happiness were perceived to be dependent on women's presence in the [conventional] home'.[33]

Like middle-class women's housing, residential clubs for working-class women socially redefined the traditional home through architectural reordering. However, working-class women's dwellings such as the Soho Club expressed this reordering differently to middle-class women's residences. Middle-class women's residences tended to employ conventional elements of middle-class domestic design, such as rooms for discrete purposes such as a library or music room, and were also designed to ensure the kinds of privacy thought necessary for middle-class women to maintain their social status. Completed in 1884, the Soho Club is more reserved than its middle-class counterparts in its use of architectural ornamentation. Built in yellow London stock brick, rather than the standard red brick more often used for residential buildings, the Soho Club is organised into four storeys of nine bays accented by red-brick banding. At ground level there is a series of pilasters, and the entrances are marked out by pediments. The stripped-down neoclassical style, fitting for the building's situation on Greek Street, also limits decorative features in view of finance. Unlike the Queen Anne style preferred by architects of middle-class dwellings, here the structure's residential purpose is only revealed at the roof-line by a series of six dormers.

In some ways the design of the Soho Club resembles model dwellings such as those of the Peabody Trust more closely than it does the buildings of the Ladies' Residential Chambers Company, which built several notable middle-class women's residences, including Chenies Street Chambers. This is evident in its use of brickwork for decorative patterning, the facade accented by fenestration, and its use of a pediment (or an entablature, which often appears on Henry Darbishire's designs for Peabody dwellings) to mark out an entrance. The Soho Club's design indicates the social group for which it was intended, but it also underscores the ways that the building was at variance with conventional domesticity. The building's size, although there was accommodation for only 33 women, emphasised by the symmetry and simplicity, contrasts with both the single-family dwelling and the more picturesque character of middle-class women's residences. The advertisement in *The Story of Old Soho* exaggerates the building's decorative aspect, and strangely offers a perspective that would have been impossible from street level. The illustration includes a steeply pitched roof punctuated by dormers to highlight the building's residential purpose. From street level, constrained on a shallow plot between two other buildings and overlooking a narrow street, this aspect would have been (and is still today) entirely obscured. If Farringdon Road Buildings was said to resemble 'terrible barracks', as George Gissing proclaimed in *The Nether World*, the Soho Club looked not unlike the pared-down factories where its residents spent the most of their time.[34]

(Ar)Tillery Mansions

Sally eventually progresses from her role at the pickle factory to become a music hall and theatrical celebrity, and each stage of her career introduces her to a different form of accommodation. After living for a time in a grimy Bloomsbury lodging house, Sally eventually rents a room at Tillery Mansions when her manager determines that she needs her own 'nice clean little flat' (212). Tillery Mansions takes as its model Artillery Mansions (Fig. 7.2), one of London's earliest blocks of flats, designed by the architect John Calder and completed in 1895.[35] Stephen Inwood notes that the 'English distaste for flats and apartments was breaking down in the later nineteenth century' and that Victoria Street was the 'pioneer of middle-class apartment blocks (or "mansion flats"), with flats of three or four bedrooms and servants' quarters'.[36] By the last decade of the nineteenth century, when Artillery Mansions was completed, Victoria Street was lined from one end to the other with apartment blocks of five to six storeys such as Grosvenor Mansions, Albert Mansions,

Figure 7.2 Front elevation, Artillery Mansions, Victoria Street, Westminster. Designed by John Calder (built 1895; photograph 1971)

Windsor House and Westminster Chambers which, as Richard Dennis notes, appeared 'Babylonian in scale but also "Babel-like" in gathering hundreds of people of different ages, experience, and origins together under one roof'.[37]

First intended as a residence for the staff of the nearby Army and Navy store, Artillery Mansions uses standard residential red brick embellished by a highly decorative neo-Gothic facade. The central bay is marked out by an exaggerated Gothic entrance arch, the broad span of which provides a perspective of the inner quadrangle and decorative fountain. The symmetrical fenestration organises the facade into seven separate vertical bays, each of which is crowned by an arch that extends into a gable that breaks the building's cornice. The building's vertical accent is heightened by the use of pilasters that frame each window, and that are crowned by a lintel with a pattern of basic tracery. The grand scale of the building, combined with its organisation around a central quadrangle as well as its use of ornament, suggests the collegiate Gothic as a model; no doubt a choice intended to play into the building's aspirations of 'old-fashioned elegance'.[38] By this point the use of neo-Gothic ornamentation – the establishment style from the point of its use in the reconstructed Palace of Westminster in 1840 – for any building, even of this scale, was not unusual. The civic improvement scheme initiated by Angela Burdett-Coutts in 1869 to build dwellings and a covered market at Columbia Road used (a considerably more abstemious) neo-Gothic style for a large-scale domestic design.[39] Artillery Mansions was also not anomalous in its use of a traditional style for a building that sought to be recognised as modern and efficient; when George Gilbert Scott's St Pancras Station opened in 1868, it was viewed in structure, style and purpose as a thoroughly modern design. Artillery Mansions aimed to communicate elegance, efficiency and what Dennis describes as 'stylish mobility'.[40] In its combination of conventional aesthetics and modern purposes, the design of Artillery Mansion offered accommodation to a new social group that, although diverse, was united by the challenge its members posed to conventional domesticity.

Advertisements, signboards and postcards for Artillery Mansions all call attention to the convenience of apartment living: it was 'the most central position in town'; it was 'close to St James Park and the District Railway, Parliament, the Abbey, Victoria Railway Station, Army & Navy Store, and the New Catholic Church [Westminster Cathedral]'; and there was even a 'French Chef'.[41] These advertisements emphasise features that would chime with potential residents' notions of middle-class domesticity, such as an 'interior decorated with palms and flowers', but at the same time acknowledge improvements and embellishments to single-family dwellings: for instance, the claim that Artillery Mansions had 'one of the most handsome entrances in London; [and a] large quadrangle laid out with tessellated paving, with novel illuminated Parisian fountain'.[42] There were electric lights and telephones, as well as 'accommodation for cycles', and even the availability of 'pure water from an artesian well on the premises'.[43]

Together with its unusually flamboyant ornamentation in design, these modern conveniences were necessary to differentiate the mansion block from the model dwelling – but such features led some critics to associate apartment buildings and their residents with a level of extravagance that was morally suspicious. In *The Heart of a Child*, the narrator is required to regularly defend Sally's pleasure in her new home:

> Sally was innately honest as she was innately pure. *But* she loved soft linings and pretty frocks. She loved, too, her new flat, a furnished bedroom, sitting-room, and bathroom, in Tillery Mansions, Victoria. She was not dull or solitary in it, there was no time. There were music lessons, and dancing lessons, she had massage to make her limbs supple, she had her rehearsals [. . .] [emphasis added] (215)

The narrator's vindication of Sally's delight in her new home, an emotion that is to be expected given that she was apparently born in London's worst slum, is in part a defence of her new career as an actress. The actress, a familiar figure in the narrative of social progress, was successful on account of her capacity for dissimulation both personally and professionally. Deborah Parsons notes that one of the period's best-known fictional actresses, the protagonist of Theodore Dreiser's *Sister Carrie* (1900), succeeds on account of having 'learn[ed] to negotiate her place in the urban world and harmonize herself within her environment', and experiences such as these led to the forging of what Parsons refers to as a new gendered city consciousness.[44] While most often the actress's flexible identity and urban sensibility were a threat to social stability (Dreiser's novel concludes with Carrie sitting alone in the penthouse suite of a glamorous New York hotel, having left a trail of financially and emotionally ruined men behind her), in *The Heart of a Child* the narrator insists that idleness and indulgence are impossibilities not in spite of but *because* of her professional life, for 'there was no time' (215). Apartment blocks like Artillery Mansions were 'disruptive of middle-class social and architectural values', whereas residences like the Soho Club were understood as part of a philanthropic project designed to correct working-class itinerancy and protect the virtue of young women.[45] Therefore Sally's move from the Soho Club to Tillery Mansions places her in a less conventional position despite the improvement to her material circumstances. This change of address requires the narrator to repeatedly aver Sally's moral goodness.

The middle-class mansion flat, a form of housing still in its infancy at the historical moment of this novel, was morally suspect for a number of reasons – and particularly so for women. The flat was a form of housing especially popular with, and most often designed for, 'well-off bachelors who preferred central to suburban living but who could not afford a flat in the West End'.[46] Most mansion flats were consequently mass congregations of young, unattached, metropolitan men, and therefore a woman who selected a flat as her residence breached the conventions of both society and gender. Being within audible range of the division bell, Artillery Mansions was especially popular as a *pied-à-terre* for Members of Parliament, which corroborated its reputation as a male space and one that was antithetical to a settled home.[47] George Bernard Shaw satirises such concerns in the opening scene of his play *The Philanderer* (1893), which is set in another of London's early apartment blocks, Ashley Gardens (1890). The unconventionality of the play's profligate bohemian protagonist, Leonard Charteris, expressed by his wardrobe which includes a turquoise ring, blue socks and leather sandals, is echoed by the setting: a flat, furnished with 'theatrical engravings and photographs and a bust of Shakespeare'. More shocking still is that the flat belongs not to this bohemian young man, but to an equally unconventional bohemian young woman, Grace Tranfield.[48] Artillery Mansions negotiated the notoriously disreputable character of mansion flats that Shaw mocks in *The Philanderer* by offering, in addition to 'Rooms for Married Couples from £75' and 'Bachelor Rooms from £42', 'Rooms for Ladies – Floors set apart for ladies only. with [*sic*] separate housekeepers: single from £25, unfurnished: or furnished if desired'.[49]

Although the flat that Sally rents at Tillery Mansions would have been located on a ladies' floor, her residence in this building still renders her character morally dubious. Sally's manager arranges for the payment of her rent directly from her own salary, but when Lord Kidderminster begins courting Sally, her career of 'honest work' (258) is doubted by Kidderminster's friends, who are sceptical about the possibility of 'platonic friendships with theatre girls' (259). Society gossip soon casts aspersions on the actress, who is believed to have been given 'a brougham and a motor to take her backward and forward' by Kidderminster, which he denies as 'a damned lie', insisting – much like the narrator – that '[s]he's a decent, straight, hard-working little girl' (258). Sharon Marcus has explored the way in which dwellings with common living areas used by individuals who were not family relations were viewed as promiscuous spaces.[50] Although common areas of mansion flats were not shared in the way that lodgers would share space in a lodging house, there remained an indeterminacy about the level of discretion accorded to different areas of the building: corridors, lifts, lobbies, courtyards and services were all communal. There were also, as Richard Dennis notes, legal questions about whether mansion blocks 'should be treated as sets of "private" dwellings or "public" buildings'.[51] Although Dennis refers specially to Queen Anne's Mansions, the unprecedented height of which produced difficulties for fire regulations, other mansion flats encountered similar difficulties as there existed no legal precedent for the delimitation of private and public spaces in these buildings. The promiscuous spaces of mansion flats extended to the inhabitants of these dwellings themselves, and in so doing engendered a charge of moral (most often sexual) impropriety.

Victoria, the small district within the City of Westminster in which London's mansion flats were located, was just as untested and indeterminate as the mansion flat itself. A major thoroughfare created by a slum clearance project that began in 1847, Victoria Street was only completed at mid-century and became defined by these experimental new mansion flats, which began to crop up near Pimlico. These unconventional buildings, which one commentator described as 'gigantic slum dwelling[s] for the rich', were criticised for what was considered to be their towering size of six storeys and irregular design.[52] Victoria was not the first district constructed in proximity to a slum clearance site that seemed to be troubled by the spectre of the buildings it replaced. In fact, Matthew Ingleby notes that the city improvement schemes that created Shaftesbury Avenue earlier in the nineteenth century had given to Bloomsbury a similarly ambiguous social position: one that was suitable for bachelors and other unconventional households, but that posed a significant challenge to conventional domesticity.[53]

The Heart of a Child draws on the social indeterminacy of both districts in a moment of society gossip, when Kidderminster is questioned by an acquaintance about his relationship with Sally:

> Oh I know all about it, everybody knows. But *why* did you take a flat in Victoria? It might just as well be Bloomsbury. Of course, when I went there, I had no idea it was your show! Who would have dreamt of your

setting up house in Tillery Mansions? You really are unconventional. Kiddie, you do impossible things. Belgravia, now, or St. John's Wood, if you must have a flat. But *Victoria* . . . [emphasis original] (289)

Kidderminster explains that he had no involvement with Sally's move to Tillery Mansions, and once again insists that she is the 'best and sweetest, and cleanest-minded, and purest girl [he's] met since [he's] been in London' (290). The moral ambiguity of the district, combined with that of the mansion flat, casts a dubious light on Sally's character.

Although Kidderminster regularly defends Sally's moral integrity, he nevertheless becomes a threat to her 'purity' himself owing to his own prejudices and expectations. After an evening of rather too much wine, Kidderminster attempts to accompany Sally into her flat at Tillery Mansions. Sally, however, demonstrates the moral integrity that is so regularly attributed to her and expresses serious misgiving when she asks, 'Are you coming in? [. . .] It's getting awfully late, isn't it?' (225). When Kidderminster first attempts to kiss her she 'pushe[s] him away with her elbow' and exclaims, 'What rubbish you're saying. What's the matter with you, you look quite pale? [. . .] I say, you are in a funny humour; what's come over you?' (225). Still resolute, despite Sally's insistence that she 'cannot abide being touched' (226), Kidderminster physically seizes her and kisses her aggressively. After 'struggl[ing], passionately, frantically, unmistakably to free herself from him' (226) she realises that

> [s]he had to fight him, she had boasted so often that she could take care of herself; now was the time to show it. And she proved it, up to the hilt; he gained nothing. The struggle was short [. . .] [he was] rejected, contemptuously and angrily scorned. It was Lord Kidderminster who flung himself on the sofa now, hid his face in the cushion, and began to sob weakly. (227)

Sally defends herself against Kidderminster's advances with her pride of strength and independence, the very qualities that have enabled her professional and social success. Similarly this scene allows Sally to redefine her flat at Tillery Mansions as a space of self-determination rather than exploitation – which is further accentuated by Kidderminster's comic defeat and emasculation. While he is sobbing on the couch, Sally states plainly: 'You've spoiled my evening [. . .] I don't want you here any more' (227). The 'promiscuous space' of the mansion flat becomes here not symbolic of its inhabitants' sexual promiscuity but instead a space of fugitive and flexible meaning that allows conventional relationships between men and women to be redefined. The social indeterminacy of the mansion flat is, therefore, marked out in this novel as the very feature that makes it hospitable to changing domestic practices and relationships.

In design, the mansion flats allowed for a woman's independent occupation of a self-contained home that differed from the conventional family dwelling, and it was therefore seen as a threat to social stability. Women who lived in flats were criticised for their unconventional behaviour at best, and branded morally reprehensible at worst. Although the Soho Club was, like Tillery Mansions, an alternative to conventional middle-class notions of domesticity, *The Heart of a Child* suggests that residences such as the Soho Club were in a sense protected by their clearly legible social status. The Soho Club was unconventional in design, but its purpose was to maintain distinctions based on class. Frankau's novel suggests that residences such as Tillery Mansions, despite the aesthetic concessions to bourgeois domesticity, were potentially revolutionary domestic spaces because they were not intensely regulated by class or gender – but equally, that such spaces potentially posed a threat to women's social and physical security.

Just as the 'meteoric' (6) narrative propels Sally away from the Soho Club, so it also predictably precipitates her towards a happy marriage to Kidderminster in which she will finally settle into a family home. The novel's subtitle, 'being passages from the early life of Sally Snape, Lady Kidderminster', assures the reader that a conclusion of domestic felicity is never in question. What the novel does question, however, are the reader's expectations of the relationship between housing and social status. This is a novel that calls attention to the social complexity generated by changing ideologies about gender, class and domesticity at the end of the century. *The Heart of a Child* is a rare account of the continuities between economically divergent forms of housing – from the slum to the mansion block – that points out their uncomfortable similarity where matters of women's domestic security are concerned.

Notes

1. The novel was also controversial on account of its thinly veiled portrait of Dr Ernest Abraham Hart, surgeon and editor of the *British Medical Journal*, and the suggestion that his wife's 'accidental poisoning' was deliberate. See Smith, *The Frankaus*, pp. 20–2.

2. Gracombe, 'Imperial Englishness in the "Book of the Jew"', p. 155.
3. *The Complete Index to Literary Sources in Film* lists two film productions of the novel: 1916 (UK; dir. Harold Shaw) and 1920 (USA; dir. Ray C. Smallwood). See Goble, *The Complete Index to Literary Sources in Film*, p. 792. The British Film Institute database lists both productions (although the former is dated as 1915), but has no further information about versions of the film made in 1911 (France), 1913 (USA), 1914 and 1925. See 'The Heart of a Child', British Film Institute Database, available at <http://explore.bfi.org.uk> (last accessed 20 January 2017).
4. Danby [Julia Frankau], *The Heart of a Child*, p. 6. Further references to this work are given in parentheses in the text.
5. Dalton, 'New Novels', *Times Literary Supplement*, 12 April 1917, p. 176.
6. For a consideration of Frankau's satire of slum fiction in *A Babe in Bohemia* (1889), see Lisa C. Robertson, 'A Babe in Bohemia', London Fictions (2013), available at <https://www.londonfictions.com/julia-frankau-a-babe-in-bohemia.html> (last accessed 14 June 2019). Tabitha Sparks has suggested that in *Dr. Phillips* Frankau makes parodic use of the conventions of sensation fiction. Sparks, 'The Symbolic Economy of Disease in Sensation and Satire: *Lady Audley's Secret* and *Dr. Phillips: A Maida Vale Idyll*', paper given at the Birkbeck Forum for Nineteenth-Century Studies, 11 November 2013.
7. Morrison, *A Child of the Jago*, 'Preface to the Third Edition', p. x.
8. Ibid. dedication.
9. Ibid. p. x.
10. Child, 'Fiction', *Times Literary Supplement*, 5 March 1908, p. 78.
11. 'Frank Danby's New Novel', *The Saturday Review*, 4 April 1908, p. 442.
12. Dolman, 'Women Workers for Women', *The Quiver*, 30 January 1895, p. 356.
13. Stanley was also manager for the Metropolitan Asylums Board from 1884 and governor of the Borough Polytechnic from 1892. Bonham, 'Stanley, Maude Alethea (1833–1915)', *ODNB*.
14. Ibid.
15. Stanley, *Clubs for Working Girls*, p. 145.
16. 'A Methodist Country Parson', 'Clubs for Working Girls', *The Wesleyan-Methodist Magazine*, July 1890, pp. 500, 506. Italics in original.
17. Stanley, *Clubs for Working Girls*, pp. 272–3.
18. Ibid. p. 4.
19. Ibid. pp. 3–4.
20. Ibid. pp. 36, 56.
21. Koven, *Slumming*, p. 198.
22. Stanley, *Clubs for Working Girls*, p. 48.

23. Ibid.
24. Ibid. p. 276. After five years, residents were given a pendant with a snowball, and after ten, another snowball.
25. There are also representations of such clubs in Walter Besant's *All Sorts and Conditions of Men: an Impossible Story* (1882) and L. T. Meade's *A Princess of the Gutter* (1895); however, Frankau's representation seems to be most closely based on a historical model. Although Sally resides at the club for only a short time, the reader is given more specific information about its operation and administration than is offered in Besant's or Meade's novels.
26. Koven, *Slumming*, p. 198; 'Short Arrows', *The Quiver*, January 1884, p. 510.
27. 'Short Arrows', p. 510.
28. 'Soho Home & Club for Working Girls', p. 26.
29. Ibid.
30. Ibid.
31. Ibid. p. 275.
32. On the novel as a middle-class literary form, see Eagleton, *The English Novel*, pp. 1–8.
33. Walker, 'Home and Away', p. 298.
34. Gissing, *The Nether World*, p. 274.
35. Weinreb et al., 'Victoria Station', in *The London Encyclopedia*, p. 975.
36. Inwood, *City of Cities*, p. 208.
37. Dennis, 'Babylonian Flats in Victorian and Edwardian London', p. 233.
38. Dennis, *Cities in Modernity*, p. 247.
39. Tarn, *Working-class Housing in 19th-Century Britain*, pp. 15–16.
40. Dennis, *Cities in Modernity*, p. 247.
41. 'Furnished London Residence, Artillery Mansions', *The Times of India*, 14 May 1903, p. 7.
42. 'High Class Residential Mansions', *The Times*, 2 September 1897, p. 12.
43. Ibid.
44. Parsons, *Streetwalking the Metropolis*, pp. 55, 29.
45. Dennis, 'Babylonian Flats in Victorian and Edwardian London', p. 245.
46. Inwood, *City of Cities*, p. 218.
47. Warman, 'Marilyn Lived Here', *The Times*, 12 July 2000, p. 20.
48. Shaw, *The Philanderer*, in *The Complete Plays of Bernard Shaw*, p. 28.
49. 'High Class Residential Mansions', p. 12. See also Dennis, *Cities in Modernity*, p. 246.
50. Marcus, *Apartment Stories*, p. 106. Richard Dennis also refers to the 'promiscuous use of space in a shared dwelling'. See Dennis, 'Buildings, Residences and Mansions', p. 42.

51. Dennis, 'Babylonian Flats in Victorian and Edwardian London', p. 235.
52. Cited in ibid. p. 238.
53. Ingleby, *Nineteenth-Century Fiction and the Production of Bloomsbury*, pp. 16–17, 79–119. See also Ingleby, 'The Bachelorisation of Legal Bloomsbury'.

Part III

'Thinking Men' and Thinking Women: Gender, Sexuality and Settlement Housing

Chapter 8

'Vital friendship': Sexual and Economic Ambivalence in Rhoda Broughton's *Dear Faustina*

Rhoda Broughton's *Dear Faustina* (1897) has been consistently interpreted as a novel that engages with, and on occasion mocks, late nineteenth-century characterisations of the independent urban working woman. The familiar narrative commences with Althea Vane's decision to relinquish the material comforts of her upper-class home and, with the guidance and encouragement of New Woman figure Faustina Bateson, embrace socially progressive causes while cohabiting with her in a 'Chelsea flat'.[1] As Althea becomes disillusioned by Faustina's political and personal infidelity, however, she exchanges her commitment to the symbolic 'higher claims' (40) touted by Faustina for settlement work and a relationship with a man of her own social status. While nineteenth-century critics identified the novel as a 'satire' of women's charitable work, modern examinations have focused on the ways in which the novel is preoccupied with recasting the independent woman's homosocial household with the more socially acceptable configuration of heteronormative domesticity.[2] Lisa Hagar convincingly reads the novel's narrative of 'inversion' as one that is linked to the themes of social work explored by the text, and suggests that the 'cross-class relationship' is one that 'imagines lesbian desire in terms of philanthropic desire'.[3] Yet *Dear Faustina* exceeds a narrative of inversion and instead complicates models of opposition, specifically those related to gender, sexuality and class. In its representation of two key forms of housing, women's residences and settlement housing, *Dear Faustina* explores the way that these new domestic forms made legible the nuanced and inextricable relationship between economic and sexual power.

Dear Faustina draws on both the traditional and modern meaning of the word 'economic'. Only in the middle of the nineteenth century did the word develop its associations with the 'science of economics' or 'political economy' that today carry its principal weight in meaning. Before this time, the word was more closely associated with its Greek root *oikonomia*, which refers to the management of a household or a family.[4] The text makes significant use of this ambivalent meaning, as it denotes the intimate relationship between the household – and the relationships that define it – and material wealth. In playing with this doubleness throughout, *Dear Faustina* generates points of opposition that are not resolved by the narrative. If the novel's plot follows a predictable pattern in which, as Hagar explains, 'degenerate sexuality' seems to be exchanged for the 'heteronormative institution of marriage', this is unsettled by these frequent episodes of textual ambivalence.[5] As a result, any exchange that occurs in the narrative is necessarily unstable and indeterminate.

The pattern of 'exchange' that Hagar identifies in the narrative's treatment of sexuality occurs also in the novel's engagement with economics, or more specifically, paid and unpaid labour. While living with Faustina, who earns her livelihood writing about controversial causes for the press, Althea assists with this work for no financial recompense. In this sense, her efforts are aligned with traditional models of nineteenth-century charity. When Althea moves to the Canning Town Settlement at the novel's conclusion, her philanthropic efforts become modernised as a form of civic engagement. Although she earns no money during her stay at the Canning Town Settlement, she gains a greater degree of independence as one of the rewards of her labour and is granted a form of citizenship. Helen Meller explains that the concept of citizenship evolved alongside the shift in status of women's work that took place over the course of the nineteenth century – from philanthropic to professional – and that the term was used to characterise women's involvement in local concerns.[6] The concept of citizenship, Meller notes, was 'uniquely adaptable':

> Citizenship became a loaded word, imbued with a meaning covering both a concern for the public sphere and altruistic concern for society's well-being. For all, suffragists, suffragettes and women opposed to female enfranchisement, the pursuit of citizenship was a way of proving their worth.[7]

In *Dear Faustina*, Althea's transition from an 'independent living arrangement' as Faustina's 'quasi-spouse' to the Canning Town Settlement is complicated by the model of citizenship that Meller identifies.[8] Although *Dear Faustina* pinpoints two distinct housing models that emerged in the late nineteenth century, the women's residence and the settlement house, it does not champion one at the expense of the other but uses both to demonstrate how different domestic forms articulate the interconnectedness of sexual desire and economic power in unique ways. If lesbian desire is reimagined as philanthropic desire, as Hagar suggests, heterosexual desire is aligned with this concept of citizenship – and in turn, greater political efficacy. The heterosexual romantic union at the novel's end is therefore as political as it is romantic: citizenship allows Althea to cultivate a public role and 'prove her worth' in a way that companionate philanthropy cannot. *Dear Faustina*'s textual ambivalence about matters of sexuality and economics, evident in both the novel's form and subject, undermines its seemingly traditional plot structure.

More Mansions: Modelling Heteronormativity

The domestic companionship that develops between Althea and Faustina in *Dear Faustina* is complicated by the social difference that exists between the two women. Yet this cross-class dynamic is employed to a different purpose than that which Seth Koven explores in his influential consideration of 'cross-class sisterhood' in *Slumming*.[9] For in *Dear Faustina*, the cross-class relationship does not favour Althea Vane, the upper-class character who might be perceived to go 'slumming'; instead, the balance of power sits perceptibly with the lower-middle-class character, Faustina Bateson. The narrative purpose of this inversion, which is part of Broughton's satirical mode, is clear: the psychological power that Faustina exercises over Althea is uncomfortable not only for its transgression of the boundaries of women's friendships, but also because this power is a threat to social stability as maintained through the class hierarchy.

It is apparent early in the text that Faustina is not bound by the same moral or social codes as those people she considers her peers. An exchange at the novel's beginning, at which point Faustina invites Althea to share a 'home where there may not be a great many silver spoons [. . .] but where work and aspiration and love will certainly not be lacking' (45), brings into collision the novel's concerns with economics and sexuality. This instance also reveals to the reader the ways in which, as Murphy explains, 'female affection is transposed from a relatively covert to an unmistakably overt plane' in order to indicate the transgressive nature of Faustina's 'social agenda'.[10] This 'social agenda' is Faustina's journalistic work of 'getting up the subject of the Housing of the Working Classes' (46) – but so too is it her desire to gain power by enlisting Althea as her 'quasi-spouse'.[11] In an oft-quoted passage, Faustina explains to Althea, 'if you bless my home with your sweet presence, your sovereignty over my heart will be absolutely unshared', to which Althea 'quivers' and replies, 'I am sure I don't know what you see in me' (47). Power, and specifically the agency attendant on Althea's higher social status, seems to be the quality that most attracts Faustina, who emotionally exploits Althea in order to put her social power to political use. To accomplish this, Faustina reproduces and exploits the gender hierarchy associated with the conventional middle-class home; and she does so with the consciousness that Althea's social status as an upper-class woman affords her weaknesses as well as liberties. The language of the passage quoted above, particularly a phrase like 'sweet presence', is reminiscent of Ruskin's description of women's domestic capacities as uniquely suited to 'sweet ordering, arrangement and decision'; and the 'sovereignty' that Althea is promised to hold over Faustina's heart recalls the 'queenly power' of women 'within their sphere' that is referred to in the title 'Of Queen's Gardens'.[12] In using such language, Faustina indicates that, despite transgressions of gender and sexuality, their relationship will be structured along traditionalist domestic patterns.

Once Althea is settled in the shared accommodation in Chelsea, Faustina demands a level of emotional and professional companionship from her that replicates the power dynamic of the heteronormative domestic conventions to which she apparently capitulates at the novel's end.[13] As Murphy acknowledges, 'Faustina addresses Althea like a smitten swain', and upon Althea's arrival at the fourth-floor flat in More Mansions, she exclaims, 'My darling! I have you at last! [. . . H]ere you are – here WE are – and can earth give anything better?' (72).[14] At this moment, Althea bursts into tears. The dialogue in this scene draws on the exaggerated emotions and archetypal characters of melodrama, but parodies these conventions for the purpose of capturing the ambivalence that is produced by such extreme representations: that is, extremes rely on difference and therefore produce their opposite as they are called into being. In *Dear Faustina*, this representational inversion produces parody – not merely to mock the women themselves, but to satirise the conventional heterosexual model that Faustina puts to her own service. Here, the text lays bare the absurdity of the forms – both literary and social – it imitates: to denaturalise conventional heterosexuality, in this context, is to expose its defects. The novel is replete with sentimental dialogue, and a style of narration that contributes to the tone of uneasiness by winking at the 'high pitch of tension' (73) that exists between the two women.

More Mansions, where Faustina and Althea share an apartment, is described as one of the women's residences or 'ladies' chambers' that were constructed during the last two decades of the nineteenth century. As the narrator comments, 'More Mansions is one of those blocks of towering jerry buildings that have sprung up within the last three years to meet the requirements and match the purses of independent female spirits, imprudent marriages and narrow incomes' (73). Broughton's pun – 'more' is here both name and description – offers a cynical although fairly accurate assessment of the origins of women's residences. While many women's residences such as Chenies Street Chambers or New Brabazon House were architect-designed and quality-built, a significant number of 'jerry-built' structures appeared during the housing shortage of the mid-1880s.[15] Most often built on speculation by enterprising individuals, such housing was constructed quickly and cheaply. These buildings were, of course, not restricted to women's housing but permeated the entire sector.

The description of More Mansions in *Dear Faustina* as a structure that is 'jerry-built' suggests the poor quality of the building, but also symbolises the domestic economy that exists within it. The language implies that, like the building itself, the relationship between Althea and Faustina is a low-rent imitation; its purpose is mere convenience, and its duration only temporary. As previous chapters of this book have examined, women's residences were culturally understood as transitional spaces that were acceptable only until a more suitable home was made available by way of marriage, even if this was not the case in practice. *Dear Faustina* makes use of the symbolic power of women's housing as temporary structures for temporary relationships, but in narrative terms the women's relationship is represented as untenable on account of its inequality. Faustina is the novel's melodramatic villain (a role made apparent not least of all by her name): she exploits Althea emotionally and sexually, it is implied, for her own professional gain.[16] Yet Althea is eager to resign her independence, feeling 'not fit to take any initiative', but wishing to 'help [Faustina] directly in her own work – [and] to "devil" for her' (85). The unequal relationship, in which both women willingly participate, exposes systems of sexual and economic power that do not merely exist in their own relationship, but define the more conventional systems on which they have modelled their household.

While terms such as 'exchange' or 'inversion' have most often been used to define the narrative pattern of *Dear Faustina*, 'ambivalence' is more accurate on account of the instability and asymmetry of romantic, political and architectural paradigms represented in this novel. Just as the relationship between the two women is not the focus of the narrative's parody, neither is it the principal threat. The figure of the 'sublimated lesbian', to use Scott Herring's term, in nineteenth-century fiction threatened to undermine the heterosexual family and along with it domesticity itself.[17] Yet characters such as Olive Chancellor in Henry James's *The Bostonians* (1886) or Bell Blount in Eliza Lynn Linton's *The Rebel of the Family* (1880) do not challenge heterosexual domestic conventions so much as they reproduce them. A related observation has achieved currency most widely through Judith Butler's analysis of drag: she points out that the power – and therefore threat – of imitation is that it reveals that there *is* no original. Not only do these imitations 'make us question what is real, and what "must" be, but they also show us how the norms that govern contemporary notions of reality can be questioned and how new modes can become instituted'.[18] What enables this imitation is what Butler describes as the 'transferability of the attribute'.[19] Faustina models her romantic relationship with Althea on heterosexual marriage for the purpose of exploiting the uneven power dynamic of this system. The formal ambivalence produced in the text by this parody functions as criticism of the original (heterosexual) model, as much as it does the (homosexual) imitation.

The reader is given a clue early in the novel that Althea's companionate role in Faustina's life may only be temporary. When Faustina offers to help Althea through the 'painful process' of 'development, [and] growth' (44) while sharing her flat, Althea asks apprehensively if there was not 'another friend [who] shared your life – lived with you?' (46). Faustina is quick to explain that she and the friend 'have agreed to part' as 'for some time [they] had been developing in opposite directions' (47). Such language is an early indication of the textual (and indeed, sexual) ambivalence that exists alongside the narrative's seemingly straightforward linear structure: Althea may be 'rescued' by the novel's hero figure John Drake, but she is compelled to repeat the same narrative function as her predecessor at More Mansions. On the first occasion of meeting Drake, who functions as Faustina's sexual and social foil, Althea asks whether he knew '[her] predecessor, Miss Lewis' (108). Drake first gives a 'helpless laugh' (108) before explaining:

> 'Oh, rather! I beg your pardon – yes, I did know that lady . . . I not only knew Miss Lewis, but *her* predecessor.'
> '*Had* she a predecessor?'
> 'Oh yes, more than one.'
> Althea starts slightly. She feels as if a sharp pebble had hit her – small, but unexpected. (108–9)

The conversation causes Althea to view her position in the household as provisional and, unsurprisingly, incites her jealousy. Murphy makes the important point that these references to Miss Lewis 'betray a note of jealousy about Faustina's erotic inconsistencies', and that Althea 'assumes the role of a jilted lover' when she realises that she herself might be replaced.[20]

However, Althea's anger and frustration result equally from the threat of losing the economic support of her relationship with Faustina – particularly after she is cast off by her family. Althea's decision to share Faustina's flat is motivated by her 'vital' (39) dedication to their friendship. The ambiguity of such a word, which Althea's sister picks up on earlier in the novel, betrays her romantic interest but also her economic dependence. Threatened with the dissolution of this support, Althea shifts her romantic and economic interests by changing her philanthropic commitment. It is in this way that *Dear Faustina* intervenes in contemporary debates about women's civic participation, and the processes by which concepts of citizenship began to translate women's domestic role from one based in the conventional home to one focused on the community. Katharine Bradley explains that '[c]itizenship was far from being a purely political phenomenon' and that although it was connected to civic participation and the right to vote, it was also associated with the 'attainment of adulthood'.[21] What has been perceived as Althea's shift in desire – homosexual to heterosexual – in this text is inextricably linked, not unproblematically, to the pursuit of 'adulthood'.[22] This notion of adulthood is understood not only in terms of sexual maturity, but also in relation to economic and political self-determination. Althea's move from More Mansions to the Canning Town Settlement – an institution that Bradley notes 'existed to expand the notion of citizenship' – must be understood to be as much motivated by her desire for civic engagement and economic independence as it is a capitulation to conventional forms of sexuality.²³

The Canning Town Women's Settlement: A Structure of 'Female Intimacy'

The settlement movement, which involved the 'location of educated workers [to] the squalid quarters of the poor, to help them by the contact of daily life', generated a substantial number of new domestic structures, both purpose-built and adapted for reuse.²⁴ These buildings are significant not least because they represent a unique attempt at desiging and implementing large-scale cooperative housing in London. While 'associated homes' that shared cooking or washing facilities gained the interest of the middle classes in the late eighteenth and early nineteenth centuries, these were often small-scale experiments involving two or three families; large-scale communal housing had otherwise been traditionally affiliated with religious groups.²⁵ The model for the settlement movement, as Henrietta Barnett explains, was initiated by university students or 'thinking men' at Oxford, some of whom left their colleges 'to spend a few weeks, some for the long vacation, while others [. . .] began their life's work, [and] took lodgings in East London'.²⁶ These 'thinking men', together with Barnett and her husband Canon Samuel Barnett, were largely responsible for conceiving of the idea of the settlement and establishing the first and most widely known example, Toynbee Hall. The collegiate origins of settlement groups influenced the design of their buildings, which were often modelled in part on gender-segregated college residences – itself the result of the monastic heritage of universities – and organised according to principles of cooperative living. In the article 'Life in a Women's Settlement', one woman reflects that at women's settlements, '[t]he life is like the life of a college – with its morning and evening prayers in a tiny chapel, its meals in common, its cheery intercourse, and mutual interests'.²⁷

Althea's departure from More Mansions to the Canning Town Settlement, according to Martha Vicinus, is a version of the 'rescue narrative' in which a 'handsome man rescues an innocent young woman from the clutches of an older woman'.²⁸ In *Dear Faustina*, John Drake functions as the 'handsome man' – but the text is not so straightforward as to place Althea entirely in his power. After all, she leaves More Mansions of her own volition and at the novel's end lives not with her 'rescuer' but in a community of women at the

Canning Town Women's Settlement, a network that Herring notes was 'structured on female intimacy'.[29] The Canning Town Settlement was, according to the American social activist and settlement worker Alice Paul, 'one of the most famous [settlements] in London'.[30] Located in London's docklands on the north side of the Thames, the settlement occupied an area notorious for its poverty and what one journalist described as 'the problem of the unemployed'.[31] When Paul arrived in London's docklands in 1907, she settled nearby in a house that was managed by the Charity Organisation Society and – after disguising herself as a member of the 'labouring classes' – found a job working twelve-hour days in a rubber factory, 'threading cords into automobile tires'.[32] The chief problem of work at the docklands, Paul discovered, was not unemployment but underemployment: the only work available was casual labour, which meant that the docklands was a neighbourhood of individuals who had no fixed income and most often no fixed address.[33] In 'The Settlements of London', an article written for *The Leisure Hour* a decade before Paul's arrival, T. C. Collings comments on the problems of the dockland's casual labour pool. The Canning Town Settlement, he suggests, was established in part to help alleviate the burdens of underemployment. At the Albert and Victoria docks, Collings notes,

> the gates used to be besieged every morning by huge armies of casual labourers, struggling for the chance of a day's work. Gasworks, ironworks, and factories of various kinds give a fluctuating demand for labour. Here the [Canning Town] Settlement was founded for practical helpfulness, in the spirit of Jesus Christ, in all that affects human life.[34]

The Canning Town Settlement, or Mansfield House as the men's settlement was also known, was not, in fact, a religious settlement. Members of the Settlement engaged in 'both secular and religious work', and much like Toynbee Hall, it resisted affiliation with a specific Christian denomination.[35] Nevertheless, much of the activity at Mansfield House was structured around religious campaigns. For instance, Collings describes the 'characteristic' activity of the Settlement as its 'Pleasant Sunday Afternoon' at the Congregational chapel, which provides local men with access to music concerts and lectures on various subjects from professors and parliamentarians.[36] Other Settlement activities included a children's 'Happy Sunday Evening', or Sunday School, a worship hour followed by Bible class and hymn singing, and a Brotherhood Society, which consisted of 'several hundred men and women bound together by a pledge "to serve humanity in the spirit of Jesus"'.[37]

Diana Maltz and Deborah Weiner have each explored how the social activities of settlements, regardless of their particular religious affiliation, were often structured on economic and social divisions. At Toynbee Hall, the project of elevating the soul through the senses – what Maltz effectively describes as 'missionary aestheticism' – relied on middle-class notions of culture in the aspiration to a 'communal aesthetic revelation'.[38] Weiner explains that Toynbee Hall's 'self-consciously paternalistic architecture' evinced the social hierarchies of the university quadrangles that had influenced its design.[39] At avowedly religious settlements such as Oxford House, which was strongly affiliated with the Anglican Church, the spiritual hierarchy on which the settlement was organised was recast and made evident in its public outreach activities. As such, settlements such as the Canning Town Settlement were often structured on similar social divisions to those that they sought to expunge. Still, the founders of Toynbee Hall, the Revd (later Canon) Samuel Barnett and his wife Henrietta, believed that settlements ought to challenge conventional models of philanthropy. The settlement movement, Barnett noted, was the first social project where reforms were not intended to '[end] in the assertion of rights over [the working] class'.[40] Thirty years after founding Toynbee Hall, Henrietta Barnett reminded readers in the essay collection *Practicable Socialism* that 'the crucial question for all social work should be "Is our aim the self-extinction of our organisation?"'[41] The foundational principles of social work upon which many settlements were based differed from earlier models of nineteenth-century philanthropy in the sense that, as Barnett remarks, the objective of these organisations was to make their very purpose redundant. In practice, however, the social customs of these settlements – steeped as they were in the ancient social and intellectual cultures of the church and the university – often abraded their egalitarian ambitions.

In *Dear Faustina*, the representation of the social divisions on which the settlement movement was based – whether between rich and poor, cultured and unrefined, clergy and lay person – helps to fulfil the generic conventions of melodrama that require the restoration of the social order. Althea's time at the Canning Town Settlement serves this purpose in the narrative by way of consolidating her authority over the working-class women among whom she lives. Yet not all of the issues and oppositions raised by the text are reconciled at the narrative's conclusion. These oppositions produce the points of textual ambivalence that interrupt and undermine the narrative progress. It is at the novel's conclusion – the point of John Drake's 'rescue', when narrative disorder seems to be corrected – that this textual ambivalence is most perceptible. The representation of the Canning Town Settlement where Drake lives 'for months at a time, organizing meetings, giving lectures, and so forth' (123), in part corrects the disorder initiated by the unconventional romantic relationship that dominates the first half of the novel.

The Canning Town Settlement was originally located in a large complex of converted buildings along Barking Road, until the construction of a new residential hall at 83–93 Barking Road in 1897.[42] The women's branch of the Canning Town Settlement, also known as Mansfield Women's Headquarters, was separated by some distance from the men's settlement at 461 Barking Road. While the men's settlement, Mansfield House, retained close connections with the Women's Headquarters, their activities were distinct and their independence was given authority by their separate operational and residential quarters. This division was typical of most settlements in the period; a survey conducted before the First World War found that twenty-two settlements were inhabited exclusively by women and seventeen by men, and only six combined men and women. The combined settlements typically distinguished between men's and women's activities, as did Oxford House and the Ladies' Branch of Oxford House.[43] The activities of the women's settlement were diverse, and included everything from lithographing sheet music and visiting on behalf of the Sick Benefit Society to classes on bandaging and poulticing, mathematics and physiology and even a system of physical drill (Fig. 8.1). There were also literary and cultural activities coordinated by the Women's Co-operative Guild, and a weekly Bible class for local residents.[44]

The representation of the Women's Headquarters at Mansfield House in *Dear Faustina* differs considerably from a contemporaneous article that describes the work of the women who 'live there and help' as 'admirable', and that gives no indication that the local women who attend its activities are anything other than cooperative and 'reliable'.[45] Althea, who has more time at her disposal on account of Faustina's growing interest in another young woman, is invited to visit the Canning Town Settlement by Drake, who 'call[s] to his aid a female friend and fellow worker of his own, who, with a newly-married and like-minded husband has pitched her tent in the settlement' (251). Althea is therefore inducted into her new position as settlement worker at the same time as she is reinitiated into a heterosocial environment that holds the promise of heterosexual marriage. This is

LONDON'S SOCIAL SETTLEMENTS.   269

it's terribly draughty." The forceful landlord's name and other essential details are gradually sifted out from among the old lady's voluble irrelevancies, and she departs happy, confident that her wrongs will be righted. Her place is taken at once by a melancholy young man, from whose Roumanian tongue rolls off another string of grievances. "He's a 'greener,'" the interpreter explains, condensing as he translates: "only been three weeks in England; thought he had left all the cheats behind him in Roumania, and finds he's mistaken. He gave a certain man of our landlord's acquaintance 10s. 'key-money' for a house that's supposed to be going to be empty, and that man's been taking 'key-money' for the same house from I don't know how many other poor people."

One of these owners of slum property actually took the roof off so as to freeze out, or flood out, his unfortunate tenant—who, invoking the authority of Toynbee Hall, got substantial compensation for this undeniable "disturbance." In a still more celebrated case this beneficent Association obtained a decision from the High Court that the "bedding" which is beyond the landlord's power to seize for rent includes the bedstead—a judgment for which thousands of unlucky folk all over the land have cause to bless the name of Toynbee.

"Before you leave Whitechapel," says our guide, "you really must pay a visit to Balliol House"—and away he hurries us over an asphalt court, where a company of the Boys' Brigade is at drill, to what at first you take for a block of "dwellings." And so it is, but the dwellers, whom you find enjoying a sociable evening in the big "common room," are young professional men, medical students, schoolmasters, clerks, and so forth, who form

CANNING TOWN WOMEN'S SETTLEMENT : PHYSICAL DRILL.

a charming little co-operative commonwealth under the mild sway of an unprofessional "Dean," instead of living isolated lives in lodgings. As we ascend a long stone stair the guide stops short on a landing. " If you had come here one night before the place was bought and christened, you might have stumbled over the mutilated corpse of a murdered woman. On this very stone one of Jack the Ripper's victims was done to death."

The Settlement for which the ground was broken by Canon Barnett's friends from Oxford and Cambridge was named after Arnold Toynbee, a still earlier pioneer in the way of living among the poor—a young man who died on the threshold of a life full of promise. And Toynbee Hall had not long been founded when another group of Oxonians, invited by Bishop Walsham How, arrived in the once rural suburb of Bethnal Green, a mile or so farther east. Their aim was to work on Toynbee lines, but under the flag of the Church of England. In an old disused schoolroom the adventurous newcomers laid the foundations of the famous Oxford House, under the guidance first of Mr. Adderley and then of Mr. Henson.

The Settlement prospered. The natives, who had been at first mistrustful of the invading "toffs," were gradually won over by

Figure 8.1 Physical drill at Lees Hall, Canning Town Women's Settlement. Photograph from George R. Sims (ed.), *Living London*, vol. 2 (London: Cassell, 1902), p. 269

a moment at which the formerly indistinct boundaries of gender and sexuality are reinscribed, and is also a point at which class divisions are rearticulated. On one occasion, after Althea visits 'each and every portion of the work – infirmary, lodging house, recreation hall, lads' club, residence, etc.' (252), she is invited to 'give tea and entertainment to the factory girls' (255). On account of her ignorance and 'prudery' (251), however, Althea has encouraged the regular attendees to bring their friends, who Drake warns are 'often job hands, [and] who are much rougher than the regular ones. They are of the class that goes hop-picking, and have not a very high-standard of politeness' (255–6). At first there is only 'a pushing and a hustling – perfectly good humoured' (258), but soon the crowd becomes uncontrollable. Althea is pinned against the tea table during a rush and, in a very literal expression of Vicinus's description of the 'rescue narrative', is saved by Drake. This dramatic crisis resolves social and sexual transgressions, for not only does Drake rescue Althea but he is also the only person who can command the room. Drake reproaches the 'rioters' and poses a series of patronising questions intended to inhibit and ingratiate the audience: 'Are you not ashamed of yourselves?', followed by 'Is this your gratitude to the lady who is so kindly giving you entertainment?', and finally, 'If this is the way that we treat her do you think that she is very likely to come among us again?' (264). Drake's questioning subdues most of the unruly attendants, but order is finally restored with the arrival of 'several male members from the Settlement' (265). The factory workers then leave, offering their apologies and appreciation to the organisers.

Much of the scholarship on the settlement movement suggests precisely what is underscored at this point in the text: that while these projects aspired to create cross-class communities and support egalitarian relationships, more often they reinforced the power structures evident in earlier models of philanthropy.[46] And indeed, the text comments explicitly on Althea's naivety in her attempt to 'humanize' (256) the factory workers, just as it acknowledges that not all attendees are 'subdued by the authority of [Drake's] tones' or his 'bracketing himself with them' (264) in the course of his questioning.

Textual Ambivalence and Ambiguity

Althea's ambivalent motive for her relocation to the Canning Town Settlement – whether it is provoked by her desire for independence or her capitulation to coupledom – expresses the doubleness that exists as a critical subtext throughout *Dear Faustina*. This ambivalence in action is communicated more subtly, but more consistently, in form throughout the novel. Textual elisions and inarticulations in the novel's dialogue confuse meaning, and consequently regularly obscure each character's motivation. These instances also give material presence to the ambivalence that characterises the textual meaning and narrative progress. It is significant that nearly all of these instances occur in conversations with Faustina, for they are evidence of the threat posed by her indeterminacy around matters of class and sexuality. While other accounts of *Dear Faustina* have called attention to these breaks and lacunae in the text, all have attributed them exclusively to the unspeakability of women's erotic desire – particularly for one another – in the period.[47] This is undoubtedly the case, but these interdictions are part of a large programme of pauses, elisions and other formal irregularities in the novel. Collectively, these textual features produce significant ambiguity around Faustina's identity.

The most apparent break with formal convention in *Dear Faustina* is its use of the present tense throughout. The use of active voice makes the novel's action feel progressive, even in those circumstances where a thought or an emotion remains inarticulate or unsaid. The effect is that the narrative is highly dramatised – or once again, melodramatic – and because this quality is sustained the narrative is urgent and uncomfortable in its expression. The use of the present tense encourages readers to anticipate or create meaning before any action has occurred and therefore relies on the reader's interpretation, just as it does in the case of textual pauses or elisions.

One of the earliest occasions where such elisions occur is the moment when Faustina invites Althea to share her flat at More Mansions. Faustina falters and stammers while posing the question:

> 'I have been the means of robbing you of one home; may not I' – sinking her voice, which has quite an un-put on tremble in it '– mayn't I offer you another – a very different one in point of luxury – but as you have often told me, the essentials of life are what you care about – you do not mind the trappings?' (45)

While the 'tremble' can be accurately read as Faustina's hesitation in proposing to establish such an intimate domestic relationship with Althea, the language is also couched in hesitation around Faustina's social and financial position. In addition to the 'tremble' there is the repetition and contraction of the expression 'may not I' to 'mayn't I', which indicates the informality of intimacy – but there is also the suggestion that this slip might indicate her want of gentility. In fact, Faustina's penchant for improper language provokes the narrator to define certain idiosyncratic terms of Althea's as 'Batesonian' (237).[48] The other unusual aspect of this extract is the narrator's acknowledgement that Faustina's tremble is 'un-put on' (45). With this claim the narrator aims to affirm Faustina's sincerity, yet the comment must also call her sincerity into question. The reader is therefore unable to read these intimations without also reading their opposite.

At the novel's conclusion Althea is given the satisfaction of believing Faustina to be duplicitous and dishonest, interested more in her own career than the condition of the people whom she purports to help. In looking more closely at how the novel's formal qualities point to the ambiguity of Faustina's past, however, it becomes clear that her ambition and self-regard are motivated by her own relative poverty. While Faustina is thought false by other characters and presumed to exploit upper-class women for their financial support or social power, she does, as outlined earlier, demonstrate a 'commitment to the working classes' (46) by way of her self-interest. When Faustina first proposes cohabitation, Althea hesitantly asks if she is to live with Faustina in the 'slums at Notting Hill' (45). Faustina anxiously explains: 'That was merely a phase through which I happened to be passing. I had to live there for a while, because – because – in fact, I was getting up the subject of the Housing of the working classes' (46). Once again Faustina's hesitancy, the repetition of 'because – because' and the interval provided by 'in fact' suggests that something is left unsaid – and in this case it is not fuelled by romantic intimacy but by the question of social position. Faustina might well have been investigating the subject of working-class housing for the purposes of earning a livelihood by way of journalism, but the method by which she expresses this suggests that she might have been compelled to live in such 'slums' for other reasons.

It is not only Faustina who hedges around in explaining her own past and financial circumstances. Drake, on the occasion of first introducing himself to Althea, refrains from elucidating any aspect of Faustina's present or past. He rather awkwardly explains that 'Miss Bateson is the daughter of – of one of [his] family's nearest neighbours' (111) in Devonshire. Yet Althea first feels that he is 'too much of a gentleman to be an intimate friend of Faustina's' (111). Once again, Faustina's identity remains indefinite. The reader can only assume that Drake refrains from stating the situation outright owing to obligations of propriety. The conversation continues in a similarly self-conscious manner when Althea refers to Faustina's family:

> 'They are, I believe, not – not at all worthy of her?'
> 'Has she told you so?'
> 'No–o – oh no, certainly not. She would not condescend to say anything in detraction of them beyond – beyond –'
> He waits, politely expectant, but not helping her to a word, as he might so easily do. She has to set off upon a remodelled sentence:
> 'I gathered it from the fact of her having had to leave home through her faithfulness to her convictions. If the species of persecution to which she was exposed –'
> '*Persecution!*'
> 'Yes, persecution' – firmly.
> He looks upon the floor, and once again she has reason to suspect that he is struggling with a laugh. (111–12)

This cryptic exchange is one of several that are marked by hesitancy and that reveal more by omission than they do by inclusion. For instance, the only information the reader is given is thrown into question by Drake's exclamation and his inability to stifle his laughter. The scene is also peculiar in that it makes use of realism in dialogue in its attempt to represent improvisational and unpolished conversation, but by so doing the conversation approaches the highly dramatised effects of melodrama. The scene, without providing the reader with any further information about Faustina's family, casts aspersions on her character by way of elision and omission.

At this stage, Althea is still of the opinion that Faustina's social position is one of elective and 'honourable poverty' (157). Her opinion shifts after she finds Faustina unwilling to abandon work for a newspaper of 'objectionable principles' (157) on account of desperately needing the money, but equally when her jealousy is incited by Faustina's increasingly close relationship with Cressida Delafield. After the young woman's mother appeals to Althea for help in saving her daughter from taking up rescue work, it is Drake to whom Althea turns for help. Only at this stage is the reader given a clearer understanding of the complexity and seriousness of Faustina's economic position. And although it is one that should at least explain, if not excuse, her ambitious and sometimes ruthless behaviour, she is unfairly and uniformly maligned by other characters for the duration of the novel.

Drake visits Faustina at More Mansions with 'one brief request – one demand to make' (350), which is that she discontinue her relationship with Cressida. Although he first reminds her of the consequences of interfering with a family of such powerful social standing, he soon threatens her with terminating their own acquaintance. Faustina realises that Drake is referring not only to his friendship, but 'the help – the pecuniary help which [he has] given [her] all these years' (355). She continues:

'[It was] given by you and accepted by me without humiliation because we were both in the same boat.'
'We were never in the same boat.'
'We were in the same boat inasmuchas [sic] we had both been turned out of doors for our fidelity to our opinions.'
'Was it for *your opinions* you were turned out of doors?' [emphasis original] (355)

In repeating the phrase 'same boat' instead of naming explicitly the situation or condition to which they refer, the dialogue continues to imbricate concerns about the way that, as Murphy comments, both Faustina's 'character and her social agenda [are] set against the rules of nature'.[49] If the reader has been led to believe that Faustina's romantic interest in Althea was only an exploitative ploy in service of her professional ambitions, it is here implied that such ambitions were a necessity for certain forms of dissident desire. This becomes clearer when Drake charges Faustina with sexual impropriety, and suggests that her convictions lead her to 'extravagant and immoral actions' (356). Yet this charge is again thrown into obscurity when he soon after refers to her objectionable 'puff and push and vulgar striving for notoriety', lamenting her lost 'selfless love [. . .] righteous anger [. . .] [and] noble faith' (357). Although Faustina is not given the opportunity for explanation or defence, it is clear that her 'striving for notoriety' was only for the purpose of escaping Drake's financial support and resultant control.

It is easy for the reader to fall into the trap of presuming Faustina to be the narrative villain on account of the ways in which her actions seem to betray a ruthless desire for power. Yet scratching the surface of each character's motivations reveals the interrelatedness of these forms of social authority. Like Faustina, both Althea and Drake act out of self-interest. Althea's fascination with the Canning Town Women's Settlement develops only once she leaves More Mansions after a lover's quarrel, during which she demands that Faustina 'choose between Cressida Delafield and [herself]' (302). Neither is narrative rescuer Drake, upon close inspection, entirely virtuous; his demand that Cressida return to her family is in no small part motivated by his own romantic interest in Althea, and his desire that she might be indebted to him for the favour. Faustina makes this very charge of him when he demands that she compose a letter to Cressida – dictated by him – designed to cut the young woman loose. Faustina calmly proclaims:

> You have interfered in a matter with which you have no smallest concern; you have stooped to be the tool of a girl as contemptible in character as puny in intellect; you have used a lever which no generous mind would have employed; and now, will you please tell me what I am to say? (358–9)

If the novel were to end here at More Mansions, rather than at the Canning Town Women's Settlement two chapters hence, both contemporary and more recent critics might have examined more closely their assumption that only Faustina is 'corrupt and hypocritical'.[50] For this is a pivotal moment in the text and one of the few instances where irony is produced not by omission, repetition or elision, but instead by the fact that – after this fully articulate and candid moment of expression – Faustina asks Drake to 'tell [her] what to say'. A reader might therefore interpret Faustina's immediate departure to America for the purposes of conducting a lecture tour not as enforced exile, but as a relocation that will allow her to speak plainly and on her own account.

Dear Faustina articulates the ways in which new forms of housing were viewed as a threat to economic stability as much as sexual convention, but that this housing could also in turn provide the means by which to manage that threat. The novel's transpositional shifts between domestic situations at More Mansions and the Canning Town Settlement express the ways in which housing that was developed in response to these new economic concerns unearthed new concerns around the complexity of sexuality and desire in the metropolis. Just as the novel's subtext works largely through elision and omission in order to question the actions and assumptions of its characters, *Dear Faustina* suggests that new architectural structures or domestic situations can only obscurely communicate their commitment to or capacity for reform as they operate within a system of economic and intellectual limitations. *Dear Faustina* suggests that examinations of narrative forms and social relationships might prove more instructive when their exclusions and inadequacies are taken into consideration.

Notes

1. Broughton, *Dear Faustina*, p. 46. Further references to this work are given in parentheses in the text.
2. 'Dear Faustina', *Bookman*, June 1897, p. 74. The review comments that Broughton 'makes her satire effective by keeping it within bounds, and keeping a few public-spirited persons and the general philanthropic idea from the lash'.
3. Hagar, 'Slumming with the New Woman', p. 461.
4. Skeet, 'Economics', in *A Concise Etymology of the English Language*, p. 159.
5. Hagar, 'Slumming with the New Woman', p. 462.
6. Meller, 'Gender, Citizenship and the Making of the Modern Environment', p. 14.
7. Ibid. p. 14.
8. Murphy, 'Disdained and Disempowered', p. 57.
9. Koven, *Slumming*, p. 183.
10. Murphy, 'Disdained and Disempowered', p. 62.
11. Ibid. p. 57.
12. Ruskin, *Sesame and Lilies*, pp. 83, 69.
13. At the end of the nineteenth century, Chelsea was a district often associated with independent professional women. See Dennis, 'Gissing and Chelsea', pp. 4–8.
14. Murphy, 'Disdained and Disempowered', p. 69.
15. Inwood, *City of Cities*, pp. 90, 184–5.
16. Hagar offers an interesting account of the names in *Dear Faustina*, and suggests that the names Althea and Faustina come from 'earlier nineteenth-century texts that deal explicitly with lesbian desire' ('Slumming with the New Woman', p. 474, n. 9). She also notes, as does Murphy, that the name evokes Swinburne's demonic woman in his 1862 poem 'Faustine' (ibid. p. 68). What passes unglossed in most studies is the allusion to the titular character of Christopher Marlowe's *Doctor Faustus* (1592). In using such a name Broughton parodies the moral dilemma presented to Faustus in the original text. The subtext of *Dear Faustina* implies that Faustina's impulse for power and knowledge is not motivated by greed and vanity, but by poverty; her 'choice' is decided for her by economic necessity.
17. Herring, *Queering the Underworld*, p. 32.
18. Butler, *Undoing Gender*, p. 29. See also Butler, 'Conclusion: From Parody to Politics', in *Gender Trouble*, pp. 194–204.
19. Butler, *Undoing Gender*, p. 213.

20. Murphy, 'Disdained and Disempowered', p. 71.
21. Bradley, 'Poverty and Philanthropy in East London 1918–1950', unpublished thesis, p. 21.
22. For an analysis of the ways in which women's emotional and sexual relationships have been interpreted as an indication of immaturity, see Marcus, *Between Women*, pp. 1–21.
23. Bradley, 'Poverty and Philanthropy in East London 1918–1950', unpublished thesis, p. 21.
24. Collings, 'The Settlements of London', *Leisure Hour*, July 1895, p. 600.
25. Pearson, *The Architectural and Social History of Cooperative Living*, pp. 3–9, 15.
26. Barnett, 'The Beginning of Toynbee Hall', *The Nineteenth Century*, February 1903, p. 309.
27. 'Where the Unmarried Live', *Woman's Herald*, 20 April 1893, p. 131; V.C.H, 'Life at a Women's University Settlement', *Temple Bar*, April 1902, p. 454.
28. Cited in Hagar, 'Slumming with the New Woman', p. 461.
29. Herring, *Queering the Underworld*, p. 32.
30. Cited in Zahniser and Fry, *Alice Paul*, p. 48.
31. 'Women's Settlements in London', *The Speaker*, 10 February 1894, p. 164.
32. Zahniser and Fry, *Alice Paul*, pp. 48–9.
33. Ibid.
34. Collings, 'The Settlements of London', p. 601.
35. 'Women's Settlements in London', p. 164. Collings explains that 'Oxford House is distinctly a centre for Christian teaching, and most other settlements avow religious aims. Toynbee Hall makes general culture its special mission and uses art, for example, as a means to refine and purify.' See Collings, 'The Settlements of London', p. 600.
36. Collings, 'The Settlements of London', pp. 602–3.
37. Ibid.
38. Maltz, *British Aestheticism and the Urban Working Classes*, p. 1.
39. Weiner, *Architecture and Social Reform in Late-Victorian Britain*, p. 168.
40. Barnett, *Practicable Socialism*, p. viii.
41. Ibid. p. x.
42. Another larger residential hall, Fairbairn Hall, was completed in 1900. 'West Ham Philanthropic Institutions', British History Online, <www.british-history.ac.uk/report.aspx?compid=42763> (last accessed 4 August 2018).
43. Beauman, *Women and the Settlement Movement*, pp. xxv, xxii.
44. Collings, 'The Settlements of London', p. 605.
45. Ibid.
46. Scotland, *Squires in the Slums*, pp. 197–210. See also Maltz, *British Aestheticism and the Urban Working Classes*, pp. 67–97. For the ways

in which these power structures are connected to sexual identities, see Koven, 'The "New Man" in the Slums: Religion, Masculinity, and the Men's Settlement House Movement', in *Slumming*, pp. 228–81.
47. Murphy, 'Disdained and Disempowered', p. 69. See also Hagar, 'Slumming with the New Woman', p. 467.
48. The term is used when Althea begins to use colloquial language: 'The phrase is Batesonian. A year ago Althea would never have thought of alluding to a footman as a "lackey"' (237).
49. Murphy, 'Disdained and Disempowered', p. 60.
50. Hagar, 'Slumming with the New Woman', p. 462.

Chapter 9

'Twenty girls in my attic': Spatial and Spiritual Conversion in L. T. Meade's *A Princess of the Gutter*

One year before Arthur Morrison's *A Child of the Jago* (1896) made infamous the East End slum neighbourhood known as the Old Nichol, the district received treatment in a novel written by an author who was a less likely candidate for representations of vice, violence and abject poverty: the popular writer of girls' stories, L. T. Meade. In *A Princess of the Gutter* (1895), Meade engages with the generic conventions of the romance novel in its narrative trajectory, but draws on modes of realism in both its discourse and subject. The novel traces the personal transformation of Joan Prinsep, a Girton graduate who is left a fortune upon her uncle's death, but who is distressed when she discovers that its source is the tenure of a series of slum properties concentrated in Shoreditch. Following the romance convention of the rescue plot, Joan is inspired to settle in the East End with the ambition of helping to ameliorate the lives and living conditions of the local population. In this sense, the novel is organised around her personal transformation but also the material transformation of the people with whom she lives: Joan's benefaction to the district is a block of model dwellings, the 'Joan Mansions', which replaces the former slum properties.[1]

The novel's subject is a familiar one and, as Lynne Hapgood notes, is based on the slum fiction of the early 1880s such as Walter Besant's *All Sorts and Conditions of Men* (1882) and George Gissing's *Workers in the Dawn* (1880).[2] Like these novels, *A Princess of the Gutter* is textured by its engagement with the conditions of urban poverty and is preoccupied by contemporaneous efforts for social justice. The novel's integration of romance and realism is not merely aesthetic; it is also political. *A Princess of the Gutter* makes use of the generic conventions of romance and realism in order to engage in contemporary debates about the settlement movement and the degree to which religious philosophy was necessary in order for this method of social action to be effective. More specifically, Meade's use of realism articulates an argument for the importance of material concerns in settlement work. These tropes of realism are, however, organised around the central structure of the novel's romance narrative, which conveys an equally weighted argument for the significance of metaphysical transcendence in effecting social change. The romance narrative of *A Princess of the Gutter* is put into the service of social and political concerns around urban poverty and social improvement schemes.

Although *A Princess of the Gutter* engages with social themes that were established a decade earlier in the pages of slum novels, it was certainly not the case that these subjects were exhausted by the century's end. The cheerless representations of the city's working classes and urban poverty in the novels of Besant and Gissing drew on contemporaneous investigative journalism into the living conditions of the urban poor by individuals such as George Sims and Charles Booth. The pervasiveness of the discourse established by such texts, coupled with the emergence and eventual ascendancy of social realism over the romantic mode in the final decades of the nineteenth century, meant that the grittier aspects of the urban environment and its inhabitants soon proliferated in the popular literary marketplace.[3] The existing scholarship that engages with Meade's *A Princess of the Gutter* focuses on the novel's use of conventions established by late nineteenth-century slum fiction – and certainly the importance of such tropes in this novel cannot be overstated. Yet to examine only the novel's successful execution of realism, or to focus on how, as a story for young people, its emphasis on romance occludes or confounds its project of social concern, is to neglect an important aspect of the novel. In fact Meade's novel shares many similarities in plot and theme with Mary Ward's *Robert Elsmere* (1888), a novel treated by scholars with more seriousness of purpose. *Robert Elsmere* follows the religious crisis of a young clergyman who denounces his orders but regains his spiritual commitment in his effort to unite the 'perpetual divorce between thought and action' by establishing the Elgood Street Settlement in London's East End.[4] Ward's novel, which was famously one of the century's best-selling, and certainly the decade's most popular, initiated important cultural debate about the relationship between religious thought and action. *A Princess of the Gutter* undertakes a similar project to *Robert Elsmere*, albeit for a different audience, in the sense that it is an intervention in concurrent debates about the relationship between religion and philanthropy. The novel engages with the conventions of both realism and romance to address the perceived conflict between metaphysical and material concerns.

Realism and Romance

Although Meade's work was characterised by contemporaries as sentimental for its adherence to the conventions of romance, Sally Mitchell points out that she wrote not only a phenomenal quantity of books – she published at least 250 novels – but also worked across literary genres.[5] In addition to school stories, tales of aristocratic life, sensation novels and books for the awards market, Meade wrote tales of the supernatural and science fiction, and she also seems to have invented the subgenre of medical mystery.[6] Nor was Meade's engagement with topical issues limited to scientific developments: she wrote a number of novels concerned with women's social and political advancement. Given Meade's engagement with girls' fiction and the attendant moral impetus that was necessarily allotted to such texts, Koven's description of her as a 'pillar of respectability, a wife and mother, [and] a staunch Evangelical' seems plausible.[7] However, Meade self-identified as a 'consummate professional', was fiercely independent, and served on the committee of the Pioneer Club, which debated social and political issues and to which Mona Caird and Sarah Grand also belonged.[8]

Between 1887 and 1893 Meade edited the magazine *Atalanta*, and transformed it into a significant resource for older girls and young women (approximately age 14 to 25) by featuring articles on women's history, schooling, women's colleges, as well as careers advice and serious fiction.[9] Among the contributors to *Atalanta* were Evelyn Sharp, Margaret Oliphant, Amy Levy and Mary Ward, who in 1888 provided an article on Elizabeth Barrett Browning to the educational feature 'Scholarship and Reading'.[10] It is likely that Meade and Ward were in communication the year that *Robert Elsmere* was published, yet the most interesting connection between these texts is not necessarily a question of influence. As William Peterson observes, the philosophical and religious questions with which Ward engages in *Robert Elsmere* had been common currency among the intellectual elite for at least a decade, and for this reason many of Ward's contemporaries derided her work as somewhat prosaic.[11] Yet the novel interpreted these debates for consideration in a new genre and in so doing cultivated a new audience for what some saw as an age-old debate. In *A Princess of the Gutter*, Meade brings these debates to a young adult audience, but does not dilute or flatten their intellectual complexity for the juvenile readership. Meade asks whether social action is dependent upon submission to religious orthodoxy and offers a response, if not an answer, in her imbrication of the conventions of realism and romance.

Jasper Court and Joan's Commitment

The protagonist of *A Princess of the Gutter*, Joan Prinsep, is the only dissident member of her upper-middle-class and conventionally religious family. Yet her family's religious principles are insincere and superficial, and scarcely disguise their materialism. Joan inherits a vast sum of money – in addition to an annual income of £3,000, she also receives a property portfolio with a realisable capital of £100,000 – with an informal stipulation that serves as the crux of the narrative. Joan discovers that the greater proportion of this money has been generated through the extortion of slum properties, located mostly in the East End but including one in Holborn, which her uncle has left to her with the request that she 'rectify [his] mistakes' (20). Joan is not legally bound to correct her uncle's unethical behaviour, but she nevertheless promises to honour his request. This is important, as Joan's conscious sacrifice plays an important role in the novel's attempt to unite moral thought and action.

After Joan's visit to Jasper Court, one of the properties she inherits from her uncle, the deplorable conditions of life in the building inspire her to devote all of her energies to improving housing for the working classes, beginning with her own properties. Meade draws on the language and imagery of slum fiction and also, as Koven acknowledges, non-fictional narratives written by reformers such as Beatrice Potter (later Webb), but combines this discourse with the romantic motivation of her moral sacrifice. While accompanying the rent collector of Jasper Court on one occasion, Joan describes the slum properties: '[N]ot a room in that wretched court was fit for habitation. The broken windows were stopped up with rags, the floors were grimy with dirt, and vermin swarmed all over the horrible place' (73). Although Meade makes use of the language of realism, which colours both slum fiction and the non-fiction accounts to which Koven refers, Meade avoids the morbid fixation on insanitary conditions and the sensationalism that it could often produce. Absent, for instance, are George Gissing's descriptions of the 'weltering mass of human weariness, of bestiality, of unmerited dolour, of hopeless hope, of crushed surrender' found in these slum districts.[12] Even when an old woman expires on a dirty pile of rags – all the while being hounded for rent by the collector – Meade substitutes sensationalism for sentimentalism: Joan, who the old woman believes must have been sent 'straight from heaven' (71), offers comfort and ensures that after her death she is 'treated with respect' (72).

As Koven explains, Meade criticised contemporaneous 'social realist novels', which in the process of reading 'could become a form of slumming, one every bit as capable of infecting the reader in the privacy of her own home as a descent into the actual filth of a slum tenement'.[13] However, it is important to recognise that Meade *uses* the conventions of 'social realist' novels, at the same time as she might denounce other more prurient aspects of these works as immoral. It may be more accurate to suggest that in this novel Meade uses social realist conventions to reposition the slum novel, which she does for the purpose of critiquing sensationalism and reinvigorating the subject with renewed moral concern. This visit to the slum district of Jasper Court not only relates the abject living conditions of the urban poor, descriptions of which even young readers would have been familiar with by the end of the century; it also justifies Joan's reform mission. The scene dramatises the complexity of religious belief and commitment in a slum district. When Joan emerges from one of the buildings in the court she is stopped by the inhabitants, who demand that she improve the buildings. One resident, 'Mad Bess', pipes up:

> I tell yer there ain't no GOD in the matter. It is hell this is. Don't talk to me of any o' your 'ells in the future. We're in hell 'ere, and so I sed to Salvation Army Captain George last Sunday. Why, we're in it, I sez. Don't you talk of no other hell. (74)

'Mad Bess', who like King Lear (or perhaps more directly, the character of 'Mad Jack' in Gissing's 1889 novel *The Nether World*) sees in madness what many others cannot see in sanity, offers a lucid argument about materialism: what effect could 'any [description of metaphysical] 'ells in the future' have on individuals who were materially already there?

This first visit to Jasper Court encourages Joan to involve herself in improving working-class housing, but it is a letter from, and subsequent interview with, Father Ranald Moore of All Souls Vicarage in Shoreditch that convinces Joan that the best course of action is for her to leave Bloomsbury and move to Shoreditch. The representation of settlements in this text differs from the university settlements referred to in Chapter 8, chiefly because they are not university-affiliated and are on a much smaller scale; but still the 'men's club' that is run by Father Moore and the corresponding 'women's club' that Joan establishes are similar in purpose and method. The diversity of settlement work represented in the text is important, for one question the novel asks is to what extent social work must be guided by religious doctrine in order to be effective. Joan's women's club treads an important middle ground between the religiously based men's club established by Father Moore and the conventional university settlement, 'Balliol House', and its affiliated women's organisation, 'St. Agnes Settlement', all of which in the novel combine social work with spiritual belief. Although John Wilson Foster suggests that the representation of Balliol House in *A Princess of the Gutter* is associated with a settlement of the same name in Belfast, it seems more likely that the settlement is based either on Oxford House or Toynbee Hall.[14] Both Arnold Toynbee, after whom the latter settlement was named following his untimely death at the age of 30, and T. H. Green taught at Balliol College, and so too was it 'the Oxford college most directly involved in Toynbee activities'.[15] Balliol House was one of two residential halls at Toynbee Hall, the other being Wadham House, both of which were established between 1887 and 1888 (although Balliol House was officially opened in 1891).[16] However, the settlement's location in Bethnal Green suggests that it may also be modelled on Oxford House, which (established in 1884) was one of the earliest settlements and was affiliated with the Church of England.[17]

While the primary objective of Balliol House in *A Princess of the Gutter* is to bring 'the university life of Oxford with its intellectual refinements into the midst of the men and women in the East End' (221), this work is understood in the manner of the New Theology advocated in *Robert Elsmere*: belief cultivated through practice. Although Father Moore's men's club is an important place of congregation for the neighbourhood, it is Balliol House, Joan acknowledges, that was doing 'exhaustive and splendid work in East London' (221). Joan describes the work of the 'brave men' (117) of Balliol House thus:

> From this centre radiated a religious, social, and educational life which was having day by day a really permanent effect amongst the poor of that part of London. Balliol House had been established in Bethnal Green in order that Oxford men might take part in the social and the religious

work of the Church in East London, that they might try to effect the mental culture as well as spiritual teaching, and might themselves offer an example of a simple religious life. (117)

The settlement is represented not just as a spiritual or educational force, but as a spatial phenomenon: a 'centre' from which radiated a diversity of influences. In this central role, and its day-to-day permanence, the settlement is an institution where spiritual work is grounded in materiality. While Father Moore, having lived in the district 'a long time' (87), is portrayed as a figure whose work in the East End has been invaluable, his proselytising and his proposal of mass emigration cannot address the city's poverty. In fact his proposal of strategic emigration for 'the right persons' (87) purports to do precisely the opposite of settlement in its aspiration towards dispersal and displacement.

Both Father Moore and his men's club, and Balliol House and St. Agnes Settlement, influence the development of Joan's women's club and her own convictions with regard to social work. It is Father Moore's personal magnetism, with his 'dark eyes that seemed to glow with a sort of inward fire' and his face 'full of energy' (86), that first persuades Joan to commit herself to settling in the East End. Sarah Wise suggests that in this scene Father Moore is cast in 'Mr Rochester mode', but there is little indication that the characterisation implies romantic attraction rather than personal charisma.[18] During this initial exchange Joan also comments that his 'features were somewhat homely' (86), and despite the narrative's reliance on certain conventions of the romance plot, no romantic relationship between the two characters develops. Father Moore does become a spiritual guide for Joan, one whose capacity for leadership – she identifies him as a 'captain in charge of a forlorn hope' (87) – and socially progressive notion of religion influence her belief and practice. Father Moore's magnetism also has a grounding in historical truth, for as Wise, Koven and Hapgood all point out, he seems to be modelled on the Revd Arthur Osborne Jay, and the neighbourhood near Frank Street in Shoreditch based on his parish in the Old Nichol.[19] A contemporary article identifies the 'well-known parish in Shoreditch', and suggests that 'no one who knows that part of London will have any difficulty in "placing" either Father Moore or the building which comprises his church on an upper floor, his boxing club for men, and his own two rooms up a spiral iron staircase, leading to a large hall devoted to his people'.[20]

The Girls' Club and Joan's Sacrifice

Joan adopts Father Moore's dedication to, and influence among, his parish; she achieves this by first opening her own flat to Martha and Lucy, two young women in the neighbourhood, in much the same way that Father Moore shares his living space with 'his people'. On the recommendation of Father Moore, Joan takes the upper floors of a building in Frank Street, which she describes as 'the reverse of inviting' (103). However, with the help of a local man, Joan has the six layers of wallpaper scraped off, the holes filled to guard against the rather indistinct *'plague of the east end* [italics in original]' (104), the floors washed with turpentine, and the woodwork treated by the mysterious means of 'a certain sanitary process' (105). This regime, together with some basic redecorating, renders the space habitable. It also allows Joan to establish a centre from which to permanently influence the residents of the East End.

After her renovations, Joan finds she has

> eight rooms in all. Two sitting rooms facing the street, and a bedroom a piece for [her]self and [her housekeeper] Mrs. Keys at the back. A large front attic was to be used as a class room [. . .] the other converted to a kitchen, with a stove and all the necessary appliances. The two back attics were furnished very simply as bedrooms. (105)

While the space is smaller than Father Moore's buildings at All Souls Vicarage, and Joan recognises that her work is 'but a drop in the ocean' (115), her tenure of this flat enables her to invite two young women to her rooms where she is able to win their interest and affection. This is crucial, as one turns out to be a character of considerable influence in the neighbourhood, the titular Princess of the Gutter, Martha Mace.[21] Once Martha is clear that Joan is not out to 'do the religious dodge' (121), she and her companion Lucy establish an intimate friendship with Joan. This relationship proves formative in Joan's ambition to organise a women's club, for it is Martha and Lucy who encourage the neighbourhood's other residents to attend its functions.

Although university settlements offered affiliates residence in the settlement buildings, and in so doing established a new method of arranging and inhabiting domestic space, in this novel Joan's living quarters remain separate from the social space of her women's club. Joan's settlement programme also differs from that of Father Moore, who lives in rooms above his boxing club. The novel adheres to convention insofar as it represents Joan's efforts among the working classes as more efficacious on account of her having established her *own* home – and thereby domestic authority – in the East End. In this sense, the novel highlights the symbolic value of settlement in the narrative; it is not only for practical reasons that Joan decides to live in the vicinity in which she works, but the organisation of her own domestic space grants her allegorical and transformative power among the other residents of the district. The transformation of her own space, that is, permits Joan to perform a similar task for the district at large. Joan's practice of settlement reveals a middle ground. Her rooms above the carpenter's shop are, by her family's standards, most unconventional; yet the space adheres to more domestic conventions than does the communal space of the residences at St. Agnes Settlement. Joan is, for instance, the master of her own domain and consolidates this by way of performing the duties of hostess when she invites Martha and Lucy for tea. Rather than jeopardise her authority by transforming her own home into public space – which she risks at one point by having 'twenty girls in [her] attic' (138) – Joan finances the construction of a purpose-built assembly hall in which to run the girls' club (134).

Establishing the meeting space outside her home allows Joan to obviate the difficulty of merging domestic and civic styles of architecture, one of the challenges encountered by architect Elijah Hoole in his proposals for the design of Toynbee Hall. Unlike the later designs by Dunbar Smith and Brewer for the Passmore Edwards Settlement, which reconceptualised the relationship between living space and working space, Hoole's design for Toynbee Hall relied on the collegiate tradition for conceiving of the ways that one building might unite both purposes. The building, which has since been considerably modified, was originally structured around a narrow central courtyard that drew influence from the collegiate quadrangle. The ground floor of the building was dominated by a large meeting hall and dining room, above which were rooms for residential workers on the upper storey. Although the settlement at Toynbee Hall had been motivated by social and political principles that gained new and important currency at the end of the nineteenth century, the building's design did not quite successfully articulate a new architectural language for this new ideological framework. In addition to the collegiate model, Deborah Weiner explains that Hoole's design relies on the architectural vocabulary of an 'Old English' or neo-Tudor style that was 'self-consciously paternalistic', and which 'tallied with the movement's nostalgic view of history'.[22] Although Weiner makes an important point about the ways in which the building's design seemed to be regressive in style, its motivations were not simply retrograde nor recuperative. The people involved in the settlement movement did aspire to generate 'new thoughts and new experiences, with new powers and new conceptions of life's uses' by way of what Henrietta Barnett describes as 'practicable socialism'.[23] What the case of Toynbee Hall makes clear is that the new social purposes for which these buildings were to be used required substantial experimentation with conventional forms. Toynbee Hall's peculiar incongruity between purpose and design gives evidence of the ways that social and domestic practices were beginning to shift in ways that were not always coherent.

While waiting for the completion of her new hall, Joan rents the basement of a shoe warehouse on 'Pink Street' that receives 'the same sort of transformation scene which [Joan's] lodgings had been subjected to' (145). Once again, the narrative draws on the conventions of realism in its representation of material detail – but also emphasises the building's modern design:

> The walls, floor, ceiling, were all thoroughly cleansed; then the ceiling was whitewashed, the walls papered with a stout washing paper, which was varnished, and the floor covered with thick kamptulicon. Venetian blinds were hung at the windows, and further curtains were added to keep out the cold. (145)

These design efforts are more in the direction of sanitation than aesthetics. Joan's emphasis on modern materials such as washing paper (waterproof wallpaper that can endure regular cleaning) and kamptulicon (a composite of rubber and cork that was a predecessor of linoleum) indicates that she is not under stress to reproduce a scaled-up version of a middle-class drawing room in the midst of the East End. Even her choice of venetian blinds, often used in commercial spaces in the late nineteenth and early twentieth centuries to regulate light and air (the most famous example being the Empire State Building in New York City), is an indication of her progressivism.[24] Like the newly invented composite materials used to give shape to the temporary space for the girls' club, Joan's efforts contribute to the development of a new religious practice that is grounded in civic and material concerns. However, her engagement with materiality is not reduced only to practicality. As at Toynbee Hall where members sought to reform by way of 'communal aesthetic revelation', as Diana Maltz notes, Joan sources 'about a dozen [. . .] good, attractive prints and engravings, cheaply framed', for she 'wanted to train [her] girls to like good things from the first' (145).[25] Joan's 'missionary aestheticism', to use Maltz's term, succeeds precisely because her efforts are grounded in practical material concerns. The renovated basement of the shoe factory is both an example of and symbol for this material engagement, in a way that the historicist design of Toynbee Hall could not be.

The girls' club is not only transformative for those who attend and duly pay their membership fee of a penny a week, but also for Joan. At the club's opening Joan recognises that in living and working in the East End it was her ambition to 'indoctrinate [the club members] with something of [Father Moore's] spirit' (149). This 'spirit' becomes Joan's working model, and one that distinguishes her from the members of the St. Agnes Settlement, who are always on hand to help out at the girls' club but who are afforded none of the moral conviction or personal magnetism of Father Moore. The girls' club becomes, quite simply, a physical manifestation of what Joan later defines as the 'universal brotherhood' (163). This term is very close both in name and idea to the 'New Brotherhood' in *Robert Elsmere*, which refers to the physical meeting place of Elsmere's disciples but also to a differently conceived Christianity that focuses on uniting thought and action. Both novels posit the advent of a reinvigorated Christianity where conventional morality is redeemed through a new commitment to social service and, correspondingly, the material effects of this service inspire a return to traditional belief systems. On the opening evening of the girls' club, Joan confesses to the reader: 'At this time in my life I did not consider myself at all religious, but I knew enough to be certain that only religion could civilise such a neighbourhood as I had found myself in' (149). The narrative shift to past voice in this instance – Joan 'did not' consider herself religious 'at [that] time in [her] life' – implies that this is a position that has since been re-evaluated. Once materiality and morality are united by the girls' club, Joan regains her religious conviction. The correlation between the novel's discourse of spatial reformation and the cultural rehabilitation that settlement work sought to achieve has been central to examinations of middle-class social work among the urban poor.[26] While such discourse is operative in *A Princess of the Gutter*, there is a spiritual transformation that occurs concurrently. Joan's spiritual rebirth is represented as a form of apotheosis: in the novel's final chapters, her sacrifice allows her to become a figure of divinity.

The 'Joan Mansions' and Joan's Apotheosis

Joan's material intervention in the East End, that is, the block of model dwellings that she commissions and sees through to completion, allows the narrative to represent her as a progressively disembodied figure whose moral influence will endure after she ceases to live physically in the East End. The specific terms of Joan's personal faith are not made explicit in the novel, and the reader is encouraged to sympathise with her conviction that conventional religious belief was most often not executed in material practice. However, Joan's religious commitment comes into focus over the course of the narrative, as her spiritual belief is reinvigorated through her dedication to social work. At its conclusion, much like *Robert Elsmere*, the implication is that a commitment to a 'universal brotherhood' that grounds metaphysical belief in material practice has the capacity to derail the emergence of religious unbelief and its political and social implications. Joan's conversion is therefore not one that maps the process of doubt to belief, but instead one that can be interpreted – like St Joan of Arc's – as the evolution from heretic to saint, where heretic is used in its standard definition of a believer at odds with conventional practice.

When Joan first meets Father Moore and agrees to settle and work in the East End, she explains:

> Now I must come to another point [. . .] I am not at all in the ordinary sense religious. The religious people I have met in the course of my life have not pleased me. I suppose there is not a man or woman living who would not believe in the real thing; but in the sort of life I live one rubs up so often against the sham, and the sham thing has put me off religion. That being the case, I don't know how I am meant to appeal to my Maker in the matter. (89)

Joan's scepticism is represented in a way that makes her more morally resolute than those people whom she denounces as Christians. Joan's 'honest doubt', to use Tennyson's phrase, is itself an act of piety.[27] While she is not religious in the 'ordinary sense' she avows her belief in 'the real thing', any further definition of which the novel purposely leaves ambiguous. Those people whom she has 'rubbed up against' and whom she considers self-serving and hypocritical are characters who the reader is familiar with and, consequently, is willing to indict in the same manner as Joan.

Joan adopts aspects of conventional religious practice as the narrative unfolds. When she confronts the 'burden [she] was to carry' in attempting to improve the properties at Frank Street and Jasper Court, the scale of her task causes her to fall on her knees and 'attempt to pray' – although she confesses to the reader: 'It is a literal fact that I had never really prayed before' (93). It is this scene that serves as the tipping point of Joan's conversion and eventual apotheosis, and thereafter the novel – using both language and image – thrusts her into a position not unlike that of St Joan, who acquired fame and a devoted following after her victories during the Hundred Years War. For instance, Joan's Uncle Bannerman understands sacrifice only in terms of foolishness and vanity, and warns her not to 'make [herself] too much of a martyr' (108). Father Moore, somewhat predictably, imagines that Joan may one day 'wear the martyr's palm' (90) as a mark of spiritual accomplishment.

It is appropriately Joan's disciples, Martha and Lucy, who make explicit this apotheosis by likening her to an 'angel'. This analogy first occurs when they visit Joan not long after she has moved to the East End. When Joan is asked by the two women how she manages to do her hair so neatly, she confesses to the reader that although she 'did not feel inclined to take down [her] hair' she 'believed the sacrifice worthy of the occasion' (131). The image beguiles Martha and Lucy:

> 'Well, ef that ain't a picter,' [Martha] said.
> 'Why, you look jest like o' the hangels in Father Moore's church,' said Lucy; 'you know 'e 'ave painted winders in the church, and one on 'em 'as an angel painted on it, with 'air like yourn – my word, is it dyed, or is it nater'l?' (131)

Joan's decision to let her hair down in the company of these women is an effort to conduct herself modestly in their company, and this behaviour gives them the impression that she is neither 'proud nor 'aughty' (130). In this scene, Joan's physical body, specifically her hair, is given prominence for the purpose of characterising her as pragmatic and down-to-earth; yet this physical act is also a 'sacrifice', language that morally elevates Joan. This is the first of many instances where the affect of Joan's body is represented as morally effective. Joan comes not merely to symbolise, but to embody the social project of her settlement. For while Father Moore is also a character whose work among the urban poor is a guiding principle of his faith, he is also embedded in structures of religious convention that moderate his influence. Even he admits to Joan that were he to be present at the opening of her club, 'all of the members would ma[ke] for the door' (149).

Each additional textual reference that describes Joan as an angel draws a connection between her material efforts among the poor of the East End and her physical presence. Martha confesses to Joan, for instance, 'it's wonderful; it's a sort of pleasure to lie 'ere and look at yer; you're like that angel – wonderful like' (194). Martha then describes how the church angel's eyes 'draw [her] out of [her]self' (229), and on one occasion Joan finds Martha in church 'kneeling under the painted figure of the angel' (231). Joan's presence, like the window itself, allows 'the soft coloured light [to steal] out on this hell on earth' (137). The conversion narrative at this point in the novel is duplicated: as Joan discovers spirituality through social practice, Martha expresses newfound religious belief by way of her commitment to Joan. On one occasion Martha remarks that she would not believe in God were it not that she could 'see Him through the angel' and 'see Him in [Joan] when [she] talk[s] werry kind' (232).

Both Martha and Lucy learn from Joan's sacrifice, and are presented with an opportunity to make their own renunciations. At the novel's climax, Joan is brutally attacked when returning home late at night after an evening at the girls' club and is only saved when a scream from a nearby murder interrupts her assailants. The scream turns out to have come from Lucy's scheming and unfaithful husband, Michael Lee, whom she has murdered in a fit of rage. This uncharacteristic action is Lucy's only display of agency or independence in the novel, and although the text condemns the murder as morally wrong, it is also an act that saves Joan's life. Martha, who recognises that Lucy would not survive prison on account of her constitutional weakness, confesses to the murder, and is convicted and sentenced to death. Yet Lucy's constitution gives way before Martha's execution and – with Joan's help – Martha is exonerated of the crime. It is Joan's role as what Koven refers to as a 'latter-day Elizabeth Fry', and her concerted efforts to have Martha's selflessness and sacrifice socially and legally recognised, that frame her final apotheosis.

The text's emphasis on the affective importance of Joan's physical body in effecting social change produces the novel's erotic charge. Just as the dynamics of interdependent sacrifice between the three women in the novel are complex, so too is the triangle of romantic friendship. In *The Blackest Streets*, Wise reads the form of friendship that exists between Martha and Lucy, which they proclaim is 'as good as bein married in some ways, an' with none o' the troubles' (127), as a historically accurate representation of mateship: an 'intense, one-on-one, non-sexual relationship between one rough gel [*sic*] and another', which Wise explains was a social arrangement not uncommon in the nineteenth-century East End.[28] For Koven, who believes the novel 'surpass[s] the boundaries of romantic friendship', it is a mystery why contemporary reviewers failed to notice what he describes as the 'frankly erotic' relationship between Martha and Joan.[29] While *A Princess of the Gutter* does not necessarily maintain the emotional or physical distance that Koven suggests is so often used to structure homoerotic relationships between women, there is – in addition to the class difference – a significant form of spiritual distance between these two characters. In fact, as the novel brings Joan into contact with women from a lower social class than her own it coincidentally establishes her difference by way of her spiritual force and thus maintains the forms of social hierarchy that might otherwise be under threat. Joan's spiritual awakening, together with her elevation to divine being in the context of the East End, also serves to diminish her corporeality and mitigate the text's eroticism. Although the spiritual distance that exists between Martha and Joan at the novel's conclusion diffuses the explicitness of their intimacy, this does not mean that the multiple registers of this relationship – or indeed the kiss to which Koven refers – were obscured to nineteenth-century audiences.

One factor that supports Joan's spiritual conversion and her transition into figurative immateriality is the architectural legacy she offers to the East End. In addition to planning a purpose-built hall for the girls' club, which is not executed within the space of the narrative, Joan also campaigns to have her own inherited property at Jasper Court destroyed. Aware that the leaseholder would refuse her the right to her own land so long as the value prevented her from buying out their lease, Joan appeals to the newly formed London County Council to have the houses condemned and pulled down. In their place, Joan commissions a block of model dwellings:

> I had very strong views on the subject of these houses. I insisted on having large windows which would let in plenty of light. I could not forget what Mrs. Keys had said about her model rooms on Saffron Hill. The rooms should have light, and should be papered with very light, cheerful paper, and should have excellent supplies of water laid on. My architect friend, Mr. Foster, informed me, with a somewhat indulgent smile, that I should certainly spoil my tenants [. . .] In my block of buildings there were ten new houses. Some were made with a

view to accommodate families – being divided into little flats of from two to three rooms or even four rooms each. The rooms had their kitchen, tiny scullery, bedrooms, and one bright little sitting-room: the sanitary arrangements were perfect; and ventilation was made not only thorough, but also of such a nature that, in spite of themselves, the tenants of the room would have a certain current of fresh air always coming in to ventilate their dwellings. (213–14)

The description of the spatial and sanitary requirements for the new lodgings are in keeping with the requirements for new houses set by the London County Council in 1889 (as is the mildly patronising tone towards the inhabitants, who shall be ventilated 'in spite of themselves'). Joan makes clear that she has gained the knowledge of experience from people such as her housekeeper, but also that her experiences in renovating her own flat and the shoe factory have allowed her insight into the particular local requirements of building in London's East End. This block of model dwellings becomes Joan's material legacy in the district in which she has worked. This is perhaps made most clear in her admission that the inhabitants of the building insist on referring to her project as the 'Joan Mansions'. While Joan is personally disembodied by her promotion to divine status, the existence of the 'Joan Mansions' ensures that she remains physically present in the East End. The unification of thought and action with the objective of a singleness of moral purpose – doing good work in a poor community – is one response that this novel offers to questions of religious doubt.

Joan's transformation into a saintly figure sets her apart from those among whom she lives, but it does not rely on her extraction altogether. Instead, it grants her a form of social and moral protection that allows her to live permanently in an unconventional household where only 'some were [flats] made to accommodate families' (214). Like *Robert Elsmere*, this novel pivots on experimentation with new forms and new practices – and the processes by which these might both be introduced to conventional society. Like Ward, Meade is careful to posit these new forms – whether they involve a new manifestation of religion or a new definition of social relationships – as part of a controlled cycle of political engagement. In this sense, *A Princess of the Gutter* seeks to curtail potentially revolutionary ideas by forestalling the very problems that might lead to major reform. Yet this is a novel that engages meaningfully with questions of religious belief and social commitment, and in so doing suggests alternative models for the family, household and community.

Notes

1. Meade, *A Princess of the Gutter*, p. 221. Further references to this work are given in parentheses in the text.
2. Hapgood, 'Circe Among Cities', unpublished thesis, p. 224.
3. For an examination of the ways in which realism and romanticism were contending for aesthetic hegemony during the period, see Leighton, 'The Trilby Phenomenon and Late Victorian Culture', unpublished thesis, pp. 15–44.
4. Ward, *Robert Elsmere*, p. 415.
5. Mitchell, *The New Girl*, p. 11.
6. Mitchell suggests that Meade's 'Stories from the Diary of a Doctor', which ran in the *Strand* between 1893 and 1897, hinged on a plot that was driven by new scientific discoveries or 'bizarre medical information'. Early stories were collected and published in *Stories from the Diary of a Doctor* (1894). See Mitchell, *The New Girl*, p. 11.
7. Koven, *Slumming*, p. 205.
8. Mitchell, 'Meade, Elizabeth Thomasina (1844–1914)', *ODNB*.
9. Ibid.
10. Brake and Demoor (eds), *Dictionary of Nineteenth-Century Journalism in Great Britain and Ireland*, p. 26. See also Wilkes, *Women Reviewing Women in Nineteenth-Century Britain*, p. 143.
11. Peterson, *Victorian Heretic*, p. 160.
12. Gissing, *The Nether World*, p. 274.
13. Koven, *Slumming*, p. 216.
14. Wilson, *Irish Novels 1890–1940*, p. 80.
15. Briggs and Macartney (eds), *Toynbee Hall*, p. 30. Koven notes that it was under the influence of Benjamin Jowett that 'the best and brightest' students were sent to Toynbee Hall. See Koven, *Slumming*, p. 254.
16. Briggs and Macartney (eds), *Toynbee Hall*, p. 30.
17. Scotland, *Squires in the Slums*, p. 17. In Meade's novel, Balliol House is characterised as a religious institution but is not explicitly given a particular Christian denomination.
18. Wise, *The Blackest Streets*, p. 223.
19. Ibid. pp. 221–5; Koven, *Slumming*, p. 217; Hapgood, 'Circe Among Cities', unpublished thesis, pp. 224–5.
20. Yonge, 'The English Clergy in Fiction', *The Gentleman's Magazine*, July 1897, p. 42.
21. Meade notes in the novel's preface that 'Martha Mace, "the Princess", is sketched from a living original'.
22. Weiner, *Architecture and Social Reform in Late-Victorian Britain*, p. 168.
23. Barnett, *Practicable Socialism*, p. 56.
24. Tauranac, *The Empire State Building*, p. 314.
25. Maltz, *British Aestheticism and the Urban Working Classes*, p. 1.

26. Koven comments on the relationship between the 'sanitary' and the 'social' throughout *Slumming*; chapter 1, 'Workhouse Nights', pp. 25–87, is especially useful in this regard. See also Nord, '"Vitiated Air": The Polluted City and Female Sexuality in *Bleak House* and *Dombey and Son*', in *Walking the Victorian Streets*, pp. 81–114; Nead, *Victorian Babylon*, pp. 150–60; and Douglas, *Purity and Danger*.
27. Tennyson, *In Memoriam*, p. 143.
28. Wise, *The Blackest Streets*, pp. 224–5.
29. Koven, *Slumming*, pp. 219–20.

Part IV

Homes for a New Era: London Housing Past and Present

Chapter 10

'To make a garden of the town': The Nineteenth-Century Legacy of the Hampstead Garden Suburb

One year before the outbreak of the First World War, Mary Gabrielle Collins penned a poetic tribute to her home: the Hampstead Garden Suburb. Situated at London's north-western limit, Hampstead Garden Suburb had been conceived by Henrietta Barnett, who had founded the Hampstead Garden Suburb Trust in 1906 after negotiating the purchase of 243 acres of land from Eton College.[1] Before this, Henrietta and her husband, the Revd (later Canon) Samuel Barnett, had made important and influential contributions to the settlement movement, which involved establishing residential buildings in impoverished districts that would, according to Samuel Barnett, 'enable the rich and poor to understand each other'.[2] For this purpose, the Barnetts founded Toynbee Hall in 1884, which was the earliest university-affiliated settlement, and certainly among the most influential. Toynbee Hall, named as a memorial to the reformer and historian Arthur Toynbee, was significant for its programme of social work directed largely by students from Balliol College, Oxford, but also because its prominence stimulated the development of a range of settlements throughout London. The Barnetts had lived at Toynbee Hall after its establishment, but towards the end of the century they moved to a property in Hampstead and became increasingly interested in the garden cities movement as laid out by Ebenezer Howard in *To-Morrow: A Peaceful Path to Real Reform* (1898) (republished under its more popular title, *Garden Cities of To-Morrow* in 1902). Howard's vision was a plan that combined the convenience and financial opportunity of the city with the peaceful and salutary nature of the country, an organised system of urban infrastructure but with an organic design that responded to rather than dominated the natural world. While the concise but comprehensive plan for urban reform set out in *To-Morrow* would prove one of the most influential for suburban development in Britain and North America, its central idea was not eccentric but rather a response to decades of writing and public debate about the improvements needed in urban spaces.

In *Practicable Socialism* (1888), Henrietta Barnett explained that her work in the East End had made apparent how greatly districts would benefit from town planning, but at that time comprehensive plans of how cities or city districts could be improved 'elicited only little interest, local or otherwise'.[3] Yet Barnett, it seems, at this early date was thinking through not only how domestic space might be redesigned in view of social problems, but how such matters might be better solved collectively through town planning. In her essay 'Of Town Planning', originally published in *Cornhill Magazine*, Barnett emphasises the importance of creating socially integrated neighbourhoods. Remembering her 'youthful indignation at the placid acceptance of stinking courts and alleys as the normal homes for the poor', Barnett claims that the philanthropic projects wrought in London's East End must be extended to the design of towns more broadly:

> No one can view with satisfaction any town [. . .] where the poor, the strenuous, and the untutored live as far as possible removed from the rich, the leisured, the cultivated. The divorce is injurious to both. Too commonly it is supposed that the poor only suffer from this separation, but those who have the privilege of friendship among the working people know that the wealthy lose more by not making their acquaintance than can be possibly computed.[4]

For this reason, Barnett's plan for Hampstead Garden Suburb was one that she believed must 'house all classes in attractive surroundings' – or as she later corrected herself: 'it would be better to say [house] different standards of income'.[5] The correction, it seems, was not made only out of delicacy: Barnett believed that the collective plan for the suburb would improve living standards for its inhabitants, but that the space itself would effect a more equitable community where a difference of income was not necessarily a difference in status.

Although the garden cities movement was conceived, as one planning report phrased it, as 'a protest against the disgraceful housing and living conditions which prevailed among the working-class inhabitants of congested industrial centres', its impulse was not at variance with nineteenth-century architectural trends. With respect to Barnett's own experience moving from social work in London's

East End to focus on town planning at its outer limits, for instance, it is clear that ideas for comprehensive town planning that included new models of domestic space were responding to specific problems of the nineteenth-century city such as overcrowding, unregulated development and slum landlordism. Yet Barnett's experience in the planning and operation of Toynbee Hall also indicates that the nineteenth century had in place its own design-led responses to these social problems, and as such, the garden cities movement is not a reversal of the period's architectural trends but rather a unification of individual schemes that had been implemented individually in the latter decades of the nineteenth century. The plan for Hampstead Garden Suburb included housing and community resources for segments of the population treated in the previous chapters of this book: dwellings for artisans and labourers, gender-segregated residences for women, collegiate-style apartment buildings with communal facilities, among a range of other community resources. The literary and architectural legacy of nineteenth-century innovation is legible in both the new forms of housing assembled by the plan for Hampstead Garden Suburb, as well as literature that responds to it, such as Mary Gabrielle Collins's collection of poems, *Garden Suburb Verses* (1913).

Building the Hampstead Garden Suburb

The masterplan of Hampstead Garden Suburb was laid out in 1906 by Raymond Unwin, who with Richard Barry Parker had developed the plan for Letchworth Garden City in 1903–04. Hampstead Garden Suburb, like Letchworth, was organised around a central square with a series of radial streets. The area around the central square included an established church (named St Jude's on the Hill after Samuel Barnett's parish in East London), a Free church, a Quaker Meeting House, a girls' grammar school (which today is the Henrietta Barnett School, a selective gender-segregated grammar school), and 'the Institute', which held a variety of lectures, classes and concerts and which was to Barnett's mind the centre of the community. Facilities further from the central square, but included in the plan, were two primary schools, tennis courts, a bowling green, a croquet lawn, a gymnasium, a smoking room, a reading room with periodicals and newspapers and a Carnegie Library.[6] While Unwin was the architect of the suburb's masterplan, he worked closely with Barnett, whose experiences working in London's East End shaped her ambitions for the suburb. In many instances, Barnett's specifications were decisive. For instance, the renowned Arts and Crafts architect Edward Lutyens had designed many of the suburb's public buildings, but was dismissed by Barnett in 1909 because she believed his designs to be extravagant and pretentious.[7]

Hampstead Garden Suburb would require a variety of housing types for the diverse group of residents Barnett wished to attract, and it was important that these buildings should avoid aesthetic uniformity. A range of architects were therefore engaged to produce a sequence of different housing types, including Courtenay M. Crickmer and J. Geoffrey Lucas, who had worked with Unwin at Letchworth, as well as MacKay Hugh Baillie Scott, C. Harrison Townsend and Barry Parker (who worked in partnership with Unwin).[8] The density of residential buildings was about half that of an urban neighbourhood, roughly eight detached houses per acre across three hundred acres, and the result was a plan that the architect Witold Rybczynski describes as one of 'great sophistication and subtlety'.[9] Despite the aesthetic variegation of its buildings, the suburb's design is stylistically coherent partly as a result of the creation of the Garden Suburb Development Company, an organisation that aimed to coordinate the townscape and ensure sufficient standards of construction.[10]

When construction began in 1907, the first sod was turned in the seventy-acre 'Artisans' Quarter', and development beyond this initial area soon produced a variety of detached homes ranging from modest cottages to rambling villas. In 'Of Town Planning', Barnett specified that the rent for such homes ranged from 'tenements of 3s. 6d. a week to houses standing in their own gardens of rentals of £250 a year, united by cottages, villas, and houses priced at every other figure within that gamut'.[11] The inhabitants of the suburb were able to purchase property assisted by what Barnett refers to as the 'welcoming system and elastic doors of the co-partners'.[12] The co-partnership scheme was a form of shareholder financing in which individuals would invest money in companies such as Hampstead Tenants Ltd, from which they would receive a dividend of 4 or 5 per cent, which would support the growth and development of the suburb. The 'tenant investors' would also be responsible for a 'modest rent'. Hampstead Garden Suburb's co-partnership brochure, 'Co-partnership in Housing', states that by 1911 three tenants' societies had emerged, and yet even so these companies struggled to 'keep pace' with demand.[13] The co-partnership scheme was not unlike earlier forms of shareholder financing, such as those that characterised the model of philanthropic capitalism favoured by the nineteenth-century model dwellings movement, with the important exception that the dividends were received by those who were themselves residents in the suburb.

Home, Landscape and Community

While Barnett desired to include at Hampstead Garden Suburb housing for all standards of income, she also saw that it was necessary to include residential buildings for groups and individuals whom she believed required differentiated domestic arrangements or services. In addition to single-family dwellings of various sizes and styles, Hampstead Garden Suburb offered innovative domestic designs intended for pensioners and single women, as well as serviced flats that catered predominantly to bachelors. One of the most significant buildings in the suburb was the Orchard, which was completed in 1909 and known originally as the 'Haven of Rest', and which provided affordable housing – at either 3s. 6d. or 4s. 6d. per week – for beneficiaries of the 1909 Old Age Pension Act.[14] Hampstead Tenants Ltd, which conceived of the scheme, commented:

> Many persons with scant means in London have to pay exorbitant rent for a single room of unwholesome size and outlook. If age has claimed them, restriction and solitude harass the evening of life. Age deprived of near kin and with insufficient money for the minimum comfort is a social dislocation that has until lately been disregarded by the nation.[15]

The 'social dislocation' – a phrase that effectively conveys the spatial effects of age discrimination – of older people is one problem that Hampstead Tenants Ltd aimed to address in the construction of the building that would become the Orchard. Designed by Barry Parker and Raymond Unwin, the purpose-built accommodation included 57 one-room flats designed to maximise living space in innovative ways: a bed-recess offered some separation of activity but did not enclose the living space, and each flat also included a scullery and an entranceway. Communal facilities included an oven, baths, laundry and drying room, 'with every convenience for washing'. The simple but tasteful two-storey brick building was organised around a quadrangle that provided 'quiet, sunny corners, and cheerfulness', as well as a space for recreation and social interaction. This design offered to its elderly residents domestic privacy with access to communal spaces that would help to prevent isolation. As well as the immediate space around the building, which was bordered with flower beds, residents had access to the 'Institute and Club, and the use of the Club Reading Room'.[16]

In planning Hampstead Garden Suburb, Unwin was unconventional in his approach to integrating buildings with the landscape. Rather than impose individual structures on to a plot of land, David Davidson explains, Unwin interpreted the existing landscape as positive space and 'carefully layer[ed] his new work onto this'.[17] Cottages were treated as features in allotment sites, and gardens and roads were designed to open up green spaces and squares.[18] For Barnett too, the preservation of open and accessible green space was central to her vision of town planning. Whereas the 'gorgeous, riotous generosity of green spaces had been realised by other countries', she explains with some exasperation that 'English people seem to have adopted the idea that it is essential to surround their parks and gardens with visible barriers'.[19] The quadrangle plan at the Orchard dispensed with visible barriers by using open arched entranceways that punctured the centre of the north and south elevations, and allowed for the glorious and generous green vistas through the quadrangle that Barnett so loved.[20]

The advantages of the quadrangle plan in view of both aspect and social purpose were put to use in other residential buildings throughout Hampstead Garden Suburb. Designed by G. L. Sutcliffe and completed in 1912, Meadway Court is another such building that is arranged in a collegiate-style quadrangle. This building's Tudor-revival design is, however, significantly less austere than that of the Orchard, which is to be expected given that this building is comprised of serviced flats that catered chiefly to bachelors and their valets. The building included communal dining facilities, as well as rear garages for those residents who owned cars.

Hampstead Garden Suburb also offered purpose-built accommodation for single women. The first building for this purpose was Waterlow Court (Fig. 10.1), which was designed by renowned Arts and Crafts architect M. H. Baillie Scott for the Improved Industrial Dwellings Company (known also as the Waterlow Company after founder Sir Sidney Waterlow) and was constructed between 1909 and 1911. Intended for professional single women with established incomes, Waterlow Court offered what Emily Gee describes as a 'sophisticated' design of a well-balanced quadrangle with an arcaded cloister.[21] Throughout the building there is the attention to detail that is common to all of Baillie Scott's work, including

Figure 10.1 Waterlow Court, Hampstead Garden Suburb. Designed by M. H. Baillie Scott (1909). Photograph by Eric de Maré, 1960

the lychgate, timbered walkway and use of half-timbering on the building's front elevation that provides visual and material continuity with the nearby Heath Close. The white lime-washed brick on the courtyard's interior modernises this aspect, and contributes to the sense of spaciousness. The arcaded cloister opens into stairwells that, like the college quadrangle system, provide access to individual flats. Interior space was generous: each flat offered between three and five rooms, including a kitchen; however, meals could also be taken in the communal dining room. Waterlow Court combines private and flexible accommodation with a more general design of open public spaces and sweeping landscapes.

Unlike earlier designs for purpose-built women's residences such as Chenies Street Chambers, discussed in previous chapters of this book, the residents at Waterlow Court were not circumscribed as closely by managerial expectations or social conventions. The building's secluded location at Heath Close granted the residents a less conspicuous position than in the city centre, and its communal gardens and dining hall allowed for but did not enforce companionability.[22] While Waterlow Court built upon the architectural precedent established by those buildings constructed by the Ladies' Residential Chambers Company that were similarly intended for independent professional women, its design offered a departure from these buildings in the greater flexibility of the internal space that allowed its residents to evince the independence they so desired. Yet this independence, as Laura Schwartz reveals, was secured by the labour of fourteen servants who lived alongside but separate from the seventy-seven 'lady residents'.[23] Waterlow Court, based as it was on the quadrangle model of the ancient universities, offered residents green vistas and open spaces – but this design also inherited ideas about social status that were, as Schwartz acknowledges, embedded in the very fabric of the building. The Oxbridge women's colleges had been designed with the intention of 'liberating middle-class women from domestic duties', but at the Oxbridge colleges and at Waterlow Court such forms of labour were transferred to servants, whom Schwartz surmises were probably living three or four to one room – and who shared a single bath and toilet.[24]

Waterlow Court, while popular among established professional women, left a perceptible vacancy for women of less comfortable means. In this sense, it may have been Waterlow Court's oversights and omissions, as much as its successes, that were the motivating factors in the design and construction of two additional residential buildings for independent women built nearly twenty years later: Queen's Court (1927) and Emmott Close (1928). Both buildings were designed by the architects Hendry & Schooling for the United Women's Housing Association. Queen's Court and Emmott Close offered accommodation for single women with less substantial funds at their disposal who were employed in careers such as nursing, retail or secretarial work. Unlike the multi-flat residential buildings built during Hampstead Garden Suburb's first phase of development, Queen's Court and Emmott Close were not built in the style of a quadrangle but rather as a series of ranges. At Queen's Court, sixteen two-storey ranges were built, each of which included a series of single bedrooms with access to shared kitchens and lavatories; at Emmott Close, four two- and three-storey irregular terraces were each divided into fifty individual rooms that had access to shared facilities. These innovative designs provided accommodation for a greater number of women than could be housed in a quadrangle-style building, but the low roof-line and punctuated red brick construction allowed both buildings to remain inconspicuous in the context of the suburb. Although these buildings provided accommodation for a greater number of women, many of whom earned fairly meagre wages, the design and management allowed for a level of privacy and enabled a degree of freedom greater than that of comparable buildings in the previous century.

While all of these buildings, whether intended for pensioners or independent working women, offered new innovations in terms of design – specifically in the way that each structure related to the local landscape – each also has its origins in nineteenth-century innovation. Whereas in the case of buildings such as Waterlow Court, Queen's Court and Emmott Close, the influence of gender-segregated women's residences offers a clear lineage of purpose, in other buildings such as the Orchard its legacy is evident in models of charitable shareholder financing that gained popularity alongside the model dwellings movement. Hampstead Garden Suburb is one example of dramatic architectural change, but it is one that directly emerged from nineteenth-century experiments in urban design. The garden city programme united these experiments from a previous century into a comprehensive plan that – drawing on the important social work of settlements such as Toynbee Hall – looked beyond individual buildings to consider the relationship between home, landscape and community.

From 'Dingy Streets' to 'Sunny Ways'

Mary Gabrielle Collins's *Garden Suburb Verses* pays homage to the visions of Barnett and Unwin in its integration of the social pleasures of metropolitan life with its celebration of the natural landscape. Collins's arcadian descriptions of the suburb foreground the salutary nature of its civic arrangements, which are a tonic for both inhabitant and reader. Yet like the suburb's variety of innovative housing schemes, Collins's poems build upon nineteenth-century discourses of urban literature for the very purpose of constructing this utopian vision. According to the *Athenaeum*, the small book included 'verses on gardening and things of local interest to the Hampstead Garden Suburb'.[25] *Garden Suburb Verses* does focus on landscape, to be sure, with poems in celebration of 'Our Hedges', 'The Old Trees' and even the 'Flowers of Almond'. However, the natural world is not only the subject of Collins's writing, but also a method by which to address what she describes as 'the vision' that is designed to give remedy to the 'waste of London streets'.[26] In this sense, *Garden Suburb Verses* relies on the language of nineteenth-century urban literature as much as it does conventional tropes of pastoral imagery for the purpose of representing the suburb.

The poem 'The Vision', which outlines the spatial and moral project of Hampstead Garden Suburb, is given further definition by a poem that details the provocation for this vision, 'As Through the Sunny Ways I Went'. The poem, which is one example of the ways in which Collins's writing draws on both rural and urban discourses, is worth quoting in its entirety:

> A horror haunted me to-day
> As through the sunny Ways I went,
> By gardens brimming o'er with flowers,
> And hedges rich with bloom and scent.
> A horror born of dingy streets,
> Too pale for drab, too wan for grey,
> Whose weary air can hardly bear
> The reek of sordid meals away.
>
> A horror haunted me to-day
> As though the sunny Ways I went,
> And saw the happy children there
> Like treasured gifts from Heaven sent.
> A horror born of torture dens
> In which, by thousands, babes are thrust,
> While Heaven is mute, and man a brute,
> And Mother Earth but mud or dust.[27]

The poem is the most explicit of the collection in establishing the contrast between London's 'dingy streets' and 'weary air', and Hampstead's 'sunny Ways' and 'gardens brimming o'er with flowers'. It is also the darkest poem of the collection, for it suggests that the prophetic 'vision' that brings salvation to the insalubrious urban landscape – figured in the poem 'The Vision' as a 'weary dove' – is matched by an equally present and haunting vision of 'horror'. The dichotomy that the poem constructs between the noxious and fetid urban environment, where nature only exists as 'mud or dust', and the salutary benefits of the natural world is a conventional one, which has its roots in much nineteenth-century poetry concerning urban industrialisation. For instance, Elizabeth Barrett Browning's 'The Cry of the Children' addresses the plight of 'weeping' children who 'drive the wheels of iron / in the factories, round and round', who should instead be 'blowing toward the west' like 'young flowers'.[28]

The clearest source for 'As Through the Sunny Ways I Went' is William Blake's 'London' from *Songs of Experience* (1794), with which it shares its loose iambic tetrameter rhyme scheme (one that Blake manipulates for effect). Both poems begin with the speaker's movement through the landscape. In Blake's 'London', this is 'each charter'd street, / Near where the charter'd Thames does flow', which Collins contrasts with the less constricted or 'charter'd' spaces of Hampstead Garden Suburb's 'sunny Ways'.[29] While Collins's poem opens with the note of sadness that characterises Blake's 'London' – the first line promises to present the reader with 'a horror' – each stanza shifts between an image of the 'dingy streets' of the city's slums and the 'gardens brimming o'er with flowers'. While Blake's poem was written at the end of the eighteenth century, its themes of urban industrialisation and their connection to the city's moral landscape would echo throughout nineteenth-century representations of urban space. Although Collins engages in explicit ways with the form and themes of Blake's work, she also offers the garden city as a restorative solution to such problems.

Garden Suburb Verses emphasises, perhaps unsurprisingly, the recuperative effects of the natural world, but equally it calls attention to the theme of kinship; and often, both themes are united through imagery. Unlike the 'new-born Infant' of Blake's poem who is 'fearful' and foredoomed by the city's 'blights and plagues', at the Garden Suburb the children 'come to know the flowers, / Not as callers once a year, / But as sisters and as brothers'.[30] *Garden Suburb Verses* uses the language of kinship throughout its poems in order to refer not to ancestral families or household groups, but the sense of fellowship present in the suburb that is apparently as natural as its hedges and flowers. It seems too that Collins was well aware of Barnett's ambition to design a 'spiritual and social community' for individuals of all income standards, for the relationship between the classes is rendered in the language of Christian egalitarianism in the poem 'With Angels in Between':

And see, the church itself is built
Of bricks and mortar mean;
And when, before the Father's feet,
Our rich and poor as brothers meet,
With angels in between,

Methinks we see the type once more
By heavenly wisdom fixed,
And, in our homes, should not disdain
To find ourselves arranged again
With classes rather mixed.[31]

The poems in *Garden Suburb Verses* are, therefore, not simply pastoral elegies for a lost arcadia. And crucially, these poems do not wish away the urban and industrial developments of the nineteenth century with the ambition of establishing an edenic paradise. In Collins's verses, Hampstead Garden Suburb is celebrated not only for its natural landscape but also for its progressiveness: its arrangement of 'classes rather mixed', and for having built upon but improved the industrial developments of a previous era to have '*made* a garden of a town'.[32]

While the salutary advantages of Hampstead Garden Suburb were celebrated in verse several years after its construction, the architectural project itself had been shaped by literature and literary culture during the process of its construction. Published in 1909 with contributions from Raymond Unwin and M. H. Baillie Scott, *Town Planning and Modern Architecture at the Hampstead Garden Suburb* introduces each of its eleven chapters and its postscript with literary epigraphs. The literary heritage of Hampstead is given colour by the work of Robert Bridges, Robert Louis Stevenson and Leigh Hunt, who describes it as a 'village, revelling in varieties'.[33] In one instance, Henrik Ibsen's *Master Builder* (1892) contextualises Hampstead Garden Suburb by decreeing that what is needed are 'houses for people to live in', while George Gissing's *The Private Papers of Henry Ryecroft* (1903) describes the necessary 'grace and order of domestic circumstance'. Other quotations from Matthew Arnold, Jonathan Swift, Samuel Pepys, Charles Dickens, Alexander Pope and William Wordsworth – to name but a few – all appear to suggest that their creative efforts were intended to herald the suburb's development.[34] As one might expect given his residence in Hampstead, the sylvan spirit of John Keats whirls through the entire volume like a 'winnowing wind', but such mystical images are balanced by the pragmatic utopianism found in the essays and fiction of H. G. Wells.[35] The reader of the prosaic-sounding pamphlet *Town Planning and Modern Architecture at the Hampstead Garden Suburb* is regularly reminded that there is 'no more intellectually active part of London than Hampstead', whose 'story' also remembers the names of 'Constable, Mrs. Barbauld, Blake and Shelley'.[36]

Town Planning and Modern Architecture offers to its readers as much of the area's literary heritage as it does practical discussion of the suburb's planning and design. Both Unwin and Baillie Scott were aware that their architectural visions for the suburb should not only be represented in a collection that includes literature, but that their project should also be shaped by literature. *Town Planning and Modern Architecture* is also clearly an effort in sales promotion. The amplification of Hampstead's literary and intellectual heritage is a clever manoeuvre designed to appeal to the self-image of potentially interested buyers, who were largely members of the middle-class intellectual elite, despite Barnett's vision of the suburb as an egalitarian community. Still, the interdependence of literature and architecture in this text cannot be reduced to mere conceit. *Town Planning and Modern Architecture* underscores the significance of literature in both conceiving of and planning Hampstead Garden Suburb. The nineteenth-century housing crisis had been shaped by its representation in literature, whether in the form of popular novels, journalism or parliamentary blue books. In *Garden Suburb Verses* and *Town Planning and Modern Architecture*, the language of those nineteenth-century representations gives shape to architectural innovation. While neither text is explicit about the way that the comprehensive plan of Hampstead Garden Suburb had its origins in the architectural innovations of the nineteenth century, each text's engagement with similar discursive forms that represented and responded to matters of domestic space reveals the influence of an earlier period.

Both Victorian and Modern

The nineteenth-century literary and architectural legacy of Hampstead Garden Suburb comes better into focus upon examination of Evelyn Waugh's reflections on the suburb, to which he lived in close proximity in his early life. In his unfinished autobiography *A Little Learning* (1964), Waugh explains that in 1907 his father moved their family further north into Hampstead when urban expansion threatened their pastoral locality. The family settled in the village of North End, Hampstead, which Michael Davis notes was built in the 1880s for the petite bourgeoise.[37] While Waugh did not live within the boundaries of Hampstead Garden Suburb, he spent his youth only a mile away, separated from it only 'by a strip of the Heath'.[38] Waugh's memories of the development of Hampstead Garden Suburb, and the broader urbanisation of Hampstead itself, follow a pattern common to those texts considered earlier in this chapter, in the sense that Waugh gives expression to the suburb's novelty using the language of nineteenth-century literature. For instance, Waugh conveys the remoteness of North End using a framework of popular nineteenth-century novels:

> I was four years old when my father built his house in what was then the village of North End, Hampstead. He was, in fact, the first of its

spoliators. When we settled there the tube reached no further than Hampstead. Golders Green was a grassy cross-road with a sign pointing to London, Finchley and Hendon; such a place as where 'the Woman in White' was encountered [. . .] North End Road was a steep, dusty lane with white posts and rails bordering its footways. North End, the reader may remember, was the place where Bill Sikes spent the first night of his flight after the murder of Nancy.[39]

In this description, Waugh invokes the novels of Wilkie Collins and Charles Dickens to establish North End as a place so remote from modernity that it could be the refuge of madwomen and murderers, character types most commonly known to legends and folk tales. Yet this description also establishes a continuity with the previous century, particularly in its emphasis on North End's literary significance.

That such popular texts appear to characterise Waugh's childhood home is perhaps no surprise, given that his father, Arthur Waugh, was editor of the Nonesuch Dickens and managing director of the publishing house Chapman & Hall.[40] Waugh's descriptions of his father suggest that he was rather preoccupied with resisting the innovation and development – architectural and otherwise – of North End, which he believed to be threatened by 'building enterprises' such as Hampstead Garden Suburb.[41] Although Waugh acknowledges that in the suburb, 'houses [. . .] were better designed' than those that had been built in North End, his father nevertheless 'had some difference' with Henrietta Barnett, the 'presiding genius' of the scheme. Waugh explains that his father 'would sometimes wander about singing a ditty of his own composition which began: "Blast it! Darn it! / Henrietta Elizabeth Barnett"'.[42] Waugh is not precise about the nature of his father's objection; clearly it did not carry deep enough for him to realise that Barnett's middle name was not, in fact, Elizabeth but Octavia Weston. Given Arthur Waugh's enthusiasm for Hampstead's 'historic associations' with 'Keats, Blake and Constable' – and that he had already moved his family on one occasion to escape urban expansion – it is not unlikely that his grievance was related to the alteration in the area wrought by the suburb. These changes were visible in its innovative design, but also in the demographic who were, Waugh comments, 'people of artistic leanings, bearded, knickerbockered, flannel-shirted, and sometimes even sandalled'.[43] Despite his disapproval, Arthur Waugh was soon drawn into the community at Hampstead Garden Suburb, where he enjoyed 'church-going and amateur theatricals'. By his adulthood Evelyn Waugh had come to realise that Barnett was an 'exemplary lady', rather than a 'ludicrous monster'.[44]

While Hampstead Garden Suburb is in Waugh's *A Little Learning* first represented as a threat on account of its innovative design and radical inhabitants, what emerges in his writing is instead a sense of discursive continuity constructed through reference to Romantic poets such as Keats and Blake, Victorian novelists such as Collins and Dickens, and the 'community of unconventional bourgeois of artistic interests' of the suburb. Not unlike Collins's *Garden Suburb Verses*, or the literary references that provide a vision of the new community in *Town Planning and Modern Architecture*, Waugh's descriptions of Hampstead indicate the ways that radical design programmes such as Hampstead Garden Suburb emerged from the discursive developments of earlier periods – just as its buildings had their origins in nineteenth-century architectural innovation. In many ways, Hampstead Garden Suburb is indisputably modern and recognisably utopian, particularly in its comprehensive design, which champions the healthful benefits of dwellings that are thoughtfully integrated into the landscape and attentive to the local community. Yet looking closely at the literature of place, together with specific architectural precedents, and the lived experience of someone such as Barnett, reveals how fully grounded these innovations are in nineteenth-century urbanism, both materially and imaginatively.

Since the emergence of garden cities at the end of the nineteenth century, they have regularly been invoked for the purposes of lampoonery. Most often, this is with the intention of pointing out the failure of these projects to achieve their social vision of more egalitarian societies. Among the most famous are John Betjeman's poems dedicated to Letchworth Garden City, the inhabitants of which he characterises as abstemious bores who lose sight of humanity in their efforts to remodel society in the promotion of health and hygiene. In 'Huxley Hall' (1953), Betjeman summarises his impressions in the final couplet by declaring: 'Not my vegetarian dinner, not my lime-juice minus gin / Quite can drown a faint conviction that we may be born in sin'.[45] The poem borrows from Alfred Tennyson's 'Locksley Hall' (1842) in both theme and metre in order to criticise Letchworth Garden City in a manner that is characteristic of Betjeman's parodic and flamboyantly derisive style.

Garden cities remained a regular subject of ridicule, particularly for writers, throughout the twentieth century. More recently, Will Self has reflected on his childhood in Hampstead Garden Suburb and focused on what he describes as the utter 'unreality' of the project.[46]

For Self, Barnett's utopian project takes on a sinister quality in his description of the 'long avenues which radiate from the chilling non-euphemism "Central Square", [and] the environs of the Suburb [that] are a reification of the social ideas of the builders'.[47] In this description, the suburb's long avenues and environs are as disciplining as the 'charter'd streets' of Blake's 'London', and the utopian ambitions of the suburb become 'chillingly' dystopian. While part of Self's dismissiveness may stem from his awareness that Hampstead Garden Suburb failed to provide housing for the working classes – 'merely "artisans"', as he remarks – his language nevertheless draws rather unimaginatively on the tropes of boredom, dissatisfaction and uniformity that so often characterise writing about the suburbs.[48] These familiar representations ignore the rich and diverse nature of suburban spaces as well as representations that – like Barnett's vision for Hampstead Garden Suburb – regularly challenge hackneyed notions of mediocrity and conformity. The literary and architectural heritage of Hampstead Garden Suburb, of which only a fragment has been considered in this chapter, offers opportunities for engaging with the mutually effective pattern of such influences, and examining how this dynamic complexity can reshape thinking about domestic space.

Notes

1. Slack, *Henrietta's Dream*, pp. 10–11. See also Miller and Gray, *Hampstead Garden Suburb*, pp. 14–16.
2. Barnett, 'The Ways of "Settlements" and "Missions"', p. 984.
3. Barnett, *Practicable Socialism*, p. 262.
4. Ibid.
5. Ibid. pp. 264, 265.
6. Slack, *Henrietta's Dream*, pp. 56–74.
7. Miller and Gray, *Hampstead Garden Suburb*, pp. 80–1.
8. For a complete list of architects involved in the design of the suburb, see Unwin and Baillie Scott, *Town Planning and Modern Architecture at the Hampstead Garden Suburb*, p. 34.
9. Rybczynski, *City Life*, pp. 184–5.
10. Davidson, 'One Hundred Years in the Making', pp. 145–6. Davidson also notes that the formation of this body granted Unwin disproportionate influence that allowed him to personally regulate the design of all buildings in the suburb, whether built for private clients or the market.
11. Barnett, *Practicable Socialism*, p. 267.
12. Ibid.

13. E.B., *Co-partnership in Housing*, p. 17.
14. Miller and Gray, *Hampstead Garden Suburb*, p. 58.
15. E.B., *Co-partnership in Housing*, p. 23.
16. Ibid.
17. Davidson, 'One Hundred Years in the Making', p. 142.
18. Ibid.
19. Barnett, *Practicable Socialism*, pp. 267, 270.
20. Slack, *Henrietta's Dream*, pp. 90–3. The Orchard was demolished and rebuilt between 1970 and 1972 after it had been left to deteriorate.
21. Gee, '"Where Shall She Live?"', p. 103.
22. Watkins, *Henrietta Barnett*, p. 159.
23. Schwartz, *Feminism and the Servant Problem*, p. 199.
24. Ibid. pp. 197, 200–1.
25. 'Books Published this Week', *The Athenaeum*, 10 January 1914, p. 449.
26. Collins, *Garden Suburb Verses*, p. 3.
27. Ibid. p. 21.
28. Barrett Browning, 'The Cry of the Children', pp. 23, 22.
29. Blake, *Songs of Innocence and Experience*, ed. Keynes, plates 46–7.
30. Collins, *Garden Suburb Verses*, p. 12.
31. Ibid. p. 7.
32. Ibid. p. 8. Italics added.
33. Unwin and Baillie Scott, *Town Planning and Modern Architecture at the Hampstead Garden Suburb*, p. 11.
34. Unwin and Baillie Scott, *Town Planning and Modern Architecture at the Hampstead Garden Suburb*, pp. 29, 43.
35. Keats, 'Ode to Autumn', in *Poems by John Keats*, p. 242.
36. Unwin and Baillie Scott, *Town Planning and Modern Architecture at the Hampstead Garden Suburb*, pp. 80, 73.
37. Waugh, *The Diaries of Evelyn Waugh*, p. 3.
38. Waugh, *A Little Learning*, p. 35.
39. Ibid. p. 34.
40. Waugh, *The Diaries of Evelyn Waugh*, pp. 3–4.
41. Waugh, *A Little Learning*, p. 37.
42. Ibid.
43. Ibid. p. 58.
44. Ibid. pp. 37–8.
45. Betjeman, 'Huxley Hall', in *The Best of John Betjeman*, p. 84.
46. Self, *Sore Sites*, p. 99.
47. Self, *Sore Sites*, p. 95.
48. Dines, *The Literature of Suburban Change*, pp. 1–27.

Epilogue

In 'The Great London Property Squeeze', an article written for the *Guardian* in 2017, Anna Minton offers a trenchant examination of the origins and effects of London's present-day housing crisis, from descriptions of 'beds in sheds' and criminal levels of overcrowding in single rooms in districts such as Newham and Brent, to accounts of 'middle-class poverty' in West Norwood where tenants – despite earning well above the national average – are forced to choose between a functional heating system and a satisfactory school catchment area.[1] While subjects such as slum landlordism, overcrowding, as well as the experiences of the 'squeezed middle' are those that characterise much writing on nineteenth-century housing, Minton's use of language equally recalls a previous era. The article opens with the author's description of her meeting with Ian Dick, the head of private housing at Newham council in East London, and follows their sordid tour through the district's illegal forms of habitation, including garden sheds and 'ramshackle outbuildings'.[2] Making their way from back gardens through the piles of abandoned mattresses, they reach 'the back of a large Victorian house, [where they] were met with a smell of leaking sewage, and the once-white walls were now filthy and soot-stained'. Peering through the bars of a 'grim-looking security gate at the back door', Minton glimpses a toddler and his mother and thinks:

> This was no place for a child – or anyone – to live, but it was also obvious that once they were evicted, their fortunes would not necessarily improve. There would be nowhere to go, and even if they qualified for social housing, they would most likely enter the world of substandard temporary accommodation.[3]

Minton's writing recalls one of the most famous pieces of nineteenth-century journalism on housing, Andrew Mearns's *The Bitter Cry of Outcast London* (1883), in several significant ways. Both

Minton and Mearns engage with forms of investigative journalism, specifically an author persona who explores an unfamiliar territory and acts as a conduit for such an experience to the reader. While Minton's article lacks the histrionic style of Mearns's pamphlet, which was designed to incite moral outrage about the forms of depravity that substandard housing might foster, both authors emphasise the sensory experience to underscore the need for improvement. While Minton speaks in measured tones about the 'smell of leaking sewage' and the 'filthy soot-stained' walls, Mearns writes of 'courts reeking with poisonous and malodorous gasses arising from accumulations of sewage and refuse scattered in all directions and often flowing beneath your feet'.[4] Both Minton and Mearns also call attention to the ways that inferior and insanitary environments impact upon the most vulnerable members of the community more profoundly. While Mearns underscores the sexual impropriety of adult men sharing sleeping quarters with women and children, Minton focuses on the plight of the toddler and his mother who – like the swift descent experienced by the eponymous character in Ken Loach's BBC television play *Cathy Come Home* (1966) – can expect no improvement in their circumstances if evicted and little help from the local council. One of Mearns's objectives in writing *The Bitter Cry of Outcast London* was to draw public attention and government interest to the domiciliary concerns of poor communities, and his descriptions end with the pointed but rather vague exhortation that the state 'secure for the poorest the rights of citizenship; the right to live in something better than fever dens'.[5] Minton is more incisive, and more precise: 'we need a new social contract', she explains, '[one] that ensures housing is once again viewed as a right for all, not just an asset for the few'. This will require nothing less than 'profound structural economic change'.[6]

Of all the books, reports and articles published in recent years on London's housing crisis – and there have been many – Minton's article, which is an excerpt from her book *Big Capital* (2017), offers perhaps the most thorough understanding of current problems and proposes the most profound solution. Until recently, debates about the housing crisis have been dominated by discussion of the quantity of homes available in the capital and the country more generally. For instance, in an article written for the *London Review of Books* in 2014, 'Where Will We Live?', James Meek opines:

> There aren't enough homes in Tower Hamlets. There aren't enough homes in London, in the South-East, in Britain. The shortage gets worse.

> Each year, population growth and the shrinking of average household size adds a quarter of a million households to the 26 million we have now. The number of new homes being built is barely above a hundred thousand.[7]

Meek is right, of course: a shortage of resources will necessarily drive up the value of that resource; and when that resource is as basic as housing, social inequity quickly amplifies owing to inequality of access. Yet in an article written for the *Guardian* the political economist Ann Pettifor demonstrates why simply building more homes will not solve the housing crisis: it is not an issue of supply and demand, she explains, but instead the consequence of a 'speculative bubble'.[8] Pettifor points out that '[h]ouse prices won't fall until the tide of cash flowing into the market abates', and one method she proposes in order to achieve this is through a system of taxation.[9] Until that point, there is clear evidence that adding to the housing stock – especially with buildings intended principally as investment opportunities – will only drive up prices on the property market. In this sense, a solution will not be achieved by building more of the 'right kind of homes', one of the solutions Duncan Bowie proposes among the broader list of reforms outlined in *Radical Solutions to the Housing Supply Crisis* (2017).[10] As Minton succinctly points out, the solution is not in building more homes, nor even is it building the right kinds of homes, but rather it is careful consideration of who these homes are built for. This is a crucial question because it has at its centre a concern not with an abstract concept of either space or economics, but with people and communities. While nineteenth-century debates about the housing crisis – and representations of living through it – might not offer clear solutions to solving the twenty-first-century housing crisis, such writing does regularly serve to denaturalise the presumption that housing is a financial asset rather than a human right, and in so doing demands that readers ask different questions than those which satisfy market interest.

The title of Meek's essay, 'Where Will We Live?', is taken from the title of a book by the early twentieth-century reformer Mary Higgs, *Where Shall She Live?* (1910), which exposed women's poverty of access to housing and aimed to provide information for women seeking accommodation in urban centres. Written for the National Association for Women's Lodging Homes, the book offers 'startling revelations of national need' but is equally preoccupied with thinking through solutions to the housing problem that also address social concerns.[11] Higgs explains of the housing crisis:

Here is a real touch. It is not a work that can be done all at once. It needs patient investigation of local need, patient adoption of means to ends, patient experiment. In the solution to this problem we shall come into real touch with many others, the problem of the sweated worker, the unemployed, the ill-used wife – in fact, all women's problems in their acutest phase. We shall get no dilettante knowledge, but real insight into the heart of things.[12]

Here, Higgs offers a method by which society might better understand for whom houses should be built: a process determined by patient investigation, an attentiveness to the relationship between means and ends, and a dedication to rigorous experiment. Combined with Minton's proposed programme of 'profound structural economic change', Higgs indicates in this book important legacies of the nineteenth century's housing crisis: investigation and innovation, both patient and persistent. Understanding the relationship between these two practices is vital now more than ever, if London is to keep pace with ever-changing patterns of life and labour.

Notes

1. Minton, 'The Great London Property Squeeze', *The Guardian*, 25 May 2017.
2. Ibid.
3. Ibid.
4. Mearns, *The Bitter Cry of Outcast London*, p. 7.
5. Ibid. p. 15.
6. Minton, 'The Great London Property Squeeze'.
7. Meek, 'Where Will We Live?', p. 7.
8. Pettifor, 'Why Building More Homes Will Not Solve Britain's Housing Crisis', *The Guardian*, 27 January 2018.
9. Ibid.
10. Bowie, *Radical Solutions to the Housing Supply Crisis*, pp. 93–8.
11. Higgs and Hayward, *Where Shall She Live?*, p. iv. For more on Higgs, see Mullholland, *British Boarding Houses in Interwar Women's Literature*, pp. 10–12.
12. Higgs and Hayward, *Where Shall She Live?*, p. 186.

Bibliography

Unpublished Sources

Archives

Passfield Papers, London School of Economics

Theses

Bradley, Katharine Marie, 'Poverty and Philanthropy in East London 1918–1950: The University Settlements and the Urban Working Classes', unpublished doctoral thesis, Centre for Contemporary British History, Institute of Historical Research, University of London, 2006.

Gee, Emily, '"Where Shall She Live?" The Accommodation of Working Women in the Capital 1875–1925', unpublished thesis for diploma in building conservation, Architectural Association, 2007.

Hapgood, Lynne, 'Circe Among Cities: Images of London and the Language of Social Concern 1880–1900', unpublished doctoral thesis, University of Warwick, 1990.

Leighton, Mary Elizabeth, 'The Trilby Phenomenon and Late Victorian Culture', unpublished doctoral thesis, University of Alberta, 2003.

Morrell, Caroline, 'Housing and the Women's Movement 1860–1914', unpublished doctoral thesis, Oxford Brookes University, 1999.

Presentations

Hewitt, Martin, 'The Poverty of Anti-Historicism', paper given at BAVS Talks 2015, Oxford Research Centre in the Humanities (TORCH), 12 May 2015.

Kroll, David, introduction given at 'Mobilising London's Housing Histories: The Provision of Homes Since 1850', Centre for Metropolitan History, Institute of Historical Research, 27–28 June 2013.

Mutch, Deborah, 'Socialist Paternalism: Fathers, Father-Figures and Guidance in Serialised Fiction, 1885–1895', paper given at conference,

'Father Figures: Gender and Paternity in the Modern Age', Liverpool John Moores University, 2003.

Sparks, Tabitha, 'The Symbolic Economy of Disease in Sensation and Satire: *Lady Audley's Secret* and *Dr. Phillips: A Maida Vale Idyll*', paper given at the Birkbeck Forum for Nineteenth-century Studies, 11 November 2013.

Primary Sources

Arnold, Matthew, *Culture and Anarchy*, ed. J. Dover Wilson (London: Cambridge University Press, 1932).

Arnold, Matthew, *Culture and Anarchy and Other Writings*, ed. Stefan Collini (Cambridge: Cambridge University Press, 1993).

Barnett, Henrietta O., 'The Beginning of Toynbee Hall', *The Nineteenth Century*, February 1903, pp. 306–14.

Barnett, S. A., 'The Ways of "Settlements" and "Missions"', *Nineteenth Century*, 42 (1897), pp. 975–84.

Barnett, Canon S. A. and Mrs S. A. [Henrietta] Barnett, *Practicable Socialism* (London: Longmans, Green, 1915).

Barrett Browning, Elizabeth, 'The Cry of the Children', in *The Broadview Anthology of Victorian Poetry and Poetic Theory*, ed. Thomas J. Collins and Vivienne J. Rundle (Peterborough, ON: Broadview, 2000), pp. 22–4.

'Beehive Houses', *The Leisure Hour*, 22 May 1880, pp. 328–30.

Besant, Walter, *All Sorts and Conditions of Men: An Impossible Story* (London: Chatto & Windus, 1882).

Betjeman, John, *The Best of John Betjeman*, ed. John Guest (Harmondsworth: Penguin, 1978).

Blake, William, *Songs of Innocence and Experience: Shewing the Two Contrary States of the Human Soul* [1789–94], ed. Geoffrey Keynes (Oxford: Oxford University Press, 1977).

'Books Published this Week', *The Athenaeum*, 10 January 1914, p. 449.

'Book Reviews Reviewed', *The Academy*, 5 March 1898, p. 269.

Broderick, W. St John, 'The Homes of the Poor', *Fortnightly Review*, October 1882, pp. 420–31.

Broughton, Rhoda, *Dear Faustina* (London: Richard Bentley and Son, 1897).

Cassan, Paul S., 'London Evictions', *Macmillan's Magazine*, October 1882, pp. 498–504.

'A Chat About Ladies' Flats with the Secretary of the York Street Chambers', *Women's Herald*, 29 June 1893, p. 293.

Child, Harold Harrington, 'Fiction', *Times Literary Supplement*, 5 March 1908, p. 78.
'A City Girl', *Time*, May 1887, p. 638.
Collings, T. C., 'The Settlements of London', *Leisure Hour*, July 1895, pp. 600–6.
Collins, Mary Gabrielle, *Garden Suburb Verses* (London: Co-Partnership Publishers, 1913).
Dalton, Frederick Thomas, 'New Novels', *Times Literary Supplement*, 12 April 1917, p. 176.
Danby, Frank [Julia Frankau], *The Heart of a Child* (London: Macmillan, 1908).
'Dear Faustina', *Bookman*, June 1897, p. 74.
Dickens, Charles, *Bleak House* (London: Chapman & Hall, 1868).
Dickens, Charles, *Little Dorrit* (Boston: Estes and Lauriat, 1880).
Dixon, Ella Hepworth, *The Story of a Modern Woman* (London: Cassell, 1894).
Dolman, Frederick, 'Women Workers for Women', *The Quiver*, 30 January 1895, p. 356.
E.B., *Co-partnership in Housing* (London: Co-Partners Publisher's Ltd, 1911).
'Editorial Notes', *Women's Penny Paper*, 5 April 1894, p. 226.
Engels, Frederick [Friedrich], *The Housing Question* (London: Martin Lawrence, n.d.).
Engels, Friedrich, 'Letter to Margaret Harkness, Beginning of April 1888 (draft)', in *Marx & Engels on Literature and Art*, ed. Lee Baxandall and Stefan Morawski (New York: International General, 1974), pp. 115–17.
'Frank Danby's New Novel', *Saturday Review*, 4 April 1908, p. 442.
'A Frenchwoman in London', *London Society*, May 1888, pp. 489–505.
'Furnished London Residence, Artillery Mansions', *The Times of India*, 14 May 1903, p. 7.
Gaskell, Elizabeth, *Mary Barton* (Leipzig: Bernard Tauchnitz, 1849).
Gaskell, Elizabeth, *Ruth*, 3 vols (London: Chapman & Hall, 1853).
Gissing, George, *The Nether World* (Brighton: Harvester, 1974).
'The Glorified Spinster', *Macmillan's Magazine*, 58 (1888), pp. 371–6.
Greenwell, Dora, 'Our Single Women', *North British Review*, February 1862, pp. 62–87.
Hardy, Thomas, *Tess of the D'Urbervilles* (London: McIlvaine, 1892).
Higgs, Mary, and Edward E. Hayward, *Where Shall She Live?* (London: King and Son, 1910).
'High Class Residential Mansions', *The Times*, 2 September 1897, p. 12.

Hobhouse, Emily, 'Women Workers: How they Live and How They Wish to Live', *Nineteenth Century*, 47.277 (1900), pp. 471–84.

James, Henry, *The Bostonians: A Novel* (London: Macmillan, 1886).

J.L. [Margaret Harkness], 'Labour Leaders II – Henry Hyde Champion', *Pall Mall Gazette*, 7 February 1891), p. 1.

Keats, John, 'Ode to Autumn', in *Poems by John Keats* (London and New York: George Bell and Sons, 1897), pp. 242–3.

Klickmann, Flora, *The Ambitions of Jenny Ingram: A True Story of Modern London Life* (London: Religious Tract Society, 1905).

Law, John [Margaret Harkness], 'The Cardinal as I Knew Him', *The Pall Mall Gazette*, 18 January 1892.

Law, John [Margaret Harkness], *A City Girl: A Realistic Story* (London: Vizetelly, 1887).

Law, John [Margaret Harkness], *George Eastmont, Wanderer* (London: Burns & Oates, 1905).

Law, John [Margaret Harkness], 'A Year of My Life', *The New Review*, 5.29 (1891), pp. 375–84.

Linton, Elizabeth Lynn, *The Rebel of the Family* (London: Chatto and Windus, 1880).

Linton, Elizabeth Lynn, 'Rights and Wrongs of Women', *Household Words*, 1 April 1854, pp. 158–61.

London, Jack, *People of the Abyss* (London: Macmillan, 1903).

Lupton, Donald, *London and the Countrey Carbonadoed* (London, n.p., 1632; republished 1977).

Marlowe, Christopher, *Doctor Faustus* (London: Edward Arnold, 1962).

Meade, L. T., *A Princess of the Gutter* (London: Wells Gardner, 1895).

Mearns, Andrew, *The Bitter Cry of Outcast London: An Enquiry into the Condition of the Abject Poor* (London: James Clarke, 1883).

Meath, Lady Brabazon, Countess of, *The Diaries of Mary Countess of Meath* (London: Hutchinson, 1928).

'A Methodist Country Parson', 'Clubs for Working Girls', *The Wesleyan-Methodist Magazine*, July 1890, pp. 500–7.

Morrison, Arthur, *A Child of the Jago* (London: Methuen, 1897).

'Novel Notes', *Bookman*, November 1896, p. 49.

'Novels of the Week', *The Athenaeum*, 30 April 1887, p. 572.

Orwell, George, *Down and Out in Paris and London* (London: Victor Gollancz, 1933).

'The Passmore Edwards Settlement', *British Architect*, 25 February 1898, pp. 125–6.

Paston, George, *A Modern Amazon: A Novel* (London: Osgood and McIllvaine, 1889).

'Petticoat Square', *British Architect*, 23 November 1883, p. 242.
Ruskin, John, *Sesame and Lilies* (New York: Henry Holt, 1901).
Ruskin, John, *The Seven Lamps of Architecture* (Orpington: George Allen, 1889).
Ruskin, John, *The Stones of Venice*, 3 vols (New York: John Wiley and Son, 1865).
Saintsbury, George, 'New Novels', *Academy*, 1 June 1889, p. 373.
Sergeant, Adeline, *Anthea's Way* (London: Methuen, 1903).
Sergeant, Adeline, *Caspar Brooke's Daughter* (London: Hurst and Blackett, 1891).
Sergeant, Adeline, *Esther Denison* (London: R. Bentley and Son, 1889).
Sharp, Evelyn, *The Making of a Prig* (London: John Lane, 1897).
Sharp, Evelyn, *Unfinished Adventure* (London: John Lane, 1933).
Shaw, George Bernard, *The Complete Plays of Bernard Shaw* (London: Odhams, 1934).
Shaw, George Bernard, *The Irrational Knot* (London: Constable, 1905; republished 1914).
'Short Arrows', *The Quiver*, January 1884, pp. 510–12.
'A Slum-Story Writer', *The Evening News and Post*, 17 April 1890.
Smith, T. Roger, 'Sanitary Houses', *British Architect*, 22.3 (1884), p. 33.
'Soho Home & Club for Working Girls', in *The Story of Old Soho* (London: C. Pettitt, 1893), p. 26.
Stanley, Maude, *Clubs for Working Girls* (London and New York: Macmillan, 1890).
Stead, William T., 'Cooperative Homes for the Unmarried', *Women's Herald*, 13 April 1893, pp. 113–14.
Strachey, Lytton, *Eminent Victorians* (Garden City, NY: Garden City Publishing Co., 1918).
Tennyson, Alfred, *In Memoriam* (London: Edward Moxon, 1851).
'*The Times* Special Correspondent', *The Story of the London County Council* (London: *The Times*, 1907).
Thompson, W., *Housing Up-to-Date* (London: National Housing Reform Council, 1907).
Tooley, Sarah A., 'Domestic Economy and the L.C.C. an Interview with Miss Pycroft', *The Woman's Signal*, 4 February 1895.
Unwin, Raymond, and M. H. Baillie Scott, *Town Planning and Modern Architecture at the Hampstead Garden Suburb* (London: T. Fisher Unwin, 1909).
V.C.H, 'Life at a Women's University Settlement', *Temple Bar*, April 1902, pp. 452–8.
Ward, Mrs Humphry [Mary Augusta], *Marcella*, 2 vols (London: Smith, Elder, 1910).

Ward, Mary Augusta, *Marcella*, ed. Beth Sutton-Ramspeck and Nicole B. Meller (Peterborough, ON: Broadview, 2002).
Ward, Mrs Humphry [Mary Augusta], *Robert Elsmere* (London: Macmillan, 1888).
Ward, Mrs Humphry [Mary Augusta], *A Writer's Recollections*, 2 vols (New York and London: Harper, 1918).
Warman, Christopher, 'Marilyn Lived Here', *The Times*, 12 July 2000, p. 20.
Waterhouse, Paul, 'The Morality of the Bay Window', *British Architect*, 2 (1898), pp. 398–410.
Waugh, Evelyn, *The Diaries of Evelyn Waugh*, ed. Michael Davis (London: Weidenfeld & Nicolson, 1976).
Waugh, Evelyn, *A Little Learning* (Harmondsworth: Penguin, 1983).
Webb, Beatrice, *The Diary of Beatrice Webb, Volume One, 1873–1892: Glitter Around and Darkness Within*, ed. Norman MacKenzie and Jeanne MacKenzie (London: Virago, 1982).
Webb, Sidney, *The London Programme* (London: Swan Sonnenschein, 1891).
'Where the Unmarried Live', *Woman's Herald*, 20 April 1893, p. 131.
'Women's Settlements in London', *The Speaker*, 10 February 1894, p. 164.
Wolseley, Frances, *Gardening for Women* (London: Cassell, 1908).
'Working Ladies' Guild', *Women's Gazette*, April 1879, pp. 56–7.
Yonge, C. Fortescue, 'The English Clergy in Fiction', *The Gentleman's Magazine*, July 1897, pp. 40–50.
Zimmern, Alice, 'Ladies' Dwellings', *Contemporary Review*, 77 (1900), pp. 96–104.

Secondary Sources

Adams, Annmarie, *Architecture in the Family Way: Doctors, Houses and Women 1870–1900* (Montreal: McGill-Queen's University Press, 1998).
Argyle, Gisela, 'Mrs Humphry Ward's Experiments in the Woman Question', *Studies in English Literature 1500–1900*, 43.4 (2003), pp. 939–57.
Armstrong, Nancy, *Desire and Domestic Fiction: A Political History of the Novel* (Oxford: Oxford University Press, 1987).
Ashton, Rosemary, *Victorian Bloomsbury* (New Haven: Yale University Press, 2012).
Balchin, Paul, and Maureen Rhoden, *Housing: The Essential Foundations* (London: Routledge, 1998).
Barnes, John, 'Gentleman Crusader: Henry Hyde Champion in the Early Socialist Movement', *History Workshop Journal*, 60 (2005), pp. 116–38.

Barnes, John, *Socialist Champion: Portrait of the Gentleman as a Crusader* (Melbourne: Australian Scholarly Publishing, 2006).

Baxandall, Lee, and Stefan Morawski, *Marx and Engels on Literature and Art: A Selection of Writings* (St Louis: Telos Press, 1973).

Bayles Kortsch, Christine, *Dress in Late Victorian Women's Fiction: Literacy, Textiles and Activism* (Farnham: Ashgate, 2009).

Baynes, Peter, *John Passmore Edwards and Mary Ward* (London: The Mary Ward Centre, 1991).

Beauman, Katherine Bentley, *Women and the Settlement Movement* (London: I.B. Tauris, 1996).

Bindslev, Anne M., *Mrs Humphry Ward: A Study in Late-Victorian Feminine Consciousness and Creative Expression* (Stockholm: Almqvist and Wiskell, 1985).

Birchall, Johnston, *Building Communities: The Cooperative Way* (London: Routledge, 1988).

Blunt, Alison, and Olivia Sheringham, 'Home-City Geographies: Urban Dwelling and Mobility', *Progress in Human Geography*, 20.10 (2018), pp. 1–20.

Bonham, Valerie, 'Stanley, Maude Alethea (1833–1915)', *Oxford Dictionary of National Biography*, online edition, 2004, <doi:10.1093/ref:odnb/45676> (last accessed 4 December 2018).

Bordain, Iain, Barbara Penner and Jane Rendell (eds), *Gender Space Architecture* (London: Routledge, 2000).

Bowie, Duncan, *Radical Solutions to the Housing Supply Crisis* (Bristol: Policy Press, 2017).

Brake, Laurel, and Marysa Demoor (eds), *Dictionary of Nineteenth-century Journalism in Great Britain and Ireland* (Ghent: Academia Press, 2009).

Briggs, Asa, and Anne Macartney (eds), *Toynbee Hall: The First Hundred Years* (London: Routledge, 1984).

British Film Institute Database <http://explore.bfi.org.uk> (last accessed 20 January 2017).

Butler, Judith, *Gender Trouble: Feminism and the Subversion of Identity* (London: Routledge, 2010 [1997]).

Butler, Judith, *Undoing Gender* (London: Routledge, 2004).

Coit, Emily, 'Mary Augusta Ward's "Perfect Economist" and the Logic of Anti-Suffragism', *English Literary History*, 82.4 (2015), pp. 1213–38.

Coleman, Deborah, Elizabeth Danze and Carol Henderson (eds), *Architecture and Feminism* (New York: Princeton Architectural Press, 1996).

Collister, Peter, 'Portraits of "Audacious Youth"', *English Studies*, 4 (1983), pp. 296–317.

Crawford, Elizabeth, *Enterprising Women: The Garretts and their Circle* (London: Francis Boutle, 2002).

Cubitt, Eliza, *Arthur Morrison and the East End: The Legacy of Slum Fictions* (Abingdon: Routledge, 2019).
Cuddon, J. A., 'Kailyard School', in J. A. Cuddon (ed.), *The Penguin Dictionary of Literary Terms and Literary Theory*, 4th edn (Harmondsworth: Penguin, 1999).
Cuming, Emily, *Housing, Class and Gender 1880–2012* (Cambridge: Cambridge University Press, 2016).
Davey, Peter, *Arts and Crafts Architecture* (London: Phaidon, 1985).
Davidson, David Andrew, 'One Hundred Years in the Making: The Creation and Protection of Raymond Unwin's Legacy at Hampstead Garden Suburb', *Planning Perspectives*, 30.1 (2014), pp. 141–52.
Dennis, Richard, 'Babylonian Flats in Victorian and Edwardian London', *The London Journal*, 33.3 (2000), pp. 233–47.
Dennis, Richard, 'Buildings, Residences and Mansions: George Gissing's Prejudice Against Flats', in John Spires (ed.), *Gissing and the City: Cultural Crisis and the Making of Books in Late Victorian England* (Basingstoke: Palgrave Macmillan, 2006), pp. 41–62.
Dennis, Richard, *Cities in Modernity: Representations and Productions of Metropolitan Space, 1840–1930* (Cambridge: Cambridge University Press, 2008).
Dennis, Richard, 'Gissing and Chelsea: An Urban Walk', *Gissing Journal*, 52.2 (2018), pp. 1–16.
Deutsch, Sarah, *Women and the City: Gender, Power and Space in Boston, 1870–1940* (Oxford: Oxford University Press, 2000).
Dickson, Beth, 'Annie S. Swan and O. Douglas: Legacies of the Kailyard', in Douglas Gifford and Dorothy McMillan (eds), *A History of Scottish Women's Writing* (Edinburgh: Edinburgh University Press, 1997), pp. 329–46.
Dines, Martin, *The Literature of Suburban Change: Twentieth-Century Developments* (Edinburgh: Edinburgh University Press, 2020).
Douglas, Mary, *Purity and Danger: An Analysis of the Concepts of Pollution and Taboo* (London: Routledge, 2002 [1996]).
Eagleton, Terry, *The English Novel: An Introduction* (Oxford: Blackwell, 2015).
Elkiss, Terry, 'A Law Unto Herself: The Solitary Odyssey of M. E. Harkness', in Flore Janssen and Lisa C. Robertson (eds), *Margaret Harkness* (Manchester: Manchester University Press, 2019), pp. 17–38.
'Farringdon Road', *Survey of London: Volume 46 South and East Clerkenwell* (2008), pp. 358–84, <https://www.british-history.ac.uk/survey-london/vol46/pp358-384> (last accessed 1 June 2019).
Forty, Adrian, 'The Mary Ward Settlement', *Architect's Journal*, 2 August 1989, pp. 28–49.

Friedman, Alice T., *Women and the Making of the Modern House* (New Haven: Yale University Press, 2006).

Gardiner, Edmund F., 'Annie S. Swan – Forerunner of Modern Popular Fiction', *Library Review*, 24.6 (1974), pp. 251–4.

Garnett, Jane, 'Feilding, Lady Mary (1823–96)', *Oxford Dictionary of National Biography*, online edition, https://doi.org/10.1093/ref:odnb/59482 (last accessed 28 May 2019).

Gaskell, S. Martin, *Model Housing* (London: Mansell, 1987).

Gee, Emily, '"Where Shall She Live?": Housing the New Working Woman in Late Victorian and Edwardian London', in Geoff Brandwood (ed.), *Living, Leisure and Law: Eight Building Types in England 1880–1941* (Reading: Spire, 2010), pp. 89–109.

Glover, David, 'The Vicissitudes of Victory: Margaret Harkness, *George Eastmont, Wanderer* (1905), and the 1889 Dockworkers' Strike', in Flore Janssen and Lisa C. Robertson (eds), *Margaret Harkness* (Manchester: Manchester University Press, 2019), pp. 91–110.

Goble, Alan (ed.), *The Complete Index to Literary Sources in Film* (London: Bauker-Saur, 1999).

Goodlad, Lauren, *Victorian Literature and the Victorian State: Character and Governance in a Liberal Society* (Baltimore: Johns Hopkins University Press, 2003).

Gracombe, Sarah, 'Imperial Englishness in Julia Frankau's "Book of the Jew"', *Prooftexts*, 30.2 (2010), pp. 147–79.

Grosz, Elizabeth, 'Bodies – Cities', in Beatriz Colomina (ed.), *Sexuality and Space* (New York: Princeton Architectural Press, 1992), pp. 241–54.

Gwynn, Stephen, *Mrs Humphrey Ward* (London: Nisbet, 1917).

Hadley, Elaine, *Living Liberalism: Practical Citizenship in Mid-Victorian Britain* (Chicago: University of Chicago Press, 2010).

Hagar, Lisa, 'Slumming with the New Woman: *Fin de Siècle* Sexual Inversion, Reform Work and Sisterhood in Rhoda Broughton's *Dear Faustina*', *Women's Writing*, 14.3 (2007), pp. 460–75.

Hamlett, Jane, *At Home in the Institution: Material Life in Asylums, Lodging Houses, and Schools in Victorian and Edwardian England* (Basingstoke: Palgrave Macmillan, 2015).

Hamlett, Jane, *Material Relations: Domestic Interiors and Middle-class Families in England, 1850–1910* (Manchester: Manchester University Press, 2010).

Hamlett, Jane, and Rebecca Preston, 'A Veritable Place for a Hardworking Labourer? Space, Material Culture and Inmate Experience in London Rowton Houses, 1892–1918', in Jane Hamlett, Lesley Hoskins and Rebecca Preston (eds), *Residential Institutions in Britain, 1725–1970: Inmates and Environments* (London: Pickering and Chatto, 2013), pp. 93–108.

Hapgood, Lynne, '"Is this Friendship?": Eleanor Marx, Margaret Harkness and the Idea of Socialist Community', in John Stokes (ed.), *Eleanor Marx (1855–1898): Life, Work, Contacts* (Aldershot: Ashgate, 2000), pp. 129–43.

Herring, Scott, *Queering the Underworld: Slumming, Literature and the Undoing of Lesbian and Gay History* (Chicago: University of Chicago Press, 2007).

Holmes, Vicky, *In Bed With the Victorians: The Life-Cycle of Working-class Marriage* (Basingstoke: Palgrave Macmillan, 2017).

Holroyd, Michael, *Lytton Strachey: A Critical Biography*, 2 vols (London: Heinemann, 1967).

Ingle, Stephen, *Socialist Thought in Imaginative Literature* (London: Macmillan, 1979).

Ingleby, Matthew, 'The Bachelorisation of Legal Bloomsbury', *Nineteenth-Century Gender Studies*, 8.2 (2012), <http://www.ncgsjournal.com/issue82/ingleby.htm> (last accessed 15 May 2018).

Ingleby, Matthew, *Nineteenth-century Fiction and the Production of Bloomsbury: Novel Grounds* (Basingstoke: Palgrave Macmillan, 2018).

Inwood, Stephen, *City of Cities: The Birth of Modern London* (London: Macmillan, 2005).

Janssen, Flore, '"What You Write Down is Going to the Press": Margaret Harkness's Accounts of the 1889 London Dockworkers' Strike', *Victorians: a Journal of Culture and Literature*, 132 (2017), pp. 162–74.

John, Angela V., *Rebel Woman, 1869–1955* (Manchester: Manchester University Press, 2009).

John, Angela V., 'Sharp [married name Nevinson], Evelyn Jane (1869–1955)', *Oxford Dictionary of National Biography*, online edition, <https://doi.org/10.1093/ref:odnb/37950> (last accessed 28 May 2019).

Johnson, Matthew, *English Houses 1300–1800* (London: Pearson, 2007).

Klaus, H. Gustav, *The Rise of Socialist Fiction* (New York: St. Martin's Press, 1987).

Kortsch, Christine Bayles, *Dress in Late Victorian Women's Fiction: Literacy, Textiles and Activism* (Farnham: Ashgate, 2009).

Koven, Seth, *Slumming: Sexual and Social Politics in Victorian London* (Princeton: Princeton University Press, 2004).

Krueger, Kate, 'Evelyn Sharp's Working Women and the Dilemma of Romance', *Women's Writing*, 19.4 (2012), pp. 563–83.

Laybourn, Keith, *The Rise of Socialism in Britain c. 1881–1951* (Stroud: Sutton, 1997).

Ledger, Sally, *The New Woman: Fiction and Feminism at the Fin de Siècle* (Manchester: Manchester University Press, 1997).

Lefebvre, Henri, *La Production de l'espace* (Paris: Éditions Anthropos, 1974).

Liggins, Emma, *George Gissing, the Working Woman, and British Culture* (Aldershot: Ashgate, 2006).

Liggins, Emma, 'Having a Good Time? The Bachelor Girl in 1890s New Woman Fiction', in Adrienne E. Gavin and Carolyn W. de la L. Oulton (eds), *Writing Women of the Fin de Siècle: Authors of Change* (Basingstoke: Palgrave, 2012), pp. 98–110.

Liggins, Emma, '"The Life of a Bachelor Girl in the Big City": Selling the Single Lifestyle to Readers of Woman and the Young Woman in the 1890s', *Victorian Periodicals Review*, 40.3 (2007), pp. 216–38.

Livesey, Ruth, 'Reading for Character: Women Social Reformers and Narratives of the Urban Poor in Late Victorian and Edwardian Literature', *Journal of Victorian Culture*, 9.1 (2010), pp. 43–67.

Livesey, Ruth, *Socialism, Sex, and the Culture of Aestheticism in Britain, 1880–1914* (Oxford: Oxford University Press, 2007).

Livesey, Ruth, 'Soundscapes of the City in Margaret Harkness, *A City Girl* (1887), Henry James, *The Princess Casamassima* (1885–86), and Katharine Buildings, Whitechapel', in Flore Janssen and Lisa C. Robertson (eds), *Margaret Harkness* (Manchester: Manchester University Press, 2019), pp. 111–29.

Livesey, Ruth, 'Women Rent Collectors and the Rewriting of Space, Class and Gender in East London, 1870–1900: The Case of Katharine Buildings, East Smithfield', in Elizabeth Darling and Lesley Whitworth (eds), *Women and the Making of Built Space in England, 1870–1950* (Aldershot: Ashgate, 2007), pp. 87–106.

Maltz, Diana, *British Aestheticism and the Urban Working Classes, 1870–1900: Beauty for the People* (Basingstoke: Palgrave Macmillan, 2006).

Marcus, Sharon, *Apartment Stories: City and Home in Nineteenth-century Paris and London* (Berkeley: University of California Press, 1999).

Marcus, Sharon, *Between Women* (Princeton: Princeton University Press, 2007).

Massey, Doreen, *Space, Place, Gender* (Oxford: Blackwell, 1994).

Matrix Feminist Design Cooperative, *Making Space: Women and the Man-made Environment* (London: Pluto Press, 1984).

Meek, James, 'Where Will We Live?', *London Review of Books*, 36.1 (2014), pp. 7–16.

Meller, Helen, 'Gender, Citizenship and the Making of the Modern Environment', in Elizabeth Darling and Lesley Whitworth (eds), *Women and the Making of Built Space in England, 1870–1950* (Aldershot: Ashgate, 2007), pp. 13–30.

Miller, Jane Eldridge, *Rebel Women: Feminism, Modernism and the Edwardian Novel* (London: Virago, 1994).

Miller, Melvyn, and A. Stuart Gray, *Hampstead Garden Suburb* (Chichester: Phillimore, 1993).

Minton, Anna, 'The Great London Property Squeeze', *The Guardian*, 25 May 2017, <https://www.theguardian.com/society/2017/may/25/london-property-squeeze-affordable-housing> (last accessed 9 July 2019).

Mitchell, Sally, 'Meade, Elizabeth Thomasina (1844–1914)', *Oxford Dictionary of National Biography*, online edition, 2004, <doi:10.1093/ref:odnb/52740> (last accessed 15 October 2018).

Mitchell, Sally, *The New Girl: Girls' Culture in England 1880–1915* (New York: Columbia University Press, 1995).

Morgan, Edmund S., *Visible Saints: The History of a Puritan Idea* (Ithaca: Cornell University Press, 1963).

Morris, Susannah, 'Market Solutions for Social Problems', *Economic History Review*, 54.3 (2001), pp. 525–45.

Mullholland, Terri, *British Boarding Houses in Interwar Women's Literature: Alternative Domestic Spaces* (London: Routledge, 2017).

Murphy, Patricia, 'Disdained and Disempowered: The "Inverted" New Woman in Rhoda Broughton's *Dear Faustina*', *Tulsa Studies in Women's Literature*, 19.1 (2000), pp. 57–79.

Nead, Lynda, *Victorian Babylon: People, Streets and Images in Nineteenth-century London* (New Haven: Yale University Press, 2000).

Nord, Deborah Epstein, *Walking the Victorian Streets: Women, Representation and the City* (Ithaca: Cornell University Press, 1995).

Norton-Smith, J., 'An Introduction to Mrs Humphry Ward, Novelist', *Essays in Criticism*, 1 (1968), pp. 420–8.

O'Day, Rosemary, 'Caring or Controlling? The East End of London in the 1880s and 1890s', in Clive Emsley, Eric Johnson and Pieter Spierenburg (eds), *Social Control in Europe 1880–2000* (Columbus: Ohio State University Press, 2004), vol. 2, pp. 149–66.

O'Day, Rosemary, 'How Families Lived Then: Katharine Buildings, East Smithfield, 1885–1890', in Ruth Finnegan and Michael Drake (eds), *Studying Family and Community History: From Family Tree to Family History* (Cambridge: Cambridge University Press, 1994), pp. 129–66.

Parkins, Wendy, *Mobility and Modernity in Women's Novels, 1850–1930: Women Moving Dangerously* (Basingstoke: Palgrave, 2009).

Parsons, Deborah, *Streetwalking the Metropolis: Women, the City and Modernity* (Oxford: Oxford University Press, 2000).

Pearson, Lynn F., *The Architectural and Social History of Cooperative Living* (London: Macmillan, 1988).

Peterson, William S., *Victorian Heretic: Mrs Humphrey Ward's* Robert Elsmere (Leicester: Leicester University Press, 1976).

Pierson, Stanley, *British Socialists: The Journey from Fantasy to Politics* (Cambridge, MA: Harvard University Press, 1979).

Pettifor, Ann, 'Why Building More Homes Will Not Solve Britain's Housing Crisis', *The Guardian*, 27 January 2018, <https://www.theguardian.com/commentisfree/2018/jan/27/building-homes-britain-housing-crisis> (last accessed 8 July 2019).

Ravenhill-Johnson, Annie, *The Art and Ideology of the Trade Union Emblem 1880–1925* (London: Anthem, 2013).

Ravetz, Alison, *The Place of Home: English Domestic Environments, 1914–2000* (London: Taylor and Francis, 1995).

Rendell, Jane, *Site-Writing: The Architecture of Art Criticism* (London: I.B. Tauris, 2010).

Roberts, David, *Paternalism in Early Victorian England* (London: Croom Helm, 1979).

Rodger, Richard, *Housing in Urban Britain 1780–1914* (Basingstoke: Macmillan, 1989).

Rosner, Victoria, *Architecture and the Modernism of Private Life* (New York: Columbia University Press, 2005).

Rybczynski, Witold, *City Life* (New York: Touchstone, 1995).

Schwartz, Laura, *Feminism and the Servant Problem: Class and Domestic Labour in the Women's Suffrage Movement* (Cambridge: Cambridge University Press, 2019).

Scotland, Nigel, *Squires in the Slums: Settlements and Missions in Late-Victorian London* (London: I.B. Tauris, 2007).

Self, Will, *Sore Sites* (London: Ellipses, 2000).

Sewell, Jessica Ellen, *Women and the Everyday City: Public Space in San Francisco, 1880–1915* (Minneapolis: University of Minnesota Press, 2011).

Shapiro, Susan, 'The Mannish New Woman: Punch and its Precursors', *The Review of English Studies*, 42.168 (1991), pp. 510–22.

Sheridan, Michael, *Rowton Houses 1892–1954* (London: Rowton Houses, 1956).

Skeet, Walter W., *A Concise Etymology of the English Language* (New York: Cosimo, 2005).

Slack, Kathleen M., *Henrietta's Dream: A Chronicle of Hampstead Garden Suburb* (London: Calvert's North Star Press, 1982).

Smith, Timothy D'Arch, *The Frankaus: Prejudice and Principles within a London Literary Family* (Norwich: Michael Russell, 2015).

Spain, Daphne, *Gendered Spaces* (Chapel Hill: University of North Carolina Press, 1992).

Stedman Jones, Gareth, *Outcast London: A Study in the Relationship between Classes in Victorian Society* (London: Verso, 2013 [1971]).

Sutherland, John, *Mrs Humphry Ward: Eminent Victorian, Pre-Eminent Edwardian* (Oxford: Oxford University Press, 1990).
Sutton-Ramspeck, Beth, 'Mary Ward and the Claims of Conflicting Feminism', in Nicole Diane Thompson (ed.), *Victorian Women Writers and the Woman Question* (Cambridge: Cambridge University Press, 1999), pp. 204–22.
Swinnerton, Jo, *The London Companion* (London: Robson, 2004).
Tarn, John Nelson, *Five Per Cent Philanthropy* (London: Cambridge University Press, 1973).
Tarn, John Nelson, *Working-class Housing in Nineteenth-century Britain* (London: Lund Humphries for the Architectural Association, 1971).
Taunton, Matthew, *Fictions of the City: Class, Culture and Mass Housing in London and Paris* (Basingstoke: Palgrave Macmillan, 2009).
Tauranac, John, *The Empire State Building: The Making of a Landmark* (Ithaca: Cornell University Press, 2014).
Thompson, E. P., *The Making of the English Working Class* (Harmondsworth: Penguin, 2013 [1963]).
Vicinus, Martha, *Independent Women: Work and Community for Single Women, 1850–1920* (London: Virago, 1985).
Von Rosenberg, Ingrid, 'French Naturalism and the English Socialist Novel: Margaret Harkness and William Edwards Tirebuck', in H. Gustav Klaus (ed.), *The Rise of Socialist Fiction 1880–1914* (Brighton: Harvester, 1987), pp. 151–71.
Walker, Lynne, 'The Entry of Women into the Architectural Profession in Britain', *Art Journal*, 7.1 (1986), pp. 13–18.
Walker, Lynne, 'Home and Away: The Feminist Remapping of Public and Private in Victorian London', in Iain Bordain et al. (eds), *The Unknown City: Contesting Architecture and Social Space* (Cambridge, MA: MIT Press, 2001), pp. 296–311.
Walkowitz, Judith, *City of Dreadful Delight: Narratives of Sexual Danger in Late-Victorian London* (London: Virago, 1992).
Watkins, Micky, *Henrietta Barnett: Social Worker and Community Planner* (London: Hampstead Garden Suburb Archive Trust, 2011).
Weiner, Deborah, *Architecture and Social Reform in Late-Victorian Britain* (Manchester: Manchester University Press, 1994).
Weinreb, Ben et al., *The London Encyclopedia*, 3rd edn (London: Macmillan, 1983).
'West Ham Philanthropic Institutions', British History Online, <www.british-history.ac.uk> (last accessed 4 August 2018).
Wilberforce, Wilfred, *The House of Burns & Oates* (London: Burns & Oates, 1908).

Wilkes, Joanne, *Women Reviewing Women in Nineteenth-century Britain: The Critical Reception of Jane Austen, Charlotte Bronte, and George Eliot* (Farnham: Ashgate, 2010).

Wilson, Elizabeth, *The Sphinx in the City: Urban Life, the Control of Disorder and Women* (London: Virago, 1991).

Wilson, John Foster, *Irish Novels 1890–1940: New Beginnings in Culture and Fiction* (Oxford: Oxford University Press, 2008).

Wilt, Judith, *Behind Her Times: Transition in the Novels of Mary Augusta Ward* (Charlottesville: University of Virginia Press, 2005).

Wise, Sarah, *The Blackest Streets: The Life and Death of a Victorian Slum* (London: Vintage, 2009).

Wohl, Anthony S., *The Eternal Slum: Housing and Social Policy in Victorian London* (London: Edward Arnold, 1977).

Yeo, Stephen, 'A New Life: The Religion of Socialism in Britain', *History Workshop Journal*, 4 (1977), pp. 5–56.

Zahniser, J. D., and Amelia R. Fry, *Alice Paul: Claiming Power* (Oxford: Oxford University Press, 2014).

Index

apartments, 120–3, 124
  Artillery Mansions, 120–7
  Queen Anne's Mansions, 125
Armstrong, Nancy, 10
Arnold, Matthew, 39
  Culture and Anarchy, 37

bachelor girl, 77, 113; *see also* bachelor woman
bachelor woman, 99–100
Baillie Scott, M. H., 178, 180–1, 186
Barnett, Henrietta, 140, 142, 163, 175, 176–7, 178–9, 180, 187–8, 189, 190
  Practicable Socialism, 142, 176–7
Barnett, Samuel, 140, 142
Besant, Walter, 23, 26, 34n, 129n, 154, 155
bildungsroman, 36, 41, 45, 114
boarding houses, 6, 14n, 40
Brewer, C. C and A. Dunbar Smith, 50–1
Broughton, Rhoda, 133, 135
  Dear Faustina, 10, 11, 133–52
Brydon, J. M., 86–9

Champion, Henry Hyde, 55–6, 57, 58, 68, 69
charity *see* philanthropy
citizenship, 134–5, 139–40, 193
Collins, Mary Gabrielle, 175
  Garden Suburb Verses, 12, 177, 183–7, 189
'Condition of England' novel, 9, 84
conservatism, 38, 47
  Tory paternalism, 38, 57
cooperative housing societies, 32, 33, 92
  Tenant Co-operators Ltd, 32
Cuming, Emily, 3, 7

Davis & Emmanuel Architects, 22, 24, 25
Dennis, Richard, 44, 121, 125
Dickens, Charles, 188, 189
  Little Dorrit, 81
dockworkers' strike (1889), 55, 56, 67–9
Dreiser, Theodore, *Sister Carrie*, 123

East End, 21, 23, 24, 31, 42, 112–15, 154–69, 176–7; *see also* London
Engels, Friedrich, 20–1, 33
  The Housing Question, 31

Fellowship of New Life, 33
Frankau, Julia [Frank Danby], 111–12
   Dr. Phillips: A Maida Vale Idyll, 111, 128n
   The Heart of a Child, 11, 111–27

garden cities, 5–6, 175–6, 189–90
   Hampstead Garden Suburb, 12, 175–90
   Letchworth Garden Suburb, 177, 178, 189
Garrett, Agnes, 86
Gaskell, Elizabeth
   Mary Barton, 84
   Ruth, 84
Gee, Emily, 7, 79, 80, 85, 95, 180
Girls' Friendly Society, 80
Gissing, George, 44, 62, 155, 157–8, 186
   Demos, 40
   The Nether World, 43–5, 120, 158
   The Odd Women, 15n, 83–4, 99
   Workers in the Dawn, 154
Glover, David, 56, 60

Hadley, Elaine, 36–7
Hagar, Lisa, 133, 134, 135
Hapgood, Lynne, 68, 154, 160
Hardy, Thomas, *Tess of the d'Urbervilles*, 27
Harkness, Margaret [John Law], 19–20, 21, 23, 37, 44, 55–6, 57, 58, 68–9, 72n
   Captain Lobe: A Story of the Salvation Army, 23

A City Girl, 10, 19–33
George Eastmont, Wanderer, 10, 11, 55–70, 101, 105
heterosexuality, 99, 135–40, 143–5
Higgs, Mary, 194–5
Hill, Octavia, 8, 24, 26, 28, 66
Hobhouse, Emily, 89, 99, 105
homosexuality, 133–40, 146, 148–9
Howard, Ebenezer, *Garden Cities of To-Morrow*, 175–6

Kailyard school fiction, 11, 97, 107–8
Koven, Seth, 41, 57, 116, 135, 156, 157, 158, 160, 167–8

labour movement, 55–7, 66–9
   Labour Elector, 37, 57
   trades unionism, 66–7, 72n
ladies' chambers *see* women's housing
Ledger, Sally, 20, 27, 29, 33, 99
lesbianism *see* homosexuality
liberalism, 36–8, 48–9, 51–2
Liggins, Emma, 77, 78, 85
Linton, Eliza Lynn, 92, 94n
   The Rebel of the Family, 91, 138
Livesey, Ruth, 22, 33, 48
lodging houses, 64–5, 80, 120, 125, 145, 194
London
   Bloomsbury, 37, 41–9, 83–6, 109, 117, 120, 125–6, 158–9

Chelsea, 76, 79–80, 133, 151n
Hampstead, 12, 175–7, 187–90
Holborn, 157
Marylebone, 78, 81–2, 86
Notting Hill, 147
Pimlico, 94n, 125
Shoreditch, 154, 158–9, 160–1
Victoria, 120–6
West Kensington, 29–30
Whitechapel, 24, 30, 42
see also East End
London County Council, 113, 119, 168–9

Manning, Cardinal Henry Edward, 59, 67–8
Marcus, Sharon, 125
Meade, L. T., 156–7
  A Princess of the Gutter, 10, 11–12, 154–69
Mitchell, Sally, 105, 156, 170n
model dwellings, 1, 5, 6, 10–11, 19–20, 26–7, 28, 32–3, 37, 41, 43–4, 53n, 62, 63, 64, 80, 96, 154, 165, 168–9, 179, 183
  Corporation Buildings (Golden Lane and Petticoat Square, City of London), 60–2, 64–5
  East End Dwellings Company, 21–2, 24–6, 28
  Farringdon Road Buildings, 43–4, 53n, 120
  Improved Industrial Dwellings Corporation, 24
  Metropolitan Association for Improving the Dwellings of Industrial Classes, 44

Peabody Trust, 24, 37, 41, 42–3, 44, 62, 114, 116, 119, 120
Morrison, Arthur, *A Child of the Jago*, 112–13, 154

New Woman, 15n, 77–8, 99, 133
Nord, Deborah Epstein, 4, 27, 72n

Parsons, Deborah, 123
Passmore Edwards, John, 42; see also settlement movement: Passmore Edwards Settlement
Peabody Trust see model dwellings
pensioners, 179–80
philanthropy, 19–20, 26–7, 31, 81, 113–14, 116, 134–5, 145
  Charity Organisation Society, 112, 141

Rosner, Victoria, 7–8, 15n
Rowton Houses, 64–5, 72n, 102
Ruskin, John, 3, 49, 50–1, 136
  The Stones of Venice, 39–40, 46

Schreiner, Olive, 57, 89
Sergeant, Adeline, 98, 99, 109, 110n
settlement movement, 6, 12, 14n, 140, 142, 145, 155, 163
  Canning Town Settlement, 134, 139, 140–5, 149–50

settlement movement (*cont.*)
  Oxford House, 142, 143, 152n, 159
  Passmore Edwards Settlement, 49–51, 162
  Toynbee Hall, 6, 41–2, 51, 140, 141, 142, 159, 162–4, 175, 177, 183
  University Hall Settlement, 42, 49–52
Sharp, Evelyn, 77, 85–6, 94n, 109, 156
  The Making of a Prig, 11, 75–92, 98, 100, 101, 105, 113
  Unfinished Adventure, 86
Shaw, George Bernard, 35n
  The Philanderer, 124
slum fiction, 112–13, 116, 128n, 154, 155, 157–8
socialism, 33, 36–7, 40, 47–8, 56–8, 59, 66, 67, 68
  Fabian socialism, 58–9, 71n, 72n
  Social Democratic Federation, 56
Spain, Daphne, 2
Stanley, Maude Althea, 81, 115–20, 128n
  Work About the Five Dials, 115
Stead, W. T., 92
Swan, Annie Shepherd, 97–8
  A Victory Won, 10, 11, 95–109, 113

Trafalgar Square Riots, 63, 68

Unwin, Raymond, 177–8, 179, 180
  Town Planning and Modern Architecture at the Hampstead Garden Suburb, 186–7

Vicinus, Martha, 6, 76, 97, 108, 140, 145

Walkowitz, Judith, 4
Ward, Mary [Mrs. Humphrey], 36, 39, 40, 41–2, 49–50
  Marcella, 36–52
  Robert Elsmere, 156–7, 169
Waugh, Evelyn, 187–90
  A Little Learning, 187, 189
Webb [Potter], Beatrice, 8, 21, 157
Webb, Sidney, 57, 62
women's housing, 11, 75–7, 79–81, 89–90, 95–7, 101–3, 119–20, 124, 137, 181–3
  Brabazon House, Home for Ladies, 86, 93–4n, 109
  Campden Hill Chambers, 79–80
  Chenies Street Chambers, 86–8, 89, 98, 99, 101, 109, 117, 120, 137, 181
  Ladies' Associated Dwellings Company, 84–5
  Ladies' Residential Dwellings Corporation, 87, 88
  New Brabazon House, Home for Ladies, 93–4n, 137
  Oakley Street Chambers, 76, 79–80, 81, 85, 95, 96

Sloane Gardens House, 85, 86, 95, 96, 101, 102
Soho Club and Home for Working Girls, 81, 114–20, 123, 124, 127
Waterlow Court *see* garden cities: Hampstead Garden Suburb

York Street Chambers, 88, 89
Women's Social and Political Union, 77, 86
Working Ladies' Guild, 79, 80, 81, 84, 95

Zimmern, Alice, 96, 101, 102–3

EU representative:
Easy Access System Europe
Mustamäe tee 50, 10621 Tallinn, Estonia
Gpsr.requests@easproject.com

www.ingramcontent.com/pod-product-compliance
Lightning Source LLC
Chambersburg PA
CBHW070351240426
43671CB00013BA/2466